THE GOOD FIGHT

Ben Lindsey

THE
GOOD
FIGHT

*The Life and Times of
Ben B. Lindsey*

CHARLES LARSEN

Chicago / Quadrangle Books / 1 9 7 2

Library of Congress Catalog Card Number: 78–152095
International Standard Book Number: 0–8129–0237–8

For GRACE, CHARLES, and DOUGLAS

PREFACE

By 1964, when I began research on Ben Lindsey, most of his contemporaries were dead. There were a few notable exceptions, however, and some of them deserve an expression of appreciation that goes beyond the acknowledgments in the text and notes that follow.

Foremost among them is the Judge's widow, Henrietta Brevoort Lindsey, who died in Los Angeles on January 4, 1969. Mrs. Lindsey played the leading role in assembling the huge Benjamin Barr Lindsey Collection, now permanently located in the Library of Congress, which is the principal collection used in the writing of this biography. Although the book is an authorized biography in the sense that Mrs. Lindsey reserved the right to approve all applications to consult the Collection, it is not an official biography in the sense that she exercised a right of veto over any part of my manuscript. She did reserve the right to read it and to make suggestions, but her final illness allowed her to see only a small portion of it in completed form.

Mrs. Lindsey's generous help went far beyond granting me permission to use the Collection. In numerous conversations and exchanges of letters between our first meeting in April 1964 and our last in August 1968, she supplied information and leads that contributed substantially to improving the manuscript. Although she was always ready with suggestions, she made only one specific request—that her own role in her husband's biography be kept to a minimum. This request I have honored, and it has not been difficult for Mrs. Lindsey's private life was largely merged with the Judge's public one. When they married in 1913, she was nineteen and he was forty-four. Temperamentally, she loved the excitement of his public life from the beginning. She brought to the marriage youth, beauty, and unswerving devotion. An amusing illustration of the last quality occurred a few years after the Judge's death, in 1943, when an old friend advised her that any future biography of the Judge, if it were to be credible, must admit his faults and mistakes and not merely portray him "as a plaster saint." In a cordial reply, Mrs. Lindsey inquired, "What *were* his faults, what *were* his mistakes? *I never knew either.*" The friend beat a hasty and judicious retreat.

Two friends and associates of the Judge deserve a special word of appreciation. Helen Mellinkoff of Los Angeles allowed me to examine letters and records in her possession and also helped to supply information about the Judge's California years that could have come from no other source. She also read the manuscript in its entirety and made numerous useful suggestions. Wainwright Evans, Lindsey's literary collaborator in the 1920's, read the chapters on that period, lent me his substantial private collection of correspondence, and gave me details concerning the writing of *The Revolt of Modern Youth* and *The Companionate Marriage* that could not have been found elsewhere.

I also owe a special debt to Judge Philip B. Gilliam, who has presided over the Juvenile Court of Denver since 1940. Judge Gilliam read parts of the manuscript dealing with the work of the Court and also allowed me to examine such records that remain of the Juvenile Court during the Lindsey era. Mrs. Evelyn Kamuck, who helped me explore these records, also deserves my thanks.

In addition to those who are named in the book, a number of persons, chiefly Denverites, were helpful in supplying useful background information. They include Dr. Ben M. Cherrington, Dr. T. D. Cunningham, Ben Draper, Mrs. Chester Elliott,

Mrs. Richard Hogue, Rabbi Charles E. H. Kauvar, Morrison Shafroth, Mr. and Mrs. Chester Smedley, and Herbert Vandemoer. Members of the staffs of several libraries gave invaluable assistance, particularly those of the Manuscript Division, Library of Congress; the Colorado State Historical Society; the State Archives of Colorado; the Western History Division of the Denver Public Library; and the Special Collections Department of the Library of the University of California at Los Angeles.

The institution to which I owe the greatest debt is Mills College. A sabbatical leave in 1965–1966 allowed me to complete the bulk of my research in the Library of Congress, and several faculty research grants supported trips to Denver and Los Angeles. Two of my former students deserve a special word of thanks—Patricia Ellis Severn, who first suggested that I begin this study, and Darlene Holbrook, who helped me during the first stage of research in the Library of Congress. Several of my colleagues have lent consistent support. Reynold M. Wik allowed me to read a relevant chapter from his forthcoming book on Henry Ford. Robert Anderson and Marion Ross have been good listeners as well as good advisers throughout the writing.

I am especially happy to acknowledge the perceptive and constructive criticisms of Ivan R. Dee of Quadrangle Books whose talents as an editor are well known to many authors.

My greatest personal debt is to my wife, Grace Hutchison Larsen, a professional historian who has made many helpful suggestions for improving the manuscript. She has also progressed from professor to academic dean while this book was being completed, at the same time having to play the occasional role of substitute father for our two children. For enduring five missed vacations, I thank all of them.

It only remains to be said that I am solely responsible for all errors of omission or commission in what follows.

C. E. L.

Oakland, California
January 1971

CONTENTS

THE GOOD FIGHT

1 / The Making of
a Reformer

OR AMERICANS WHO WISHED TO ENJOY THEIR AFFLUENCE
without unpleasant intrusions, the last third of the
twentieth century began as an unhappy aftermath of the
somnolent Eisenhower years. In 1970 the president of Columbia
University declared that society was in a period of transition as
profound as the Renaissance or the Industrial Revolution. At
home, one-tenth of the population was struggling to erase the
last vestiges of slavery, legal and *de facto*. Abroad, the nation
was engaged in a conflict which even historians, by nature a
cautious breed, were calling the most unpopular in American
history. These events were unsettling enough, but they were
compounded by a questioning of the entire value system of
American society by some of the most articulate of the younger
generation.

Most of the younger people did not break openly with society, but even those who played the game sometimes let it be
known that they were fairly skeptical about the rules. In April
1968 a senior student at the University of California, chosen by
his peers to represent the newly elected members of Phi Beta
Kappa, startled his audience by asserting that his straight "A"
record was won at too high a social cost to have been justified.
The young man went on to recommend the abolition of the
grading system. Here was no unkempt, bearded lout who could
be sneeringly dismissed as just another incompetent who had
no chance of making it because he lacked intelligence and self-
discipline. If the best practitioner of the system, by the system's

· 3 ·

own standards, was angry enough to want his denunciation proclaimed by news media throughout the country, perhaps the time had come to take a look at the whole college scene from a social, as well as an academic, standpoint.

The revolt against traditional college patterns was not confined to demands for modification or elimination of the grading system. Inside academic walls, faculty members and administrators were exploring ways to make higher education more "relevant," as the saying went, to the twentieth century. Independent study, tutorials, and credit for work in the urban ghettos often seemed more meaningful than traditional lecture courses. Joint faculty-student committees were becoming widespread as students insisted on participating in curriculum planning. On the social side, there was a growing demand by the students that the colleges reject the *in loco parentis* concept and its attendant rules on such matters as drinking, sign-in sheets, overnight "privileges," and dormitory visits. The more sophisticated institutions were usually only too glad to be relieved of such obligations, especially as far as off-campus conduct was concerned, and approached the issue of student behavior chiefly as a public relations problem involving those whose good will they must cultivate—principally parents, donors, and (especially for state-supported institutions) the general public. Of the three, the public sometimes gave administrators the greatest headaches, since student demands for less surveillance strengthened the belief among those who traditionally suspected colleges as hotbeds of political subversion that they were dens of promiscuity as well. The suspicion was heightened by accounts in the public media of a growing number of undergraduates who were experimenting with "trial marriages."

The so-called sexual revolution was not confined to the campus, or even to youth. Hollywood, that staid self-censor of the thirties and forties, now officially recognized a class of adult films that would have passed for pornography a generation earlier. In every major city, bookstores displayed magazines and paperbacks ranging from the prurient and sensational to the serious and analytical concerning the state of manners and morals. A recurrent theme was the psychological and social aspects of premarital and extramarital relations. Scientific developments during and after the Second World War had gone a long way to demolish two pragmatic arguments against such conduct. The ancient fear of venereal disease was weakened by the discovery of penicillin, and the invention of the Pill came close to achieving the goal of several generations of birth-control advocates—a contraceptive that was at once scientifically and aesthetically satisfactory. Fear, ignorance, and apathy still prevented the dramatic decline in venereal disease that was technically possible, and a variety of personal and social factors kept the rate of illegitimacy high; but it was almost certain that the growing diffusion of information, combined with such expected improvements as a morning-after Pill and a vaccine against syphilis, would eventually put those twin enemies of mankind in the same limbo occupied by polio after the mid-fifties. Given their continuing decline, no end seemed to be in sight to the debate over standards of sexual conduct.

Another upsetting area for those Americans who yearned for peace, quiet, and an absence of controversy in the 1970's was juvenile crime. In 1965 a special Task Force on Juvenile Delinquency was created by the President's Commission on Law Enforcement and the Administration of Justice. In 1967 the Task Force confirmed what social workers and law enforcement officers had long known: one in every six boys was being referred to a juvenile court before his eighteenth birthday. Between 1960 and 1965, arrests of boys and girls under eighteen for serious crimes increased by 47 per cent, more than double the rate of population increase in that age group. The Task Force went on to call juvenile crime "the single most pressing and threatening aspect of the crime problem in the United

States." To some alarmed observers, the revolt of modern youth appeared completely out of control. What was to be done?

Some found in the slogan "law and order" a simplistic solution to many of the problems besetting America in the late twentieth century. Often the cry for law and order was merely a transparent euphemism for keeping the blacks in their place, or rather for putting them back into it. Sometimes it was invoked by others, however, who were not racists but who were confused and frightened by the growing use of drugs, the symbolic burning of draft cards and flags, and increasing violence—a problem dramatized by scores of killings whose victims ranged in power and status from a President of the United States to four black children attending Sunday school on a September morning in Birmingham, Alabama.

The country was as divided over the causes of unrest as it was over proposals for dealing with it. Many Americans felt that law and order was no more than a shibboleth employed as a substitute for the hard task of dealing constructively with the accumulated shortcomings of a whole society. Law and order would win acceptance only if it were coupled with justice, they warned. Violence would not subside as long as racism and poverty were tolerated in a country that prided itself on being the richest in the world. A few critics of the law and order approach also doubted that harsh measures really constituted a deterrent in any event. They pointed out that although mutilation and the death penalty were allowed for more than two hundred offenses in eighteenth-century England, London at that time was no safer at night than twentieth-century Chicago, and probably less so. The Great Society would need more than support of its local police to achieve security and safety.

Most memories are short, and the day-to-day reporting of the public media encourages the fallacy that the challenges of the present are unique. At least a few Americans in the 1970's were able, however, to recall a controversial judge who once had a great deal to say about law and order, juvenile crime, the war against poverty, and even a sexual revolution. Hardly any of them remembered that he specifically mentioned the birth-control pill in 1927, but it was generally recalled that he advocated something called "companionate marriage," a proposal sometimes discussed in the sixties and seventies as if it were a novel idea. In the 1920's no literate American would have had trouble telling a great deal more about Judge Ben Lindsey. (His legal name, Benjamin Barr Lindsey, was rarely used.) For twenty-five years his name had been a household word in the United States, and it is safe to say that he was better known by the general public than many of the national political figures of his time. As early as 1914, in a poll conducted by Hearst's *American Magazine,* he won the ambiguous honor of tying with Andrew Carnegie and Billy Sunday for eighth place as the "greatest living American." Lindsey's rise from an obscure county judgeship in Denver to national fame in less than a decade had been as remarkable as it was meteoric.

It all began on a wintry Denver afternoon, early in 1901, in the drab old Victorian courthouse at 16th and Tremont Streets.* In one of the smaller courtrooms, a new judge, barely more than thirty, with intense brown eyes and a rather restless manner, was presiding. If it had not been for his full moustache and prematurely receding hairline, a spectator might have thought for a moment that some adolescent prankster had climbed into the judge's chair, for Ben Lindsey had reached his full stature of five feet, five inches and weighed, at this time, approximately ninety-eight pounds. A few years later, Theodore Roosevelt, who was quite fond of him, recalled that the little Judge's enemies were maliciously referring to him during the 1912 election campaign as "the Bull Mouse."

In the midst of the court proceedings, which involved "some musty old mortgaged furniture," an assistant district attorney interrupted to ask the Judge if he would mind taking a couple

* It is now the site of the May D. and F. Department Store in downtown Denver.

of minutes to dispose of a simple case of theft. Judge Lindsey agreed, and a trembling teen-ager named Tony Costello* was brought before him. Tony was accused of stealing coal alongside the railroad tracks on the outskirts of town. The complaining witness was a railroad detective who had caught him red-handed. The boy clearly had no defense against the charge and was silent when asked what he had to say for himself. Lindsey, seeing no alternative, sentenced him to a term in reform school. As the Judge turned back to hear the argument about the furniture, the air was suddenly rent by what he later described as "the most soul-piercing scream of agony that I ever heard from a human throat." Unknown to Lindsey, Tony's mother had been sitting in the back of the courtroom. The pathetically dressed woman tore her hair and continued to shriek as a bailiff forcibly removed her to another part of the building. Lindsey, badly shaken, dismissed court and retired to his chambers. With the memory of the mother's screams still agitating him, he phoned the district attorney and obtained his consent to suspend Tony's sentence, even though they were both aware that there was no legal basis for such action.

Tony's case did not end there, however. On the same night that he suspended sentence, Lindsey decided to pay a visit to Tony's "home." There, in a miserable hovel, he found the boy's father dying from lead poisoning contracted while working twelve hours a day in a smelter. The large family lived in two cold, filthy rooms which Tony's stolen coal might have helped to warm. Somewhat at a loss for words, Lindsey gave Tony a gentle lecture about obeying the law and informally placed him on probation, a second step that had no legal foundation at the time. The Costellos' friends, unaccustomed to having a judge visit their neighborhood, crowded into the Costellos' shack to meet him and give their thanks. Tony's mother emotionally kissed Lindsey's hands. As the Judge left, he felt little satisfac-

* In his writings, Lindsey used pseudonyms to conceal the names of actual children who came before his Court.

tion at the warmth of the gratitude he had received. Rather, he felt an overwhelming sense of shame to know how the Costellos of the world must view his court and its pretense as a seat of justice.

There were many Costellos in American courts in 1901, but only a few judges felt a compulsion to do something about them. Ben Lindsey was in the vanguard of those who cared. In many ways his entire past had been a preparation for the afternoon when Tony Costello appeared in court. For the Judge, who was scarcely larger than Tony himself, could never forget his own poverty and despair only twelve years earlier, close to the same railroad tracks where Tony had been arrested.

The suffering that young Ben had experienced in adolescence and early manhood was accentuated by the memories of a lost happy childhood spent mostly in Tennessee. He was born in Jackson, November 25, 1869, the first child of Landy Tunstall Lindsey, a former Confederate Army captain now turned telegraph operator, and Letitia Barr Lindsey, daughter of Benjamin Barr, a plantation owner who had managed to keep his property and now sheltered his two daughters, their husbands, and their growing families. The patriarchal arrangement worked well for several years and the families lived comfortably, if not luxuriously, in a rambling house on a broad expanse of land dotted with great elms. Five decades later Ben Lindsey would reminisce about the Tom Sawyer style of living he and his younger brother enjoyed in the river country around Jackson, the dogs they loved, the horses they rode, and the great log fires in his grandfather's house. It was, as he remembered it, "a veritable paradise."

Relations among the adults in the Barr household were not idyllic, however. When Ben was about five, his father, a devout Episcopalian, became interested in the Oxford Movement and eventually became a Catholic convert. Ben, his younger brother and sister, and their mother immediately followed suit. The Barr side of the family, which already considered Landy

Lindsey a rather moody and erratic character, regarded his conversion as one more proof of his bad judgment. Although the Lindsey children apparently did not suffer from any withdrawal of affection, a growing coolness developed among the rest of the family. In 1879 Landy Lindsey, accompanied by his wife and daughter, moved away from Jackson permanently.

The ostensible reason for Landy's move was a good job offer in Denver, where he assumed charge of telegraph operations of the new Denver and South Park Railroad. He also spoke glowingly about the great economic opportunities in the American West. Perhaps hostility to his religion, both in the Barr household and in the community, made Jackson unattractive. There is a further hint in the few scraps of evidence regarding Landy Lindsey that a deeper dissatisfaction may have led him to seek contentment in a change of scene. He was apparently a person who never fully accepted the workaday world in which he lived. As a young man in Mississippi before the Civil War, he had dreamed of finding a way to attend the University of Virginia. In a letter to a former war comrade in July 1865 he revealed his yearning for "a classical education" and lamented the fact that he would have to "drag out a miserable existence" and "enter as a performer on the great stage of commercial life." He melodramatically confided to his friend that he wished he had been killed in the war so that he would not have to endure a society where it was not possible to be concerned with "first principles."[1]

These attitudes had an impact on Landy Lindsey's roles as husband and father. Even before he left Tennessee, his alienation from his surroundings was evident in his tendency to spend more money than he could afford on books, chiefly religious tracts and romantic historical fiction. He was a good storyteller. Ben loved to hear him describe his wartime exploits in tales that invariably extolled the virtues of bravery and loyalty. In later years the son looked back fondly on his father's qualities of gentleness and idealism. The only hint of a complaint that his father's zeal for devotional reading and church activities was a little unfair to the family appeared in Ben's later comment that the elder Lindsey "gave [the Church] much of his time and money in that formative period of my childhood."

Almost a year after he settled in Denver, Landy arranged for Ben and his brother, Chal, to join the rest of the family. The boys arrived, just after Ben's eleventh birthday, in a mood of keen disappointment at not having seen a single Indian or buffalo on the train ride from St. Louis to Denver. Ben was enrolled in public school and began to get acquainted with the sights and sounds of the Colorado metropolis, which boasted a five-story building among its outstanding attractions. Ben's first Denver period was short but pleasant. The family was together again, his father had a good job, and he and his brother were free, when school was out, to explore the bustling silver-mining center that would triple its population during the next decade. Although the boys were inclined to think that Jackson was more fun, Denver had its strong points too.

The Denver stay was soon interrupted. Father Zahm, a visiting recruiter for the elementary school department of Notre Dame University, arrived in Denver a year after Ben's arrival. His campaign to persuade Catholic parents to send their boys to his school was enhanced by a bonus of free transportation for all who would go. The appeal worked, and the priest soon convinced a sufficient number of Denver families, including a few Protestants, to fill the special Pullman car which took Ben, Chal, and the other boys to Indiana.

Although he was homesick for a few months, Ben always looked back "with an abiding affection" on the two years of his early teens in the "minim department" of Notre Dame. He enjoyed playing baseball and football, hiking and skating, and going on long rides to the local farms, where he and his classmates would gorge themselves on mince pies. On the academic side, he was outstanding in the debating society and even won a gold medal for his proficiency. In later years he liked to recall

the time that he and young Ed Costigan,* another Denver re-
cruit, argued affirmatively for the proposition "that Denver
was the most progressive city and Colorado the greatest state in
the Union." On the other hand, Lindsey was critical, at least in
retrospect, of certain features of Notre Dame. Religious indoc-
trination sometimes included a generous dash of bigotry. He
remembered a class in which a priest claimed that he had once
looked through a window into a room where a Masonic lodge
meeting was being held and saw the Devil, replete with tail
and cloven hoof, sitting among the Masonic brethren. "The
report was not to be questioned," Lindsey sarcastically recalled,
because "the good father had seen it." The lurid descriptions
of Hell which young Ben heard resembled those which frightened Stephen Dedalus in James Joyce's *Portrait of the Artist as
a Young Man*. He remembered being so terrified of eternal
damnation that he would wait until Sunday morning to go to
confession in order to allow the shortest possible interval in
which a sinful thought might cross his mind before receiving
Communion. He later wondered whether a lifetime tendency
toward morbidity may have been caused by his excessive concern with Hell during his formative years. He observed that
his younger brother, whom he could not induce to read *The
Lives of the Saints,* never suffered in this way. In late middle
age Ben Lindsey conjectured, "I am not sure that a dime novel
would not have been better for me."

Lindsey's memories of his Catholic education were not all
unpleasant. The aspects of religion which were stressed in the
classrooms depended in part on the personalities of the nuns
and priests. When young Ben once served as messenger from
his favorite nun to the president of the University, the priest
engaged him in conversation and recommended that he read
about St. Francis of Assisi. Ben immediately became infatuated

---

* Edward P. Costigan (1874–1939) later became active in Colorado politics and was a leading supporter of New Deal legislation in the United States
Senate, where he served from 1931 until his death.

with St. Francis and "could not get enough" of the saint who loved all living things. He also formed several close attachments to his teachers and corresponded with one of them, Sister Aloysius, for more than forty years. In the 1920's, when Lindsey clashed bitterly with Church spokesmen over his advocacy of birth control and liberalized divorce laws, he nevertheless continued to defend the character and integrity of the priesthood and sisterhood as he had known them during his childhood.

At the end of Ben's second year at Notre Dame he learned that his father had lost his job as a result of the railroad's change of management. A family council was held by mail and it was decided that Ben and Chal would go back to Tennessee, where Benjamin Barr was enthusiastic about the prospect of having his teen-age grandsons live with him again. Ben's mother, his sister Mary, and young Tunstall, last-born of the Lindsey children, would stay in Denver while the father looked for a new job. Ben stayed in his grandfather's home until he was sixteen. His mother's sister, whom the family called Aunt Pat, and her husband, C. T. Bates, who owned a hardware store in Jackson, still lived in the Barr house. Grandfather Barr took care of most of Ben's and Chal's expenses, with some help from "Uncle Bates." Since Ben's parents were unable to contribute to his support, they did not make the decisions about his schooling. As a result he was enrolled in Southwestern Baptist University, which amounted to a preparatory school, where he remained for three years.[2]

Ben had a winning personality, and he found the transition from a Catholic to a Baptist environment not painful. At first he tried to defend his Catholicism against the arguments of his new classmates and teachers. The defense must have been good-natured, for it did not prevent his active participation in college affairs or his election as recording secretary of the debating society in his second year. A few months after his return to Tennessee he was writing enthusiastically to his parents about school activities. His letters were those of a happy, gregarious boy. If he missed his parents, there was compensation in the affection of his grandfather, his aunt, and Uncle Bates. When Ben left Jackson three years later to return to his parents in Denver, he did not know that his boyhood was over.[3]

Ben's first shock on returning home was to discover that his father's health was so poor that he and his brother would have to supplement the family income immediately by taking on full-time jobs. His hope of entering the new East Denver High School was dashed. But the worst was yet to come. One morning, shortly after his eighteenth birthday, Ben Lindsey discovered his father's body in the family coal cellar. Despondent over his poor health and accumulating debts, Landy Lindsey had committed suicide by cutting his throat with a razor.[4]

His father's suicide confronted Ben and his family with a long-term crisis. The relatives in Jackson could help a little, but Ben would have to be the economic mainstay of the family, with some aid from Chal. Just before his father's death Ben had found a job keeping abstract books for a real estate company. Since he was paid only $10 a month, he found it necessary to earn extra money by delivering the *Rocky Mountain News* in the early mornings and working evenings as a janitor. He began to discover that the fruits of Denver's much-touted boom economy were not easily or evenly shared.

The next three years were bleak. The only bright spot, and that a mixed one, was an agreement with his younger brother to swap jobs. Chal had found work as an office boy with R. D. Thompson, a successful Denver lawyer. Ben, who had left the real estate office for a better job clerking for a mining company, was anxious to read law. Chal was quite amenable to the exchange, and the boys persuaded their employers to agree. Ben's first step on the road to a legal career was soon interrupted, however, by a severe personal crisis.

The crisis resulted partly from sheer exhaustion. Ben's duties for lawyer Thompson included running errands, carrying books to and from court, and copying letters. The position also involved some rudimentary legal research. Although he had given up carrying newspapers, Ben still had to earn additional money by scrubbing floors and performing other janitorial services at night. Ambitious to win admission to the bar and to save a small portion of his earnings in order to set up practice, he got little sleep and ate only molasses and gingerbread for lunch. Physically spent, he became "dopey," as he put it, and sometimes researched a case for hours only to discover that he had built his entire legal argument on some basic misapprehension of the law. Gradually he began to struggle with the fear that he was worthless and would always remain so.

Conditions at home—a wretched shanty on lower West Colfax Avenue—in no way assuaged this crisis of confidence. The pall of poverty hung heavily over the household, and uncertainty about the future lent an air of pervasive gloom. Family tempers were short. An evening at home became one of "exasperated misery." Convinced that he did not have the talent ever to extricate himself from a labyrinth of failure at work and acrimony at home, young Ben, at the age of nineteen, locked himself in his room one night, placed the muzzle of a revolver against his temple, and pulled the trigger. Twenty years later, when his fame had spread to four continents, he recalled what happened next:

> The hammer snapped sharply on the cartridge; a great wave of horror and revulsion swept over me in a rush of blood to my head, and I dropped the revolver on the floor and threw myself on the bed. By some miracle the cartridge had not exploded; but the nervous shock of that instant when I felt the trigger yield and the muzzle rap against my forehead with the impact of the hammer —that shock was almost as great as a very bullet in the brain. I realized my folly, my weakness; and I went back to my life with something of a man's determination to crush the circumstances that had almost crushed me.

After a few more months in lawyer Thompson's office, the fog began to lift. Ben continued to apply himself to the study of law, reading Blackstone, Kent, and Parsons, and accustoming himself daily to the jargon and folkways of judges and lawyers. He soon joined a small group of young men similarly situated in setting up a moot court which they held in a rented room on the campus of the University of Denver. There, in the gaslight after working hours, they quizzed one another and held make-believe trials. Ben gradually became "more of a clerk and less of an office boy." Under the rather easygoing rules of Colorado law practice in the 1890's, he was occasionally allowed to appear in court and make more or less *pro forma* motions for his employer. On two occasions before his admission to the bar, he was permitted to argue cases that had an impact on his views in later years.

The first episode concerned one of Thompson's clients who had been defrauded by a man who used forged credit references. A deputy district attorney had given up the effort to prosecute the man after a jury had freed him on two counts and failed to agree on a third. Thompson's firm was on good terms with the district attorney's office, and when young Lindsey begged to be deputized to win a conviction on the third count, the district attorney agreed. Lindsey was persuasive; the jury brought in a verdict of guilty. The victory gave him such a sense of confidence that he later called it a turning point in his life. But there was another side to the story. Almost as soon as he had won, Lindsey decided that it was a Pyrrhic victory. In his anxiety to win, he did not consider the consequences. The defendant, a married man with dependent children, had no means of supporting his family other than his earning power. A prison sentence would punish the guilty but would also throw the innocent into the streets. Lindsey was so overwhelmed with the recognition of the cruelty of "criminal justice" that he pleaded with the judge to suspend sentence. His silence about the aftermath of the case suggests that he was less successful with the judge than he had been with the jury. He later recalled the judge's friendly advice: "Son, your *forte* will never be that of a prosecutor. . . . I think you would be much happier defending people than convicting them."

The judge did not forget the young law clerk, and shortly afterward asked him to come to his chambers. Lindsey was flattered to learn that the judge wanted to assign him to the defense of two indigents accused of burglary. The court paid only a nominal fee for such services, but the opportunity to make oneself known was an appealing prospect. When Lindsey told the judge it was a great compliment to be given the task of defending *two* accused criminals, he thought that the judge smiled rather enigmatically. Lindsey obtained the numbers of the cases from the court clerk, looked over the pleadings, and went to the West Side jail to confer with his two "clients." He followed the warden through huge iron doors to the back of the room where he found two grown men—as it turned out, a safecracker and a horse thief—playing poker in a cage with two hero-worshiping boys about twelve years old. For a moment Lindsey feared he had a very difficult assignment since the older men had the look of hardened criminals and the encouragement they were giving two little boys to gamble hardly improved the impression they made. Lindsey was relieved when the warden advised him that the men were to be defended by "a real lawyer" and that the children were his clients. Then he was angry. The children, who were accused of breaking into a railroad section house and stealing some tools, had already been in jail for two months. Why, Lindsey demanded of the warden, could they not be released until the fall term of court opened? The warden admitted it was "a damned outrage," but pointed out that the boys' parents could not afford bail. Why, Lindsey persisted, were the boys put into a cell with older men who were teaching them how to gamble and, perhaps, other vices as well? The warden tried to find excuses, declaring that often there were children in the jail and that there was not enough space to accommodate all the prisoners properly. As the warden continued his feeble defenses, Ben Lindsey's sense of outrage swelled. He concluded that the wrong parties had been indicted. Irrespective of any technical guilt on the part of the boys, the greater criminal was the State of Colorado:

Here were two boys, neither of them serious enemies of society, who were about to be convicted of burglary and have felony records standing against them for the rest of their lives. And, pending the decision of their cases, they were associating generally with criminals and particularly with a horse thief and a safe-cracker. The state was sending them to a school for crime—deliberately teaching them to be horse thieves and safecrackers. It was outrageous—and absurd.

My first fight, then, was with the state of Colorado. I was determined that these boys should have their chance. I saw only vaguely then what afterward became clearer to me—that my first fight with the state was not just for those two boys but for millions like them. Even then, however—before I had formulated any plan to change the things that were or had written any of the hundreds of laws I afterward wrote for my own and other states and foreign countries—I had made up my mind to smash the system that meant so much injustice to youth.

Lindsey returned to the chambers of the judge who had given him, almost whimsically, his role as public defender. The judge was apparently moved by the young law clerk's eloquence and concern, and used his influence to have the boys released on condition they would periodically report to Lindsey and satisfy him that they were mending their ways. Thus, as Lindsey commented with some amusement, did he first become a "juvenile judge" and "probation officer," a decade before either office existed in Colorado.

In 1894, just before his twenty-fifth birthday, Ben Lindsey was admitted to the bar. He pooled his resources with another beginning lawyer, Fred Parks, and they rented rooms in an old building on Champa Street in West Denver, just north of the civic center. Lindsey and his partner promptly became aware of the injustices that occurred under the rules of the game as it was played in Colorado around the turn of the century.

The first case that came to them involved alleged malpractice by a surgeon. Lindsey was convinced that it was an open-and-shut case of a faulty diagnosis. The plaintiff, a boy named Smith, had suffered a fractured thigh and had been treated for a bruised hip. The case aroused an unusual amount of local interest because the surgeon, whose brother owned one of the largest smelting companies in the state, was represented by a prominent corporation lawyer. Word soon got around that the biggest show in town was in a dingy courtroom where "two kids [were] fighting the corporation heavyweights." At an early stage in the case, the young lawyers won their first triumph when the judge denied the defendant's lawyer's motion to dismiss the complaint. After a dramatic trial that lasted three weeks, Lindsey and Parks were confident they had won. The jury, however, hung by a vote of eleven to one. Convinced that they could not lose in the long run, the young lawyers pressed for a new trial. Again everything seemed to go their way during the trial, but again the jury hung.

At this point Lindsey and Parks were visited by A. M. Stevenson ("Big Steve"), a powerful political figure and an attorney for the Denver City Tramway Company.[5] Stevenson, "a heavy-jowled, heavy-waisted, red-faced bulk of good humor," a perfect model of the genial corruption of the gaslight era, began the meeting with some flattering remarks about the favorable press the young lawyers were getting. Then he came to the point. Would they be willing to agree to an out-of-court settlement? Lindsey refused, asserting that their client would eventually win in the courtroom.

> "We got eleven to one each time," I said. "We'll win yet."
> "Uh-huh. You will, eh?" He laughed amusedly.
> "One man stood out against you each time, wasn't there?"
> There was.
> "Well," he said, "there always will be. You ain't going to get a verdict in this case. You can't. Now I'm a friend of you boys, ain't I? Well, my advice to you is you'd better settle that case.

Get something for your work. Don't be a pair of fools. Settle it."
"Why can't we get a verdict?" we asked.
He winked a fat eye. "Jury'll hang. Every time. I'm here to tell you so. Better settle it."

Lindsey and Parks advised their client to fight the case again in court, but he decided to do without their services.

Two other early cases brought home to the fledgling lawyers the nature of the prevailing injustice under law. Like other states, Colorado was wholly innocent of any employers' liability or industrial accident statutes. The harsh common-law doctrines of contributory negligence, fellow servant, and assumption of risk prevailed.[6] When Lindsey and Parks took the case of a twenty-one-year-old factory worker whose face had been badly mutilated by a bursting emery wheel, they lost on the ground that the young man had continued to work at the wheel after he knew it was defective. Lindsey argued to no avail that the young man had good reason to believe he would have been fired if he complained about the wheel. When the two young lawyers tried to win a suit on behalf of a mother whose child had been hit by a streetcar, they discovered that the court was unable to compute the value of the dead child's prospective "services," and that no statute allowed any compensation for the mother's mental anguish. About this time Lindsey and Parks began to formulate a plan. If it was hopeless to fight for good causes under the existing rules of the game, why not try to change the rules? They embarked upon a scheme to send Parks to the state legislature.

Fred Parks was an ideal candidate for elective office. He was personable, extroverted, and ambitious. With the backing of George Graham, Silver Republican leader, in 1898 he won a nomination for state senator on a fusion ticket supported by Silver Republicans, Democrats, and Populists. In the expectation that Parks could push reform measures in which they were interested, and with an eye to increasing their professional contacts, the partners split the burden of the $500 assessment that was expected of Parks as his contribution to the costs of the campaign. When Parks won handily, the two lawyers went to work on three bills that Parks would introduce in the first session of the new legislature. The first bill—the so-called three-fourths jury bill—would provide for verdicts by less than a unanimous vote in civil suits, thus making it impossible to create a hung jury by simply bribing one member. The other bills Lindsey prepared would modify the common-law rules favoring employers in industrial accident suits and allow parents to be compensated for mental anguish resulting from the injury or death of a child. On the advice of "Boss Graham," Lindsey and Parks decided against scattering their initial efforts in too many directions and put all their energies behind the three-fourths jury bill.

Corporation lobbyists promptly descended on the legislature, using every means, legitimate and otherwise, to oppose the bill. Their chief legitimate tactic was a motion seeking a declaratory judgment from the state Supreme Court holding that the Lindsey-Parks proposal was unconstitutional. Lindsey and Parks appeared as friends of the court and rejoiced when the justices refused the request and intimated that they would probably approve the bill if passed.[7] This victory enabled Parks to have the bill reported favorably by the Senate judiciary committee. It was passed by the legislature at the end of its first session. The triumph was brief, however, for the next year the Supreme Court, purporting to draw a distinction between the measure and earlier laws it had upheld, declared the statute unconstitutional.[8] Lindsey was convinced that the justices' action was influenced by the pressures of the utilities companies rather than their scrupulous regard for the constitution.

Lindsey's political education began in earnest during his support of Parks's campaign and while lobbying for reform legislation. He quickly modified some of the stereotyped ideas of his youth. As a boy Lindsey believed that the Democratic party was the source of all political virtue and the Republicans the embodiment of evil. When he first came to Denver he recalled wondering vaguely why Republicans never seemed to be wearing the bloody shirts that a Confederate veteran in Tennessee had assured him they all waved. Actually, his opinion of Republicans did not change much, but he soon decided that in Colorado, at least, the Democrats were not much better. The leadership of a major segment of his party, Lindsey became convinced, was simply the reverse side of the coin of the hated Republicans, equally eager to do the bidding of "the interests" that poured needed funds into their coffers. Lindsey nonetheless believed that the greater hope for reformation lay with the Democrats and gave his support to Charles S. Thomas' successful campaign to become governor in 1898.

Lindsey's first political appointment was to a precinct committee. His district was the fashionable Capitol Hill area which was the social as well as the political capital of Colorado. Democrats usually did not do well in the precinct, but the young campaigner worked hard, using the servants' entrances of the wealthy homes to plead with the domestics, whom he often found cynical and indifferent nonvoters. On election day, one poll-watcher was heard to observe, "Good heavens! Lindsey's got all the servant girls in the country here." Though Lindsey's efforts did not carry the precinct, the Democrats did much better than usual. As a reward for his services to the Thomas faction, Lindsey was appointed early in 1899 as Public Administrator and Guardian. For two years he served in this county office, acting as guardian of orphans and other dependents of deceased persons who had left no competent relatives or executors to look after their interests.

A promising young lawyer and a diligent worker for his party's interests, Lindsey was soon under consideration for more important posts. Chances of his becoming a district judge or even district attorney were lost on two occasions because of previous commitments by party leaders to other candidates. In 1900, however, a vacancy in a county judgeship occurred when Judge Robert W. Steele was elected to the state Supreme Court.

Lindsey's relations with Judge Steele were especially cordial as a result of a long association that went back to the days when Lindsey was a law clerk with R. D. Thompson. Lindsey easily won Steele's backing as well as that of Governor Thomas and Senator Thomas Patterson. As a result he was appointed to fill the unexpired term of Judge Steele. It was a position he was to hold, with slight variations in title, for the next twenty-six years.

When he became a judge, at the age of thirty-one, Ben Lindsey had developed certain traits of personality, temperament, and intellect that stayed with him for the rest of his life. They made him one of the best-loved, as well as one of the most hated, men of his times. Perhaps his outstanding characteristic, and one that even his enemies often conceded, was an almost uncanny ability to empathize, not only with young people but also with a wide variety of adults. Closely related to this quality was his sense of drama, a talent he knew intuitively how to invoke to accomplish his ends. Since he believed that his actions were motivated by a highly developed sense of social idealism, he had the satisfaction of always being the hero in the historical drama that was perennially unfolding. Although an occasional intellectual leaning toward objectivity might allow him to be temporarily convinced by a Lincoln Steffens that "good" and "evil" were relative terms, in his heart the Judge always regarded the history of mankind as a struggle by the advocates of justice, compassion, and amelioration against the forces of greed, bigotry, and hatred. If his detractors sometimes caricatured him as a Don Quixote, Lindsey was equally confident that he was a St. George. As a boy he won several prizes in elocution and debating and remembered best those occasions when he pleaded passionately for an underdog. After winning a debate at Southwestern Baptist University in which he pleaded for the independence of Ireland, he "resolved to become a lawyer because the profession seemed . . . to offer opportunity to express the burning passion within me to fight for justice."

Lindsey's ardor for social justice found expression in a temperament that was, in his words, "moody, melancholy, and sensitive." He attributed these traits to poverty and to the uncertainty about his future that haunted him during his young manhood. His very size was a source of embarrassment to him in his early years. Certainly his father's suicide may well have exacerbated the self-doubt and feelings of insecurity that apparently led him to try to take his own life. In his struggle to conquer himself, Lindsey decided that the best defense was a good offense, and the targets of his offensives in his mature years were those who opposed the reform measures he advocated. In attempting to analyze his own motives in his public career, he wrote of the aftermath of his purported attempt at suicide:

> I was never afterward as afraid of anything as of my own weakness, my own cowardice—so that when the agents of the Beast in the courts and in politics threatened me with all the abominations of their rage if I did not commit moral suicide for *them*, my fear of yielding to them was so great that I attacked them more than ever.

His attacks were brutally effective, partly because they were so specific in their details of the crimes and misconduct of his opponents, partly because the drama of confrontation was invariably enhanced by Lindsey's portraying his opposition as the embodiment of pure evil. Not surprisingly, the Judge's attacks provoked the tenacity of his enemies so that they pursued him beyond Colorado in later years, almost to the time of his death.

Clues to intellectual influences on Lindsey in his early years are scanty. In his published accounts of the reform campaigns he waged, notably *The Beast* (1910) and *The Dangerous Life* (1931), he accounted for his social philosophy chiefly on the basis of his own bitter exposure to poverty and his first hand experiences with political corruption in Denver. His disillusionment with organized religion he attributed to the family bickering it caused during his childhood. Only a few preserved letters shed any light on Ben's intellectual development during his teens and early twenties. During his teens his Uncle Bates wrote letters to Ben's father which showed a strong affection for the boy. Bates particularly admired Ben's strong and independent spirit, which he compared invidiously, on one occasion, to that of Ben's brother, Chal. Uncle Bates's feeling for Ben was apparently reciprocal, for they corresponded regularly after the boy left Tennessee and became self-supporting. Bates was a skeptic in religious matters and may have influenced Ben's gradual drift away from the Catholic Church. In politics, Bates advised Ben that the major parties always put votes ahead of principles, and urged him to read the works of Henry George. Perhaps, as was true of other followers of George, Bates found the single-tax advocate's opposition to the status quo as appealing as the specific economic measures he proposed. A few months before the older man's death in 1895, Ben sent him copies of the popular Free Silver movement tract *Coin's Financial School,* and the utopian fantasy *A Traveller from Altruria,* reflecting, perhaps, their bond of disenchantment with the world as it was.[9]

In many ways Ben Lindsey did not have a "judicial temperament," even though he spent almost half a lifetime as a judge. A comment about Ben by Uncle Bates when the boy was only sixteen showed considerable insight and predicted with uncanny accuracy Lindsey's love-hate relationship with the law in later years. Ben might succeed as an editorial writer or actor, Bates wrote to Ben's father, "or his application as a student might possibly make a passable lawyer out of him. But being visionary, dreamy, and very sensitive, I hardly think that the law profession would suit him."[10] Ben Lindsey must have found this letter among his father's effects, or perhaps his mother gave it to him, for it was preserved among his papers. Undoubtedly he would have concurred to a large degree in Bates's judgment and would even have taken a certain pride in it.

The young Judge often found the routine of court work

tedious and trivial. A considerable amount of the litigation to which he had to listen dealt with squabbles over property worth no more than $2,000. The judgeship hardly seemed the most suitable forum for the talents of an ambitious, idealistic, and socially concerned young man with a flair for drama. Actually, unknown yet to Lindsey, there was present in his Denver courtroom one wintry afternoon in 1901 an almost perfect concatenation of the time, the place, and the characters from which history can be made. When a trembling teen-ager named Tony Costello was brought into the little Judge's courtroom, the concatenation was complete.

2 / The Kids' Judge

A T THE TURN OF THE CENTURY THE STATUS OF THE CHILD IN Anglo-American criminal law was not so different from that of an adult. The common law of England, which was frequently followed in American courts, had held for centuries that seven was the "age of reason." Colorado, by statute, had generously raised it to ten. Thereafter the child might be held responsible for criminal acts. Until the age of fourteen, however, the law presumed that the child did not understand the nature of his offense. But this presumption could be rebutted; that is, the state could attempt to show that the child was mature beyond his years and should be held responsible. After the age of fourteen, an accused youth was legally on the same footing as an adult. Children were also tried in the same courts as adults, although Boston pioneered in hearing charges against them separately in 1869, and Chicago established the first formally organized juvenile court thirty years later.

The treatment of children after conviction of crime was as harsh as the legal principles by which they were tried. Until the nineteenth century, juvenile offenders went to the same jails as adults and were even mutilated or executed as were adults. A number of humanitarian reformers, shocked by the conditions to which children were exposed in jails and prisons, were responsible for the modern "reform school" movement. In England a Reformatory School Act was passed by Parliament in 1854. In 1825 a private House of Refuge, a rough precursor of the modern reformatory, was established in New York City. Various states and counties gradually followed suit, and by the end of the century the principle that young offenders should be segregated from adult convicts had won general acceptance in the United States. In Colorado a state industrial school was established at Golden in 1881, and a reformatory for more incorrigible boys was opened at Buena Vista ten years later.

In Colorado as elsewhere, however, the picture was not so bright as the existence of such institutions might suggest. Inadequate appropriations, the lack of any theoretical framework for "reforming" the inmates, and the usual deficiencies of the spoils system under which the schools were administered, combined to reduce them to a status little better than junior prisons. And, as Ben Lindsey had discovered in the case of his two youthful clients, accused youngsters often spent many months in ordinary jails before being sentenced. Although conditions in Colorado were no worse than the national pattern, and were even slightly mitigated by the absence of the large industrial slums found in eastern states, it was clear that Lindsey's campaign for the children of Colorado would have to be fought on many fronts.

By the end of his first year on the Bench, Lindsey was ready to fire his opening broadsides. The first task was to discover a legal basis for taking special steps on behalf of children. The *ad hoc* arrangements between the Judge and the district attorney had not been challenged, but both officials felt uneasy about using such a frail legal edifice each time a new case came along. In trying to find a solution, Lindsey came across a law of 1899, popularly known as the School Law. The statute was intended to deal only with school attendance, but the unorthodox Judge found room for creative opportunities in Section 4 of the law:

> Every child between the ages of 8 and 14 years, and every child between 14 and 16 years, who cannot read and write the English language or is not engaged in some regular employment, who is an habitual truant from school, or who is in attendance at any public, private or parochial school and is incorrigible, vicious,

or immoral in conduct, or who habitually wanders about the streets and public places during school hours, having no business or lawful occupation, shall be deemed a juvenile disorderly person, and be subject to the provisions of this act.

Lindsey enthusiastically recalled his discovery:

A juvenile disorderly person! Not a criminal to be punished under the criminal law but a ward of the state to be corrected as *parens patriae*. The law was a school law, intended only for the disciplining of school children; but it could be construed as I proceeded to construe it. It was not a steel fire-escape built according to the statutory regulations. It was merely a wooden ladder rotting in a back yard. But it would reach the lower stories—and I asked the District Attorney in future to file all his complaints against children under this law, in my court, according to a form which I furnished—and he agreed to do so. Thus our "juvenile court" was begun informally, anonymously, so to speak, but effectively.[1]

Lindsey's genius as a reformer was not limited to a talent for legal improvisation. He was an artist at public relations with a sure instinct for dramatizing his cause. Recognizing that the campaign for children would have to involve the active participation of many segments of the community, he carefully cultivated private charitable and religious groups as well as public agencies and lawmaking bodies. Knowing that he would have to step on toes occasionally, he saw the urgency of building mass public support to counteract the efforts of political enemies who would try to oust him in every succeeding election.

Two episodes in Lindsey's early career demonstrated his talent for using his judicial forum with the greatest effectiveness in mobilizing popular support. The Judge saw his first chance to expose the alliance between saloon owners and politicians by riding the crest of a reform wave already under way against the "wine rooms," as the saloons of Denver were called. The wine rooms were commonly used as much for gambling and prostitution as they were for drinking. Dancehalls were often attached to them, and little or no effort was made to discourage minors from using all the services available. Lindsey knew firsthand the consequences of these wide-open arrangements. In his courtroom he found prostitutes who had learned their trade as teenagers, and young men who were being prosecuted by their employers for stealing to cover gambling losses. In the privacy of his chambers the Judge heard mothers make futile pleas that a way be found to recover money lost by their sons and husbands. From younger confidants he learned that even newsboys were encouraged to play "policy" with their meager earnings. In regard to minors, especially, here was a situation that would be seen as morally indefensible if brought dramatically to the public's attention.

At first Lindsey tried to get action by pleading with the district attorney, the chief of police, and the police board. Several officials tried to humor him with promises that were quickly forgotten. A few more candid politicians tried to explain that "business" helped everybody, including the Judge's own Democratic party, which depended on contributions from the "liberal" element. When a token arrest was made of a dive keeper who had illegally served a woman, a magistrate held that such ordinances as the one involved deprived women of their equal rights. Lindsey, whose court had appellate jurisdiction in the matter, reversed the judgment, fined the dive keeper $100, and publicly excoriated the magistrate for his decision.[2] The *coup de grâce* was yet to come, however. Lindsey invited all members of the police board to come to his court on Saturday morning, May 24, 1902. When the commissioners arrived they found the courtroom filled with the Judge's "kids" as well as a number of reporters. Though they were invited to sit in the jury box, it soon became apparent that the commissioners were unwittingly in the dock. Lindsey proceeded to let out all the stops. Lincoln Steffens later remembered the Judge's description of the scene:

"I have asked you gentlemen to come here and look at these boys," he said. "There are also girls in this city who report on Friday," he added. The Commissioners looked at the boys, and the Judge went on to say that while these children were brought there as delinquents, it was not the children alone who were delinquent. "Parents, in many cases, and adults who violate the law, and particularly police officials who refuse to enforce the law, they are more responsible than the children," he said.

He illustrated: "It became the duty of this Court recently to send a young girl to the Industrial School. She was not depraved or vicious; she was capable of being a good, pure woman with any kind of favorable environment. But she was subject to temptations. What were these temptations? The wine-rooms; not one, but many. She was induced to enter such places. You knowingly permitted them to run in violation of the law. Yet the child is punished and disgraced. You and the dive-keeper, the real culprits, you go scot-free."

". . . I know it is unusual to speak thus publicly, but all things usual have been done, and something unusual is justifiable. I therefore beg of you in this public manner, in the presence of these children, for their benefit, that you earnestly and diligently war upon these places. . . . I assure you that you will have then the good will and respect that are denied you now. That is worth more than all the vaunted boastings of all the devil's agents in this town. It is to these that you are catering now, and until you break the spell they have over you, you will be storing up misery, hell, and damnation for the present and future generations."[3]

The newspapers had a field day. The *Denver Post* carried a front-page cartoon portraying the commissioners as hypocrites sweating in the jury box under Lindsey's public exposure, and followed up with stories under such banners as "The Wine Room Is the Gateway to Hades." Clergymen contributed to the avalanche of criticism of the dive keepers and praised the Judge for his unique method of hitting at them. The wine rooms were hopelessly on the defensive. They were not yet destroyed, but a climate of opinion had been created that made it impossible for them to continue to ply their wares to adolescents. A year later Lindsey and others insured that the new conditions would not be temporary by successfully lobbying for legislation that made enforcement procedures against saloon keepers meaningful. There were times, Lindsey concluded, when it was necessary to "grandstand with a megaphone."[4]

The Judge used similar tactics to good effect in his campaign against the city and county jails. Persuaded by Harry Wilbur, a reporter from the *Rocky Mountain News,* that he would not see a juvenile detention home in Denver until public sentiment was aroused, Lindsey asked boys who had been in his court to describe their experiences in jail.[5] The conditions they described were common enough in the United States at the turn of the century (and not unusual now in the seventh decade of it). They included kangaroo courts, sadistic jailers, and sexual perversion. The story in the *Rocky Mountain News,* printed in red in the form of an interview with Lindsey, had a unique impact because it was endorsed by the Judge, who, in a characteristic tone of moral outrage, demanded an end to "the abominable pollutions that had been committed on [the] little bodies" of the children. Against such charges only one response was possible—denial. Police Commissioner Frank Adams did just that and intimated that the "little Judge" had "gone batty" on the subject of the children. Lindsey proceeded to play his trump card by offering to prove everything. He invited the police board, the governor, the mayor, other officials, and fifteen clergymen to come to his chambers and hear the stories from the lips of the children themselves. The police board, having learned its lesson from the wine rooms episode, failed to make an appearance, but Governor James Peabody and the others came. On this occasion reporters were not present, and Lindsey urged the boys to tell their all-male blue-ribbon audience details that not even the *Denver Post* would have printed. After an attempt to impugn a young witness failed disastrously, the audience fell into silence. As the session neared its end, a priest found the testimony so revolting that he left the room, saying that he could not take any more of it. The governor then declared that he believed what he had heard and would fully support the "Lindsey bills" that had been stalled in the legislature. Thus by 1903 the Judge's campaign for a new deal for children bore its first legislative fruit.[6]

The 1902–1903 campaign set the pattern for Lindsey's style as chief lobbyist for children's legislation in Colorado. At every stage from drafting to final enactment he played a key role. Much of the legislation he wrote with his own hand. He studied the laws of other states, notably Illinois and Massachusetts, sent numerous letters to other judges, and conferred with Colorado legislators on the political strategy of moving the bills along. Nor did he stop when the bills were finally passed. There was always more to be done, and new campaigns would be helped if the public could be convinced that the reforms adopted to date were a success. The legislative victories won by the Judge in his first decade as children's lobbyist deserve inspection.[7]

On July 3, 1903, Lindsey spoke at the annual conference of the Colorado Bar Association and reviewed the triumphs of the early spring. He recalled the meeting in 1902 when a number of county judges determined to work for a revision of the probate code and for several laws to protect children. The laws enacted in March 1903 accomplished all the goals substantially as they were proposed.

The new probate code, a highly technical legal document, aimed to reduce charges on estates of deceased persons by consolidating old statutes and eliminating red tape. The "law's delay" was no mere literary allusion in this field, and the reforms were widely recognized as long overdue. Lindsey, though no "lawyer's lawyer," had observed, while serving as Public Administrator and Guardian, some of the practical defects of existing laws. He was personally responsible for drafting those sections of the new law that put an end to two inequities. Not surprisingly, both concerned the interests of children. The first gave widows more significant rights in their husbands' estates. Under the old rules, a widow whose inheritance consisted

THE GOOD FIGHT · 34

almost entirely of real estate would find herself at a disadvantage because of legal delays and encumbrances regarding any transfer of real property. By contrast, a widow whose inheritance was chiefly money, stocks, or bonds, was in a favored position. By putting realty and personal property on an equal footing in determining widows' allowances, Lindsey ended an invidious distinction that made little sense. The other item of Lindsey's own handiwork was a provision for an orphan's allowance in those cases in which the mother predeceased her husband. The old law provided a lien for widows but gave no similar benefit to orphans. Lindsey proposed giving the orphans an equal lien of $2,000. The new code included the change.

In one sense the real significance of the movement for the new probate code was that it gave Lindsey a handle to use in pressing for other legislation that was of deeper concern to him. Although his committee work dealt chiefly with probate matters, he managed to use it to enlist the prestigious support of his fellow judges for the first "Lindsey bills." He suggested that the probate legislation was part of a package deal of legal reforms which all public-spirited citizens should endorse. The result was the adoption at a single session of the Colorado legislature of a greater number of laws concerning juveniles than had been passed during the entire history of the state.[8]

The most comprehensive of the "Lindsey bills" was "An Act Concerning Delinquent Children." In it the Judge candidly and forcefully stated the philosophy of the juvenile court movement:

> [The] care and custody and discipline of the child shall approximate as nearly as may be that which should be given by its parents, and . . . as far as practicable any delinquent child shall be treated, not as a criminal, but as misdirected and misguided, and needing aid, encouragement, help and assistance.

The Juvenile Delinquent Law, as it was popularly called, applied to children sixteen years or younger. It spelled out in some detail the acts that would bring a child within its purview. The law could be enforced against any child

> who violates any law of this state or any city or village ordinance; or who is incorrigible; or who knowingly associates with thieves, vicious or immoral persons; or who is growing up in idleness or crime; or who knowingly visits or enters a house of ill-repute; or who knowingly patronizes or visits any saloon or dram shop where intoxicating liquors are sold; or who knowingly patronizes or visits any policy shop or place where any gambling device is or shall be operated; or who patronizes or visits any public pool room or bucket shop;* or who wanders about the streets in the night time without being on any lawful business or occupation; or who habitually wanders about any railroad yards or tracks, or jumps or hooks on to any moving train, or enters any car or engine without lawful authority; or who habitually uses vile, obscene, vulgar, profane or indecent language, or is guilty of immoral conduct in any public place or about any school house.

For the first time the term "juvenile court" was used in a Colorado law, even though Lindsey had already used the broad language of the 1899 School Law to apply some of the same principles and procedures which were now given formal recognition. Technically the Juvenile Delinquent Law did not create a juvenile court but merely required county courts in the larger counties to keep a separate set of records for all cases arising under the law, called "The Juvenile Record," and a separate calendar called "The Juvenile Docket." The county court, when hearing such cases, might be called, "for convenience," a juvenile court. Clerks of the courts were to submit annual statistical reports on their "juvenile divisions" to the State Board of Charities and Corrections, but it was forbidden to disclose the names of any children or parents who had come before the court.

The core of an effective juvenile court system is its probation department. For several years Ben Lindsey had used truant officers and a few cooperative school teachers as unofficial proba-

---

* A bucket shop was a place where betting was conducted on the prices of stocks, grains, etc., without actually dealing in the securities or commodities.

tion officers. In many ways the Judge was his own chief probation officer, but he recognized the need for more formal arrangements. The Juvenile Delinquent Law broke ground by providing for salaried probation officers. The number was based on county population, and Denver was entitled to three.

Two abuses which had troubled Lindsey for a long time were curtailed by the new law. A fee system, which had encouraged law enforcement officers to arrest children, and petty magistrates to try them, was eliminated by giving exclusive jurisdiction in such cases to the county courts, which would be served by the probation officers and a deputy district attorney. Finally Lindsey attacked his old enemy, the jail. The statute forbade putting children under fourteen in jail "under any circumstances," and required that every effort be made to get the consent of a parent or other responsible person that any child under sixteen who was arrested would appear in court at the proper time, thus avoiding "temporary" lock-ups pending trial. In counties of the first class (Denver), a detention home was to replace the jail for all minors under sixteen. In Denver, at any rate, the state would no longer force children "to consort with horse thieves and safecrackers."[9]

Although the Juvenile Delinquent Law made it no longer necessary for Lindsey to rely on the School Law of 1899, the old statute was still useful. A Lindsey amendment of 1903 changed it by raising the age of compulsory school attendance from fourteen to sixteen. The revision was, in effect, a child labor law, though certain exemptions were allowed, notably in situations where a child over fourteen had to contribute to the support of a parent. The Lindsey bill retained the term "juvenile disorderly person" for truants. Parents or employers who chose to ignore the school attendance law were subject to fine or jail sentence.

The most unusual feature of the Lindsey legislation of 1903 was the so-called Adult Delinquency Law, an original contribution of the Judge which soon won national recognition. Its purpose was to fill a gap in the law in regard to adults who contributed to the delinquency of a minor. To a limited degree, existing laws dimly recognized the general principle. The sale of liquor and tobacco to minors was already illegal, for example, though the penalty, a fine of $100, was cynically regarded by sellers as a kind of unofficial business expense levied sporadically to appease reform groups. The principle of adult responsibility also was applied against parents and employers, but only in cases in which they were responsible for a child's nonattendance at school. The unique aspect of the Adult Delinquency Law was that it applied to *all* persons "causing or contributing to" the delinquency of a minor. Penalties could include a thousand-dollar fine and a jail sentence up to one year. No sooner was the new statute on the books than a "Lindsey Ultimatum," as the *Denver Post* described it, was issued, warning tobacco and liquor dealers that the harsher penalties would be fully enforced.[10]

The capstone of the 1903 legislation was a general law allowing the county courts to hear cases in which the defendant was under twenty-one. Minors between sixteen and twenty-one found guilty of a crime could, at the discretion of the court, be placed on probation on the same terms that applied to children covered by the Juvenile Delinquent Law. With this feature added, the "Juvenile Court" of Denver acquired a larger potential docket of children's cases than any comparable court in the country, including the original Chicago Juvenile Court. The main outlines of the new system were now drawn. But the system was not yet complete.

In March 1907 Lindsey enthusiastically wrote to Lincoln Steffens that he had won a major victory on the court front.[11] The Judge had in mind the Juvenile Court Act which he had just lobbied through the legislature. Lindsey was pleased that the new law, which finally instituted a separate juvenile court in each county and called it so officially, also endowed it with all of the rule-making powers vested in other courts of record. There would be more clerks and probation officers, and their salaries and appointments would no longer be subject to the patronage of the county Board of Commissioners. Best of all, Lindsey informed Steffens, the legislature gave the juvenile courts the sweeping jurisdiction he had proposed. In broad language, the latest "Lindsey bill" gave the courts original jurisdiction

> in all criminal cases or other actions or proceedings in which the disposition, custody or control of any child or minor, or any other person, may be involved under the acts concerning delinquent, dependent or neglected children, or any other acts, statutes, or law of the state now or hereafter existing concerning dependent, delinquent, or neglected children, or which may in any manner concern or relate to the person, liberty, correction, protection, morality, control, adoption, or disposition of any infant, child, or minor, of any parent, guardian, or any other person, corporation, or institution whatsoever.

In most respects Lindsey's elation over the Juvenile Court Act was justified. The law did establish his Juvenile Court formally as a part of the Colorado judicial system, where it has permanently remained. Ironically, however, one of Lindsey's chief aims under the law was repeatedly frustrated by the state Supreme Court. Lindsey maintained that the statute gave the juvenile courts jurisdiction over every case in which the offense involved the morals of a minor. Yet in 1915, in *Colias v. People,* a case involving an act of pederasty between father and son, the Supreme Court of Colorado held that it was uncertain that the legislature meant to give juvenile courts a general right to try adults for crime when the custody of the child was not technically under consideration.[12] When three years later the high court reaffirmed its *Colias* decision in a case involving statutory rape,[13] Lindsey decided it was time for a campaign to "clarify" the intention of the 1907 law. After a hard fight he believed he had won when the legislature, in 1923, adopted an amendment which seemed to remove any possible ambiguity in the 1907 law by providing that the Juvenile Court would have concurrent jurisdiction in "any criminal case ... concerning any adult person for the violation of any law of this state where the offense charged ... shall be against the person or concerns the morals or the protection of a person under 21 years of age." During the Judge's remaining few years on the Colorado bench, the Juvenile Court of Denver again tried adults in cases involving incest, statutory rape, and "indecent liberties." In 1932, however, the Supreme Court, in another statutory rape case, again showed its resistance to any effort to give the Juvenile Court felony jurisdiction over adults. The court declared that the language of the 1923 amendment still was not strong enough to give a general criminal jurisdiction over adults, even when minors were involved as victims. In view of the fact that the amendment had used the word *any* three separate times, a dissenting justice asked, "If, by the language used, the Legislature has failed to accomplish its purpose, pray what language could it select in order to make its will effective?" The question may have had weight in logic, but it was only a dissenting opinion in law.[14] At least there was consolation in the fact that the juvenile courts of Colorado continued to keep their adult misdemeanor jurisdiction in contributory delinquency cases and in dependency situations where parents or other responsible persons neglected or failed to support a child.[15]

As a result of his experiences in the courtroom, Lindsey eventually concluded that the various laws he was required to enforce, including some of those he had personally drafted, did not always achieve substantial justice. The adult contributory laws were a case in point. Lindsey had been responsible for putting two such laws on the books. The first was his 1903 statute providing for a fine of $1,000 or a one-year jail sentence, or both, for any adult who contributed to the delinquency of a minor. The other was a 1905 law applicable to parents or other responsible persons who contributed to juvenile dependency or were guilty of child neglect. The original bill drafted by Lindsey provided the same penalties for contributing to dependency as to delinquency, but the legislature reduced them to a fine of $100, ninety days in jail, or both. By 1909 Lindsey was ready to be even more flexible than the legislature had been. After all, putting a father in jail for ninety days or taking $100 from him did not help to feed or clothe his dependent children. To be sure, both the contributory delinquency and dependency laws allowed the judge to suspend sentence, but they remained *criminal* statutes, and a suspended sentence was applied only to someone who had just been given an indelible criminal record.[16]

The alternative Lindsey now proposed was a civil proceeding in equity, an idea that had been introduced in some discussions he had held earlier with other authorities in juvenile court matters such as Judge Julian Mack of Chicago and Bernard Flexner, whose articles in the leading journal of the settlement and charities organizations, *Charities and the Commons,* had further publicized it. Under the more flexible rules of the branch of law known as equity or chancery, the courts were free to consider all the factors in a particular situation and formulate an "equitable decree." When the hearing was over, the court kept jurisdiction over the parties and could see that its orders were carried out. Yet in the whole process *nobody got a criminal record.* There was, however, a "gun behind the door." A person who failed to comply with a directive of the court could be fined or imprisoned for civil contempt. In 1966 Judge Philip Gilliam of the Denver Juvenile Court said that Lindsey's 1909 civil contributory law was his greatest single accomplishment in the field of juvenile legislation. Although an occasional criminal prosecution for contributing to juvenile delinquency or dependency is still heard in the Denver Juvenile Court, Lindsey's 1909 civil statute continues to be the basis for several hundred petitions each year, chiefly in contributory dependency cases against fathers for nonsupport. Aside from petitions filed against boys for misconduct (the main business of the court), the "Lindsey petitions" constitute the largest category of proceedings before the Denver court.[17]

In the Master of Discipline Act of 1909, Lindsey made further use of flexible equity procedures when he sponsored a bill involving appointment of masters or referees of the kind familiarly used in bankruptcy proceedings. The statute permitted judges to appoint a responsible adult, with the power of a court clerk to issue orders, who would have the right to investigate cases of juvenile delinquency and child neglect. If necessary, the master could be authorized to superintend a child's probation. In Denver, Lindsey used the law to appoint a woman clerk of the court as referee or "assistant judge" in charge of girl delinquents. Outside Denver the law helped to relieve overburdened county judges by permitting them to delegate authority to teachers, principals, social workers, and other laymen who served as masters.[18]

A child-support law successfully sponsored by Lindsey in 1911 gave two forms of protection to *all* children. The statute eliminated the distinction between legitimate and illegitimate offspring as far as the duty of support was concerned, and imposed a further duty on the father of an illegitimate child to contribute to the support of the mother during childbirth and any attendant illness. In order to make extradition possible if the father moved to another state, violation of the statute was made a felony. A conditional suspended sentence was usually invoked when the father resided in Colorado.

A final legislative victory achieved by Lindsey in the years before World War I involved newspaper publicity in children's cases. For several years the Judge's personal appeals to editors had helped keep the names of children in trouble out of the Denver papers.[19] There were occasional lapses, however, when a dramatic situation made the temptation to break a story too great. A 1913 Lindsey bill made it a misdemeanor to publish the name of any child who was called as a witness in any rape case, delinquency or dependency proceeding, or in any other case concerning the protection or correction of children. The bill also made it unlawful to photograph or make any kind of drawing of a child for any purpose covered by the act. Lindsey tried to make the bill palatable for the press by emphasizing that newspapers were still free to cover such stories as long as they did not divulge children's names or identities. The law was generally regarded as a success, though its spirit could sometimes be evaded by publishing information about children immediately after they were arrested but before they were arraigned.[20]

Lindsey did not confine his activities on behalf of children to lobbying for legislation, any more than he restricted his role as a judge to the conventional scope of the courtroom. During his earliest years on the bench Lindsey became the instigator of what might be called Denver's first anti-poverty campaign. He organized a Juvenile Improvement Association to gather statistics, call meetings, and publicize the needs of underprivileged children. Funds were raised to send orphans and slum children who had never been outside of downtown Denver to summer camps in the mountains, which for all their visibility might have been a thousand miles away as far as the street urchins of West Colfax Avenue were concerned. The association also worked with a sympathetic member of the Park Board in helping to get a grant from the city council to build public playgrounds. The Judge personally organized a Juvenile Athletic Association in which boys between the ages of ten and sixteen played at various field sports under the guidance of a court officer. Nor was Lindsey unwilling to resort to unorthodox methods to achieve his purposes, as the episode of the public baths demonstrated.

For more than two years the Judge had campaigned for public baths for newsboys and others who did not have decent facilities in their own homes. When the Board of Commissioners continued to procrastinate, Lindsey advised the boys in the neighborhood to play in the courthouse fountains, remarking that "if the citizens of Denver could afford a perpetual shower bath to a few bronze painted cherubs in a fountain, they could afford it to these more sensitive and grateful cherubs of flesh and blood, who were coated with dust and dirt." When policemen chased the dripping boys into the Judge's court-room, Lindsey noted that they had followed his advice to wear swimming trunks and refused to reprimand them. The board got the point. The "kids" soon had their regular public baths.[21]

Another aspect of Lindsey's activities as "Kids' Judge," as he was now popularly called, did not always appear in the newspapers but was known well enough by those who were touched by it. The Judge's bitter experience with poverty as an adolescent had made him acutely aware of the importance of a job in the development of self-confidence and self-respect in a young man. He made strenuous efforts to find jobs for boys when they were released from Industrial School, and wrote letters to those not yet released promising his support if their records showed they were "proving up." The boys' letters to the Judge suggested that something more than mere apple-polish-ing motivated them to correspond with him. The details they gave of life at the Industrial School demonstrated their belief that the Judge cared about them. The Judge's letters to them, though they invariably contained homilies, managed to avoid a sanctimonious tone by including bits of humor and trivia. The same qualities were revealed in Lindsey's numerous friendships with boys who were guilty of nothing more than swiping some ice cream or fruit. The Judge delighted in taking them to shows, going on weekend outings, and talking sports with them. The boys, in turn, found it easy to identify with the Judge.

The reason for the identification was not hard to find. There was always something of the child in Lindsey himself. In spite of the hard knocks of his youth and the grim in-fighting of Colo-rado politics, the Judge represented a curious combination of idealism, enthusiasm, and pragmatism that rarely failed to strike a responsive chord in his young friends. It found expression in a gamut of actions that ranged from participating in free-for-alls on country outings to earnest discussions of public issues with adolescents making their first fumbling efforts to understand the great world. On another level it was reflected in a romantic temperament which was expressed in an intense devotion to the theater. Whenever he was in New York, Lindsey found time to see a great number of plays and subsequently amazed his friends with his ability to mimic actors and re-enact scenes. A distinguished federal judge caught something of Lindsey's appeal to young people in a letter of condolence to Mrs. Lindsey just after the Judge's death in 1943:

> There is a recollection of him, personal to myself, which might be described as a sort of modest footnote to one stage of his career. I think that I should tell you of it.
> In the summer of 1907, during my student days, I was tent boss of a chautauqua circuit conducted by the Redpath Bureau in various Iowa towns. There were several of us, all students, employed about the tent. Each week Judge Lindsey came to us to lecture. At the close of the sessions he would almost invariably invite us to go along with him for a soda, and we would talk for a long time, becoming eventually well acquainted.
> He was then very slight of figure but of an energy almost too great for his frail body. We grew to love him for his toughness of mind, his utter sincerity, and the warmth of his heart toward humanity generally and especially young people. We looked forward each week to his visit. Doubtless he forgot those occasions, for he had so many like them through the years. But while I never saw him afterwards, my recollection of him is as vivid as though the time were yesterday.[22]

Lindsey's ability to relate to children was manifest in his conduct of the Juvenile Court of Denver. A juvenile court is not like an ordinary court. The fact that it is not so hamstrung by rules of procedure gives a presiding judge unique opportunities to make his influence felt at every stage of the proceedings. The style of the court inevitably reflects, for good or ill, the judge's personality and social outlook. The "Lindsey style" was especially striking in the Judge's treatment of juvenile delinquents.

As early as 1903 Lindsey asserted that the essential requirement for dealing effectively with juvenile delinquents was "to establish communication." To do so it was necessary to put oneself in the place of the child. Although adolescents did not speak about distrusting everybody over thirty in those innocent days, the viewpoint would not have been alien to many of them. Children in trouble, Lindsey believed, usually felt that the adult world was indifferent at best, hostile at worst. In all probability their contacts with their own parents (or parent), the "cops," and the ordinary run of judges made their viewpoint entirely reasonable. In an interview with a visiting journalist, Lindsey described the case of a twenty-year-old prisoner in another state under sentence of death for committing murder. The young man had been in and out of jails since the age of twelve. His first conviction was for stealing a razor to whittle kite sticks. Lindsey recalled his description of the courtroom scene:

> "It was this way," he explained. "The guy on the high bench with the whiskers says, 'What's the boy done, officer?' And the cop says, 'He's a bad kid, your Honor, and broke into a store and stole a razor.' And the guy on the high bench says, 'Ten dollars or ten days.' Time, three minutes; one round of a prize fight!" "I couldn't forget those dramatic last words," added [Lindsey,] "and I decided his story wouldn't be duplicated in Denver if I could help it."[23]

Lindsey "established communication" in a number of ways. To remove the physical barriers that separated judge and defendants, he lowered the court bench and discarded his judicial gown. Much of the work of the court was carried on in his private chambers, and Lindsey soon demonstrated his talent for achieving rapport with the boys.* A major reason for his success was his willingness to accept the boys' own values as a basis for appealing to them. The matter of "snitching" was a case in point.

Early in his judicial career Lindsey was struck with the fair-

* Girls' cases were usually handled by a woman who served as court clerk.

ness of a question asked by a small boy who had been brought to his court: "Say," the street gamin asked, "do yuh t'ink a fellah ought to snitch on a kid?" There was something about the way it was asked that made the Judge ashamed. After all, most respectable people had little love for a tattletale. Loyalty was generally counted a virtue. Furthermore, among boys at least, there was a very practical additional argument against "snitching." The snitcher, when discovered, would be held in utter contempt by his fellows and probably have his face "mashed in" for good measure. Lindsey resolved that no child in his court would ever be asked again to give the names of his accomplices.

Lindsey was well aware that this first step was not enough. He thought it essential to make the boys active allies of the court. They must not snitch on others, but they must be persuaded to snitch on themselves. The Judge believed that the new probation system would be crucial in persuading the boys to own up. Fear was the father of lies, and the knowledge that honesty might involve pleading guilty to an offense that would lead straight to a correction institution like Golden or Buena Vista hardly encouraged candor in the criminal courts. Lindsey was able to dispel this fear by convincing the boys that if they would be square with him they would receive a sympathetic hearing. When accomplices were involved, playing square required an earnest effort to persuade one's erstwhile partners in crime to snitch on themselves. The Judge's role in the process can be seen in a characteristic note to some anonymous addressees:[24]

Dear Boys:

    Earl _____, Frank _____, Joe _____, and Clarence _____ were told to come to this Court because they have been taking papers that did not belong to them. We know that there are eight or ten other boys who are taking papers that don't belong to them or who have been taking papers in the last year. I did not ask the boys to tell the names. They did not "snitch" on any of you, because I did not require them to. I supposed that you would come here without the officer coming after you.

    If you will come to court and promise to "cut it out," we won't send you up this time, but give you a chance to go home and behave yourselves and never take papers again. I have asked these boys to tell you to come here at four o'clock, Tuesday, January 25th, 1910, after school and I shall expect you to come.

Ben B. Lindsey
Judge of the Juvenile Court

That the "Lindsey system" worked was attested by the growing number of boys who came to the Court on their own, convinced that the Judge would give them a square deal. One hard-bitten Denver cynic, obviously a W. C. Fields prototype, observing Lindsey's success in bringing a tough gang of boys to the courthouse, reluctantly admitted to a reporter, "I don't see how he does it. The little rats fairly swarm up there."[25]

The secret of Lindsey's success was no mystery. In addition to the appeal of self-interest which he used, the Judge's empathy and imagination guided him in making a court session almost an entertainment. His techniques were most evident in the probationers' meetings held every other Saturday. Lincoln Steffens, sent out by *McClure's* in 1906 to cover "the Lindsey story," described a typical Saturday morning session:[26]

> The boys assemble early, two or three hundred of them, of all ages and all sorts, "small kids" and "big fellers"; well-dressed "lads" and ragged "little shavers"; burglars who have entered a store, and burglars who have "robbed back" pigeons; thieves who have stolen bicycles, and thieves who have "swiped" papers; "toughs" who have "sassed" a cop or stoned a conductor, and boys who have talked bad language to little girls, or who "hate their father," or who have been backward at school and played hookey because the teacher doesn't like them. It isn't generally known, and the Judge rarely tells just what a boy has done; the deed doesn't matter, you know, only the boy, and all boys look pretty much alike to the Judge, and to the boys. So they all come together there, except that boys who work, and newsboys when there's an extra out, are excused to come at another time. But nine o'clock Saturday morning finds most of the "fellers" in their seats, looking as clean as possible, and happy.
>
> The Judge comes in and, passing the bench, which looms up

empty and useless behind him, he takes his place, leaning against the clerk's table or sitting on a camp-chair.

"Boys," he begins, "last time I told you about Kid Dawson and some other boys who used to be with us and who 'made good.' Today I've got a letter from the Kid. He's in Oregon, and he's doing well. I'll read you what he says about himself and his new job."

And he reads the letter, which is full of details roughly set in a general feeling of encouragement and self-confidence.

"Fine, isn't it!" the Judge says. "Kid Dawson had a mighty hard time with himself for awhile, but you can see he's got his hand on his throttle now. Well, let's see. The last time I talked about 'snitching,' didn't I? Today I'm going to talk about 'ditching.'" And he is off on the address with which he opens court. His topics are always interesting to boys, for he handles his subjects boy-fashion. . . . "To ditch" a thing is to throw it away; and the Judge, starting off with stories of boys who have ditched their commitment papers, proceeds to tell about others who, "like Kid Dawson out there in Oregon," have "ditched" their bad habits and "got strong." I heard him on Arbor Day speak on trees; how they grew, some straight, some crooked. There's always a moral in these talks, but the Judge makes it plain and blunt; he doesn't "rub it in."

After the address, which is never long, the boys are called up by schools. Each boy is greeted by himself, but the Judge uses only his given or nickname. "The boys from the Arapahoe Street School," he calls, and, as the group comes forward, the Judge reaches out and seizing one by the shoulder, pulls him up to him, saying:

"Skinny, you've been doing fine lately; had a crackerjack report every time. I just want to see if you have kept it up. Bet you have. Let's see." He opens the report. "That's great. Shake, Skin. You're all right, you are." Skinny shines.

Pointing at another, he says: "And you, Mumps, you got only 'fair' last time. What you got this time? You promised me excellent and I know you've made good." He tears open the envelope. "Sure," he says. "You've done it. Bully for you." Turning to the room, he tells the "fellers" how Mumps began playing hookey, and was so weak he simply thought he couldn't stay in school. "He blamed the teacher; said she was down on him. She wasn't at all. He was just weak, Mumps was; he had no backbone at all. But look at him now. He's bracing right up. You watch Mumps. He's the 'stuff,' Mumps is. Aren't you Mumps? Teacher likes you now all right, doesn't she? Yes. And she tells me she does. Go on now and keep it up, Mumps. I believe in you."

"Hearts and flowers!" "Lindsey's Sunday School!" the cynics scoffed. The Judge was accused of being an easy mark by those who were confident that the answer to juvenile delinquency was stricter enforcement of the laws. If their premise were true, their conclusion was sound, for the basic method of the court was not the enforcement of the laws but the suspension of them through the probation system. The humane theory underlying juvenile probation (and adult probation too, for that matter) was that most offenders were more likely to be reformed by being given a chance to live under unobtrusive supervision within society than by being forced to live exclusively with convicted criminals, even in the best-run correctional institution. With Lindsey this belief was an article of faith. But it was not a blind faith, and he did not forget that it applied only to *most* offenders. Similarly, his willingness to give delinquents a second chance, and sometimes even more than that, was not grounded on mere sentimentality. The court, working with the community, must become an educational force for the building of character, he wrote to a fellow judge in Georgia who solicited his views on the proper role of juvenile courts. In building character, trust was usually the best method, but sometimes the child was not ready for it. A juvenile court must take many factors into account, Lindsey advised, because "it is only through a system of this kind that we can avoid the dangers of the old jail methods, on the one hand . . . and probably just as great dangers, on the other hand, of kindness, frequently mistaken for weakness—or, in short, the effects of seeming leniency which, strange to say, seems to produce much the same results as those of brutality, although in my judgment not quite so bad."[27]

The phrase "seeming leniency" epitomized Lindsey's conviction that though there was no justice without love, conversely there could be no love without justice. In practical terms, commitment to the Reform School or the Industrial School was sometimes the only answer. Lindsey reached such decisions reluctantly because he considered commitment never a very good answer. Once made, however, he was ready to defend such decisions. His reaction when Governor J. B. Orman pardoned two young offenders whom he had sentenced to Golden showed that the Judge was not the mindless do-gooder his critics sometimes accused him of being. Lindsey assured Orman that he had no doubt that the governor's action was motivated by a "kindly and humane spirit," but he reminded Orman that he never sent a boy to the Industrial School until "we have exhausted every power to help him at home." Both boys, the Judge pointed out, had repeatedly violated their probation, and their home surroundings provided no basis for expecting a change of heart. Finally, Lindsey warned, their careers had been so notorious that their unmerited pardons had a demoralizing effect on the other boys at Golden and weakened the entire probationary system. Though the governor could not undo the pardons, Lindsey's realistic appeal had its effect when he replied to the Judge, "I have noticed all you say and will, in future, before pardoning any one from that institution, refer the matter to you for such facts and recommendations as you may desire to make."[28]

Among Lindsey's accomplishments as Judge of the Juvenile Court of Denver, one especially caught the popular imagination: his creation of an honor system whereby certain boys who were sentenced to the state Industrial School were allowed to carry their own commitment papers and report there unaccompanied by an officer. The "Lindsey Honor System" had two goals in mind. The first was to diminish petty graft under the fee system that gave the sheriff's office a fixed amount for taking each prisoner to a correctional institution. Since no proof was required of the number of trips made, it was in the interest of the sheriff and his deputies to take as many prisoners as possible in one trip and charge the county separately for a larger number. In this respect Colorado practice was not unique. The amount of graft enjoyed by the sheriff's office under the widely prevalent fee system, which often also included paying a fixed fee for the maintenance of each prisoner in the county jail, was so great that it was a common practice in many parts of the country to make the sheriff ineligible to succeed himself in office. Lindsey resolved that the fee system, which he had already attacked in regard to child arrests and trials in magistrates' courts, would be further weakened in cases involving transportation and commitment.

Lindsey's second motive in establishing an honor system was even more fundamental. The Judge considered it an important technique in the character-building role of his court. A boy who "made it" from Denver to Golden won a double moral victory. He proved his loyalty and his strength as well. The loyalty was to the Judge who trusted him and who would be hurt by his political enemies if the boy violated his trust. Lindsey freely described his appeal to the boys he put on their honor, and consciously injected a sportsmanlike challenge into the entire procedure. The "cops" and other law enforcement officers were betting against them, Lindsey told the boys. But the Judge was gambling that they had enough "sand" not to "let him down." Thus Lindsey attempted to use the boys' respect for strength—which they had often identified with defiance of law—as a motive for obeying the law.

Lindsey began the practice in 1903. At first his critics said it would never work. By the middle of 1905 the Judge claimed to have sent forty-two boys to Golden without losing one of them. A visiting hypnotist in Denver won brief notoriety by suggesting that Lindsey's amazing record proved that the Judge had mastered the art of hypnotism. The Judge disavowed this dubious compliment from the "professional Svengali" with the comment that the simple truth was more interesting. As the years went by, Lindsey continued to send some of the boys he committed to the state Industrial School without a guard. By the time he left the Denver court in 1927, he had sent several hundred boys to Golden without escort and claimed to have lost only five of them. The Judge's pride in this accomplishment was evident in his practice of including it in every entry of his biographical sketch in *Who's Who* until the time of his death.[29]

On one dramatic occasion in 1915 the honor and loyalty that Lindsey advocated for youngsters was tested when the Judge found himself in the unusual position of being a defendant. The case involved a charge of criminal contempt and challenged one of Lindsey's most cherished principles. The specific issue was the Judge's refusal to testify in a murder trial about a confidential talk he had held with a young boy concerning the murder of his father. Apparently the father, John Wright, was a brutal drunkard who regularly beat his wife as well as their twelve-year-old son. After one particularly vicious beating, Bertha Wright bought a revolver "for self-defense." Her husband had allegedly threatened to return and "throw her out of the house." When he did return, he was fatally shot just after he entered the family living room. He lived long enough to sign a statement that his wife had shot him.

The case for the prosecution looked easy until the Wright boy went to the district attorney and claimed that his mother was withholding information in order to shield him. The twelve-year-old declared that his mother was threatening to kill herself when his father entered the house, that he was trying to wrest the revolver from his mother, and that it fired accidentally while they were struggling. The district attorney refused to believe the boy's story, regarding it as a typical defense lawyer's trick to save a guilty client. The prosecution of the mother would continue.

Shortly after the boy's "confession," Judge Lindsey had a private talk with the boy. Apparently, after Lindsey assured the boy that he, as a judge, could not be compelled to testify about their conversation, the boy repudiated the story he had told the district attorney. In the subsequent trial of Bertha Wright, the district attorney called Lindsey as a witness for the prosecution to discredit the boy's story. Judge Lindsey refused to testify, claiming that the boy was now within the jurisdiction of his court and that any prior conversation between them was a privileged communication. Besides claiming a right not to testify, Lindsey declared that important moral and practical considerations were at stake. The effectiveness of the juvenile court system depended to no small degree on young people's confidence that a judge would not betray their trust. If a judge "ditched" them at the first threat of a legal reprisal, how could they ever trust him or the system again?

The jury acquitted Bertha Wright. It was widely believed that her son's testimony was a major factor in the result. For his refusal to testify, however, Ben Lindsey was fined $500. Lindsey's role in the case was widely discussed. A sympathetic Upton Sinclair proposed that newsboys all over the country contribute a penny apiece to pay the fine of "the Judge who would not snitch." Lindsey was delighted with the idea, and thousands of pennies were soon arriving in the mail. An anonymous poet in the *Brooklyn Eagle* celebrated "Ben Lindsey's Fine":

> There's loyalty when kids combine
>   More strong than that of men is;
> And boys will pay Ben Lindsey's fine
>   With fifty thousand pennies.
>
> The judge but scorned the latest sign
>   Of hatred and of grudges;
> And stands erect, although the fine
>   Is backed by other judges.
>
> He wouldn't "snitch upon a kid"
>   Whose words were confidential;
> His mood is pride in what he did
>   And never penitential.
>
> All Denver loves a curveless spine;

Hate smothered in her den is;
And boys will pay Ben Lindsey's fine
With fifty thousand pennies.

Lindsey did not accept defeat without a fight, and challenged the fine all the way to the Supreme Court of the United States. The Supreme Court of Colorado first gave the appeal a full hearing. Four members of the court, a majority, held that the doctrine of privileged communications did not apply and the fine must stand. The remaining three justices joined forces in a dissenting opinion based on Lindsey's view that the fine was a blow at juvenile courts everywhere. The majority opinion, they declared, was "technical in character, narrow in construction," and "not in harmony with modern and enlightened jurisprudence." Commentators in the *Harvard Law Review* and *Yale Law Journal* agreed, siding with Lindsey and the dissenting Colorado justices. The Supreme Court of the United States refused to pass on the merits of the conflicting claims, however, on the ground that it had no jurisdiction in such a case. Thus the 4 to 3 decision of the Colorado Supreme Court stood, and Lindsey paid the fine after almost six years of litigation.[30]

By the end of his first decade on the court, Lindsey had made remarkable progress in winning acceptance for the underlying goal of his court—"to put a little love in the law," as he expressed it to the English theosophist Annie Besant. From a county court that heard a few cases involving children on the basis of a strained interpretation of a school law, he had transformed the Juvenile Court of Denver into the best-known court of its kind in the world and the first juvenile *and* domestic relations court in the United States. At the same time Lindsey was becoming increasingly convinced that enlightened legislation for children was not enough. The protection of children was part of a larger problem. It could only be meaningfully achieved in a just and humane society. When the Judge therefore began to fight the necessary battles to win "the war against privilege," he became the most controversial figure in Colorado.[31]

3 / Fighting the Establishment

AS LAWYER AND JUDGE, LINDSEY CAME ACROSS MANY EXAMPLES of the corrupting influence of "the interests" on American society. As a teen-ager in Tennessee he had been moved by Victor Hugo's *Les Misèrables,* and the similarity between Jean Valjean's theft of a loaf of bread and Tony Costello's theft of a few lumps of coal did not escape him. How different, after all, from nineteenth-century France was a "democratic" society that allowed the representatives of corporate greed to use a man twelve hours a day until he was too old or sick to go on, and then leave his family to the ignominy of the poorhouse or the dubious bounty of private charity? How different from justice handed down by an absolutist regime was a system of law that could be circumvented by the bribery of a single juror?

At the same time he was fighting the saloon-keepers of Denver, Lindsey uncovered quite by accident a spectacular case of graft involving a more sedate business. On a Saturday morning in May 1902 the Judge noticed a package of ledger sheets lying on a chair in his clerk's office. They came from the Smith-Brooks Printing Company, which by contract supplied stationery to county offices. On top of the package was a bill for $280 for a thousand sheets of paper. Lindsey sent the clerk, Thomas Bonfils, to Smith-Brooks to ask if a mistake had been made. The Smith-Brooks representative refused to comment on the price of the ledger paper and told Bonfils that the bill had been sent to him by mistake. It should have gone to the clerk *of the Board of Commissioners,* "as usual." On hearing this,

Lindsey's suspicions were aroused. He decided upon a ruse to discover the charges for other items. He sent a message to Smith-Brooks claiming that he had reason to believe that his court was being charged for supplies it had never received. Possibly, the Judge suggested, his accounts were mixed up with those of some other courts. Would it be possible to see the bills? On this occasion Smith-Brooks was apparently less cautious and sent Lindsey a sheaf of bills. They confirmed his suspicions that the company was following a consistent pattern of gross overcharging. Lindsey now wrote to the Board of Commissioners and asked if they knew what was being charged for county office supplies. He received no answer. After ten days he wrote again. Another week later he wrote a third letter threatening a public investigation. This produced results.[1]

Lindsey was visited by Tom Phillips, chairman of the Board of Commissioners. Phillips assured the Judge of his own innocence but pointed the finger at two of his colleagues, Fred Watts and Frank Bishop. Phillips gave Lindsey access to county records which revealed an extensive system of graft based on fake bids and trick specifications as well as inflated prices. When rumors about Lindsey's investigation began to spread in political circles, the Judge soon discovered that he was up against the same alternating pattern of cajolery and threats that he was encountering in his campaign against the wine rooms. First there was the dual appeal to party loyalty and personal obligation. The commissioners were Democrats, part of the same faction that had put Lindsey himself on the bench. "Don't be an ingrate," pleaded John T. Bottom, attorney for the commissioners, who urged the Judge to spare "the boys." A minor official told Lindsey that these men had appointed him to office and that he did not "give a damn if they stole the county blind." When pleas failed they were followed by threats of political ruination and social ostracism to make it plain that the Judge would not have an important friend left in Denver if he persisted in his folly. Nevertheless, Lindsey passed the incriminating evidence to the *Rocky Mountain News,* thus forcing a reluctant district attorney eventually to indict the commissioners.[2]

The aftermath was an anti-climax, at least as far as the fate of the commissioners was concerned. District Attorney Harry Lindsley, a prominent Democrat, chose to indict them only for a misdemeanor, and an amiable judge who was brought in from out of town in order to give them an "impartial" trial imposed a fine of $10 on each of them. More constructively, the affair put an end to at least one of the more outrageous forms of bilking the public treasury. Perhaps the episode's greatest significance, however, lay in the part it played in developing Lindsey's ideas about the relationship between crime and economic privilege. In the process he developed a style and vocabulary which placed him squarely in the muckraking spirit of the age and helped build his national reputation.

For Lindsey the printing scandal came to epitomize the operations of the corrupt alliance between business and government. It took nearly a year to bring the commissioners to trial. In the meantime they continued in office, and during the period gave a rebate of $70,000 in back taxes to the Denver Tramway Company. A citizens' reform organization, the Municipal League, had attempted to enjoin the commissioners from granting the rebate but had been rebuffed by Judge Peter L. Palmer.* John T. Bottom, who allegedly urged Lindsey "to go easy on the boys" in the printing scandal, argued on behalf of the commissioners' right to grant the rebate. Charles J. Hughes, Jr., a prominent Democrat, served as attorney for the tramway company in the proceeding. He had simultaneously begun to represent the commissioners in the pending criminal trial against them for their role in the Smith-Brooks deal. "Is it possible," the *Denver Post* speculated, "that the fact that Charles J. Hughes, Jr., is also attorney for the Commissioners in the crim-

---

* Palmer was the same District Judge who had held the ordinance forbidding women to be served in the wine rooms to be an unconstitutional infringement of their equal rights.

inal cases brought against them in connection with the county printing steals, has had anything to do with the Board's action in this matter of tax compromise with the tramway?" "It *was* faintly possible," Lindsey commented sarcastically.[3]

Lindsey's views were strengthened when he attended a meeting of the Democratic executive committee after the commissioners' trial began. The Judge was no longer a member of the committee and soon discovered that his presence was most unwelcome. District Attorney Lindsley, after glancing pointedly in the Judge's direction, made a successful motion that only members of the committee be allowed to speak. Lindsey recalled that it was the same Harry Lindsley who had procrastinated when he had sought his help in prosecuting the saloon-keepers. Charles J. Hughes, Jr., a member of the committee, made an impassioned plea against a resolution which called for honesty in public officials. The principle was admirable, Hughes asserted (he was soon on his way to the United States Senate), but its adoption under the circumstances would be regarded as an attack upon loyal members of the party who had "faithfully served the county" for many years. The resolution was defeated.[4]

As Lindsey reviewed the first decade of his career in Colorado politics, he thought of the many instances of corruption he had encountered. He recalled the time when a prominent Republican politician had attempted to bribe him and his law partner with a promise of "legitimate" legal fees from the Denver Tramway Company if they would stop their campaign on behalf of the three-fourths jury bill. He remembered how his ambitious partner was warned that he must not offend the Denver Union Water Company, or the Denver Gas and Electric Company, or the Mountain States Telephone and Telegraph Company, if he wanted the further support of Republican leaders in Denver. He learned firsthand, as a member of the finance committee of his own Democratic party, that the utilities companies were the most truly nonpartisan elements in Colorado, supporting with fine impartiality any politician from either party who would help to maintain or enlarge their franchises. Lindsey also remembered an occasion when he mentioned to a Denver banker the name of an attorney whom he wished to suggest to the governor for a newly created vacancy on the state Supreme Court. "The Governor?" said the banker. "Why, he hasn't anything to do with it. Don't you know the deal is to let the committee name the judges?" The banker went on to explain that a candidate who did not have the support of an informal group representing the public utilities, the railroads, and the Colorado Fuel and Iron Company would not have a "show." The support of William G. Evans, president of the Denver Tramway Company, could be crucial. And what were the criteria for winning their support? The candidate must be able to convince these gentlemen that he was "sound" on matters that concerned their interests. The record of the Colorado Supreme Court in cases involving such matters as the eight-hour law, the use of martial law during strikes, and the fraudulent conduct of franchise elections satisfied Lindsey that "the system" did indeed embrace even the highest court in the state.[5]

Lindsey was never a passive onlooker in Denver politics. As the occupant of an elective office, he soon discovered that he could not be. Either he must play the game by keeping silent about certain matters, or risk having his judicial career brought to an abrupt end. His "troublemaking" during his first year in office, when he began to wage war on the wine rooms, had led to an attempt by other Democratic officeholders to knife him. Reluctant to launch a frontal attack on him because of the favorable publicity his work with the children was getting, they gave him a nomination but tried to make it worthless by passing the word in the downtown wards that Lindsey's name should be scratched from the ticket in favor of his Republican opponent. Their efforts in the lower wards were successful, but Lindsey did so well in the residential and higher-income districts that he ran ahead of the Democratic ticket in the city as a whole and defeated his Republican opponent by more than two thousand votes. Among the Judge's supporters were those who did not yet realize that his attacks would not always be confined to saloon-keepers and petty politicians.[6]

Until 1904 Lindsey had not met head on the political power of the utilities companies of Denver. The first clash came as a result of the apparent jurisdiction* of his court over certain disputes growing out of the notoriously fraudulent conduct of the election in the spring of that year. At that time Robert W. Speer, a Democrat, had supposedly defeated Republican John W. Springer in the mayoralty campaign. Springer filed suit in Lindsey's court, claiming he would have won if the honest ballots only were counted. The Speer-Springer contest was no simple bipartisan affair, however. A strong faction in the Republican party, headed by William G. Evans (usually called "Boss" Evans by the Democratic *Rocky Mountain News* and the independent *Denver Post*), had supported Speer. Evans was president of the Denver Tramway Company and had reason to believe that Speer would be less hostile to the utilities companies than Springer, who was identified with the clean-government element in the Republican party. The utilities companies had been under fire for several years and had managed, only after a bitter fight in 1902–1903, to defeat a liberal charter which would have substantially limited their franchises. They were now determined not to let an "unsound" man sit in the mayor's office.

The whole matter was first broached to Lindsey in June 1904 by Milton Smith, chairman of the state Democratic Central Committee. Smith asked the Judge to make a ruling that his court had no jurisdiction over the disputed election. Lindsey might feel embarrassed, Smith suggested, at having to pass on controversies about an election in which he himself had been a candidate. The Speer forces hoped to have a change of venue

* The Supreme Court ultimately held that county courts such as Lindsey's did not have jurisdiction over these disputes.

and had lined up a friendly judge elsewhere. Lindsey refused to accede to Smith's request, even though he was not unmindful that his uncooperative attitude, following closely his open conflict with the party leadership over the printing scandal, probably branded him a hopeless maverick.

Shortly after his unpleasant interview with Smith, Lindsey had a visit from his former law partner, Fred Parks, now a successful Republican state senator.[7] Parks, in Lindsey's opinion, had reached the conclusion some time ago that the only way to get ahead in politics was to sell out to "the interests," and had proceeded to do so. The two men had dissolved their partnership, but they were not yet enemies. Parks indicated that he had been in touch with Mayor Speer, as well as "Boss" Evans, and that it had been agreed that he would serve alongside Democrat Charles Hughes as counsel for the mayor. The arrangement would give Speer's defense a bipartisan look, according to Parks. Parks then made his proposition to his former partner. His appointment as Speer's counsel, Parks confided, depended upon his ability to persuade Lindsey to dismiss the case on the ground of jurisdiction. He implied, but did not directly state, that Lindsey would share in the large legal fee he had been promised if the Judge would consent. He also argued, at considerable length, that Lindsey would never have another chance of winning a Democratic nomination if he declined the offer. The Judge, apparently feeling that a refusal based solely on moral grounds would be incomprehensible to Parks, tried to show his former partner how he would be permanently vulnerable to blackmail if he agreed to such a scheme. But Parks was not persuaded by this argument and left the Judge's home angry and empty-handed. It was the end of their friendship.[8]

Whatever his opinion of Parks, Lindsey was now certain that one part of his ex-partner's analysis was correct. His chance of being renominated by the Democrats was probably nil. On his return from a month's lecture tour in the East, Lindsey began to cultivate his friendships within the liberal faction of the Republican party. In the Judge's favor was the prestige and popularity he enjoyed as a result of his Juvenile Court work. His name on the Republican ballot might strengthen the whole ticket. Also, reform elements among the Republicans were impressed by his denunciation of graft by fellow Democrats. By late summer Lindsey was convinced that he had clinched the Republican nomination when he was privately assured by party leaders that the "old guard" had decided not to oppose him. The Judge was soon in for a rude shock, however.

On the evening that the Republican caucus met to send its nominations to the party convention, Lindsey learned from a friend that the word had been quietly passed to endorse Hubert L. Shattuck for the judgeship. Lindsey panicked as he feared he would not be nominated on either party ticket. He sought counsel from his young Republican friends, who advised him to appeal to David H. Moffat, president of the First National Bank of Denver, a man considered influential in Republican circles. The Judge declined on the ground that he did not know Moffat. Instead he decided to try his luck with Walter S. Cheesman, president of the Denver Union Water Company, who had given him financial help in his earlier campaigns for public playgrounds and baths. Cheesman was polite but immovable. He confirmed the rumors Lindsey had heard that "Boss" Evans had sent a telegram from New York firmly opposing the Judge's nomination on the Republican ticket. Cheesman confided to Lindsey that he had discussed the matter with E. B. Field, president of the Mountain States Telegraph and Telephone Company. They were sorry, Cheesman said, that Evans' stand would almost certainly mean an end to the Judge's career. "But," he went on, "Mr. Evans represents our interests and we cannot very well question his judgment. If Mr. Evans were here, I'd make an exception in your favor and see him about it. But he's in New York. . . ." Lindsey pleaded to no avail with Cheesman to send a telegram to Evans, requesting him to reconsider.

Finally he asked Cheesman if he would personally support him as an independent candidate. Cheesman said he was sorry, but it was impossible.

Lindsey weighed the obstacles facing an independent candidate in a straight-ticket election system and decided that his only chance of winning was to obtain the Republican nomination. He began an all-out effort in this direction. The *Post* and the *Rocky Mountain News* lent their support, accusing the Republican leadership of treachery for having led the Judge to believe that they would not oppose him in his effort to continue his good work with the children. More important, perhaps, such young Republican comers as Edward P. Costigan, James C. Starkweather, and James H. Causey stuck by him and worked hard to win the support of doubtful delegates to the convention. Finally, Lindsey's friends helped fill the galleries of the old Coliseum Hall with hundreds of supporters, including many children who cheered for the Judge's name and booed his opponents. And it worked. Lindsey's opponent, "Bert" Shattuck, finally withdrew his name, and Lindsey was nominated by acclamation. The Democrats, fearing the Judge's popularity would be a powerful asset for the whole Republican ticket, grudgingly gave him their own nomination, thus ironically guaranteeing his bipartisan 1904 election victory.[9]

The years that followed were no more tranquil. In 1906 the Judge ran as an independent candidate for governor.* By 1908 he had sufficiently alienated the leadership of both parties that neither would give him a nomination. On this occasion Lindsey ran for re-election as an independent. It would be a prerequisite for victory, he decided, to explain to the voters the corrupting influence of "the interests" on both major parties. At his own expense he printed an exposé which he called *The Rule of the Plutocracy in Colorado: A Retrospect and a Warning*. The sixty-eight-page booklet traced in considerable detail the in-

* For Lindsey's gubernatorial campaign, see Chapter 5.

fluence of public utilities companies on the government and politics of Denver and Colorado over a period of eight years. It attacked the same politicians and corporation officers whom Lindsey had so often blasted in the press. Its importance might have been confined to helping Lindsey win the 1908 election were it not for one happy coincidence.

Just after the printing of *The Rule of the Plutocracy*, Upton Sinclair was making his first cross-country trip. The well-known Socialist writer had heard of Lindsey and stopped in Denver to meet him and watch his Juvenile Court in action. When Sinclair left for California, the Judge gave him a copy of the manuscript account of his war with "organized corruption." Sinclair read it on the train and enthusiastically wired *Everybody's Magazine* in New York that here was a story with possibilities. The magazine opened negotiations with Lindsey and soon sent out Harvey O'Higgins, one of its bright young men, to expand the story, rewrite it, and put it in a national context. Lindsey and O'Higgins worked well together and formed a lifelong friendship. O'Higgins added his characteristic literary flourish to the Judge's efforts, and in October 1909 *Everybody's* began serial publication of what was now called "The Beast and the Jungle." A year later, Doubleday, Page and Company published the articles in book form as *The Beast*.[10]

"The Beast" was but another name for "the system" excoriated by Lincoln Steffens, Ida Tarbell, Samuel Hopkins Adams, and other muckrakers in *McClure's, Everybody's,* and *Cosmopolitan*. Metaphorically, Lindsey compared it to the hidden tiger in a child's picture puzzle. On the surface there would appear to be merely a forest of trees and dense underbrush. The problem was "to find the cat." The child would gradually see emerging a tail among the branches, an ear in the underbrush, a paw in the crook of a tree limb. Finally, upon completing the picture, the child discovered not a gentle domestic pet but a crouching beast of the jungle with bared fangs, ready to leap upon the unwary.

The Judge and O'Higgins warned their readers in the heady prose of the day:

> There is hidden in our complicated American civilization just such a beast of the jungle. It is not a picture in a picture puzzle. It is a fact in a fact puzzle. There is no man among us, in any sort of public business or profession, who has not seen its tail or its paw concealed among the upper branches, or its eyes and ears watching and listening in the lowest underbrush and fallen timber of our life. It is there—waiting. To some it has appeared to be a house cat merely; and it has purred to them very soothingly, no doubt. But some have come upon its claws, and they have been rather more than scratched. And others have found its teeth, and they have been bitten—bitten to the soul. A few, who have watched it and stalked it carefully, know that it is, at the last, very like the dragon in the old fable of Greece, to whom some of the people were daily sacrificed. For it lives upon us—upon the best of us as well as the worst—and the daughters of the poor are fed to it no less than the sons of the rich. If you save your life from it, it is at the price of your liberty, of your humanity, of your faith with your fellows, whom you must hand over to it, helpless. And if you attack it—![11]

The Beast was Lindsey's story of what happened when he did attack it. It was a conflict that could not be avoided, the Judge asserted. The "interests" always recognized the reformer as their implacable enemy. The chief source of the sickness of society was the greed of entrenched economic privilege. It was the root cause of juvenile delinquency. To attack one was to attack the other, for

> criminals are born *and* criminals are bred, but the conditions of which they are born and under which they are bred in Denver are the same conditions that debauch our Legislature, our judiciary, our press, our business life, and our poor. I found no "problem of the children" that was not also the problem of their parents. The young bud was blighted by the same corruption that infected the twig, killed the branch and ate out the heart of the trunk. The rule of the plutocracy in Denver was the cause of three-quarters of the crime in Denver. The dependent and delinquent children who

came into my court came almost wholly from the homes of dependent and delinquent parents who were made such by the hopeless economic conditions of their lives; and those conditions were made hopeless by the remorseless tyranny of wealthy men who used their lawless power to enslave and brutalize and kill their workmen. Legislatures, corrupted by corporate wealth, refused to pass the eight-hour law that would give the child's home a parent able to fulfil his parental duties—refused to pass the employers' liability law that would save the widows from starvation and the children from the streets—refused to pass even a "three-fourths jury" law that would allow the victim of corporate greed to obtain a little pittance of justice in the courts. . . . I could not do my duty toward the children without attacking the conditions that deformed the lives of the children. And when I tried to do *this* . . . the Beast replied: "Then you shall not be allowed to save even the little children."[12]

Lindsey was an inveterate correspondent, and his private letters also reflected his liberal belief that crime and "sin" were usually caused by economic injustice rather than Adam's fall. "The kingdom of God on earth must come," he wrote to William Allen White, "but I do not believe it ever can come until we deal not only with the hearts of men, but [also with] those conditions . . . which are more or less responsible for the kinds of hearts they have. . . ."[13] Similarly, though the Judge flirted with the Prohibition movement, he was impatient with reformers who talked as if the "evil of drink" were the chief trouble of the times. He gently chided Billy Sunday and other clergymen for seeming to blame social ills exclusively on saloon-keepers and the like while neglecting to point to a more important cause of much human suffering, "the system." He privately urged Billy Sunday:

If you could only point out a little more definitely the fundamental causes of poverty and injustice and therefore one of the chief causes of sin, you would perhaps be doing in this world one of the greatest works since Christ came on earth. I wish you would read "Social Problems" and "Progress and Poverty" by Henry George.[14]

At times the Judge's conviction that juvenile delinquency was the inevitable corollary of an unjust economic system led him to question the worth of the work of his own court and others like it. In a letter of October 1907, which he asked Julia Lathrop, the social reformer, to share with her colleague Jane Addams, he expressed dissatisfaction "with the kind of palliatives we are dealing with in the juvenile court" and mused whether "we are [only] travelling in a circle." Indeed, he surmised, modest reforms under existing circumstances perhaps even encouraged "the Guggenheims, Evanses and Rockefellers" of the world by giving the general public the illusion that conditions were improving. The cold fact, he said, was

> [that] we are not getting anywhere. So long as present industrial, political, social and economic conditions exist, we cannot, in my judgment, make any permanent progress. We can only furnish the salve for the sores as they develop; but we cannot prevent the sores.[15]

Although Lindsey seemed to put his best hopes for defeating "the system" in such typically Progressive political reform measures as the initiative, the referendum, and the recall, he sometimes went further and argued that public ownership of at least a part of the economic structure was an essential condition for social justice. Returning to Denver from one of his early national lecture tours in 1906, he declared that he had found a growing sentiment in favor of public ownership of utilities, particularly "in the better-governed cities." In a similar vein he bluntly predicted to Governor Joseph W. Folk, whose attacks on graft and corruption in Missouri had attracted favorable notice across the country, that the time would come when "the people must own all these natural resources upon which [they are] absolutely dependent ... and, perhaps, eventually, the land itself—at least that part of it that has to do with these resources."[16]

The Judge's widely publicized battles with the utilities companies and his excoriations of "the system" led a number of Socialists to write to him, expressing their gratitude for his role in the good fight. At the rank-and-file level, a worker from Mobile, Alabama, wrote:

> Please consider this as a handshake for your expression of "The Beast." I am only a motorman but I realize that I contribute twelve hours of my life daily to appease his appetite. Success to the "struggle." ... I didn't vote an old party ticket—*guess*.[17]

Anna Louise Strong, then in her salad days as a social worker, was moved to tell Lindsey of her own conversion to socialism. She had first met the Judge in 1904 in St. Louis, when she helped arrange the Juvenile Court exhibit for the great fair held in celebration of the centenary of the Louisiana Purchase. Their paths crossed subsequently at various social welfare conferences. In 1911 she described to Lindsey an incident which finally caused her to become a Socialist "in five minutes." It happened, she said, when she was called upon to obtain the services, for a brief period, of an architectural draftsman. A qualified and personable young man appeared for an interview. In the course of their talk he told of his concern over finding long-term employment, mentioning that he had a wife and child to support and that no other work was in sight. "Then and there," Miss Strong emotionally affirmed, she decided to become a Socialist. Any system which failed to provide a decent living for a self-respecting husband and father who was willing and able to work did not deserve to survive, she declared. Although she did not couple her testimonial with a plea to the Judge to join her, other correspondents did. As early as 1908 Upton Sinclair had urged Lindsey to get out of Denver and become a national figure in the Socialist party. A year later Carl D. Thompson, a national leader in the party and its national committeeman from Wisconsin, admitted the shortcomings of the Socialist leadership in the United States but pleaded that the talents of people like Lindsey were all the more needed for that reason.[18]

Unlike some middle-class reformers of old American stock, Lindsey was not horrified at the thought of socialism. His own early brushes with poverty and despair always caused a part of him to identify with the have-nots and to reject the view that poverty existed simply because "poor folks has poor ways." He was also sensitive, as men like Theodore Roosevelt rarely were, to elements of smugness and hypocrisy in the "privileged classes," and did not balk at publicly denouncing them. His rhetoric reflected this attitude when he commented on the cries for law and order that arose when the IWW resorted to violence in labor disputes in Colorado and the Pacific Northwest. A ruthless capitalist who murdered his workers on the installment plan by long hours and unhealthy conditions, Lindsey declared, was morally as guilty of violence and lawlessness as an IWW assassin. Lindsey made it clear that he was not merely speaking in generalities by citing Simon Guggenheim, mine owner and United States Senator from Colorado, as an example of the kind of capitalist he had in mind.[19]

Lindsey's sympathies never led him all the way to socialism. Like many Americans, it was more his style, as Mr. Dooley put it, to beat a carpet than to make a revolution. Perhaps the hardheaded, pragmatic side of his nature warned him that a reformer had enough problems without being saddled with a third-party tag that would alienate even some of his supporters in the working class, whose ethnic or religious loyalties were stronger than any class-consciousness. It is also possible that Lindsey had some ideological reservations about socialism, but he did not state them very strongly. In 1907 he privately expressed his "kindly feelings" toward the Socialists but added that he could not become one because he believed that men's hearts, as well as their institutions, had to be changed—a statement that contrasts interestingly to his comment to William Allen White four years later that "conditions" are largely responsible for the kinds of hearts men have. In reply to Anna

Louise Strong's letter about her conversion to socialism, he replied:

> What you say interests me more than I can begin to tell you. I think we are going that way. I have been willing to take one, two, three and the Lord knows how many steps for the Socialists, but somehow I haven't yet come to accept everything they stand for. Perhaps that isn't necessary, for it will be a long time before any of us are asked to do that.²⁶

Interested as he was in large ideas about the society of the future, Lindsey spent most of his time when he was away from court lobbying for specific practical measures. Sometimes his role as a judge helped pave the way for new legislation. One of his earliest fights with "the Beast" took place during his second year on the bench. Around the turn of the century some cotton mills had been built on the outskirts of Denver. Their owners recruited families from the Old South, chiefly Alabama and the Carolinas, to migrate to Colorado. On his own initiative the "Kids' Judge" visited the factories, went to the homes of the newcomers, and talked with the children. He found that some of the worst conditions he had heard about in the South were being visited upon Colorado in the name of "enterprise" and "progress." "These imported people were practically slaves," Lindsey told Lincoln Steffens. "They had come out under contracts, and the children, unschooled, toiled at the machines first to liberate their parents, then to support them."

The Judge resolved that he would act against the Overland Mills, one of the worst offenders, even though Colorado's rudimentary child labor legislation permitted no penalty more severe than a small fine. Lindsey dramatized the situation by levying the fine not only against the company superintendent but upon the president of the company as well. Such an action in the political and social climate of 1902 was unusual, to say the least, and was tantamount, in the eyes of some of the outraged business community, to *lèse majesté*. "We have never had any trouble until this fight started," the injured president informed Lindsey. "We're helping Denver and we ought to be encouraged instead of being persecuted. I warn you . . . that if this thing is kept up, we'll shut down the mills and you'll have to take the consequences."[21]

Lindsey continued his "harassment" of the mills, and eventually they did go out of business, although the Judge's campaign played a relatively minor part in their demise. The political consequences were not disastrous for Lindsey, as the mill owners predicted. Indeed, the favorable publicity given to the Judge's crusade in Denver and other parts of the state helped put the legislature in a receptive mood for passing a new Child Labor Act in the spring of 1903. Within two years Lindsey felt able to assure the National Child Labor Committee at its annual meeting in New York City that "Colorado claims the proud distinction [in the West] of being twin sister to Illinois in acknowledging superiority to no state in advanced child labor laws as well as other laws for the protection of her children."[22]

But the Supreme Court of Colorado was to demonstrate again to the Judge that his confidence was unwarranted. Justice Campbell, an ultra-conservative whose Social Darwinist philosophy was written into numerous judicial opinions striking down laws designed to ameliorate economic and social ills, found the 1903 law unconstitutional on the ground that it gave the courts too much power in deciding which occupations were "dangerous" for women and children. The legislature was improperly attempting to delegate powers to the judiciary which it alone should exercise. *Burcher v. People* was a model case, in the minds of reformers, for illustrating the "economic freedom" that employers and their lawyers sought to protect. The object of their solicitude on this occasion was a washerwoman whose freedom to work fifty-five hours a week was now affirmed by the Supreme Court of Colorado just as the Supreme Court of the United States, two years earlier, had affirmed the right of bakers to work more than ten hours a day over the ringing dissent of Justice Holmes. In *Burcher,* Judge Lindsey must have found it singularly appropriate that the attorney who represented the laundry was his old partner and present political enemy, Fred Parks.[23]

The Judge now added a stronger child labor law to the bulk of bills for whose passage he campaigned. On the public level he addressed meetings in churches and schools and gave interviews to the press. Behind the scenes he wrote letters of exhortation and advice, gave counsel on tactics, and worked closely with legislators, especially the small number of women members of the general assembly who could be counted on to support humanitarian measures encompassed in the "Lindsey bills." The campaign was long and exhausting, and victory was not won until the second biennial session of the Colorado legislature following the Supreme Court decision in *Burcher.*

The Lindsey-Jones Bill of 1911, so known in Colorado history in recognition of the Judge's personal drafting of the bill and his efforts in securing its passage (even though he was never a member of the legislature), was the most comprehensive law dealing with child labor in Colorado until that time. It met the objections of the *Burcher* decision by expressly providing a legislative categorization of "dangerous" and "injurious" occupations. Some of its prohibitions amounted to an eloquent commentary on events. For example, no child between the ages of fourteen and sixteen could be employed at all if he (or she) could not "read at sight and write legibly simple sentences." Children between fourteen and sixteen were generally forbidden to work except in the most harmless occupations. A child labor registry was to be maintained, and a chief factory inspector was delegated responsibility for enforcing several provisions of the law. If these relatively modest innovations hardly seemed to embody the "creeping socialism" that opponents of the bill found implicit in it, they could point to a new provision which raised from fourteen to sixteen the age at which boys might be employed to work in mines and smelters. As Morison and De Soto, conservative annotators of the Colorado statutes, bitterly complained:

> The central idea of the Act seems to be that education will preserve the morals and health of the child, without the necessity of food or clothing, which when the child is homeless and destitute, can be provided only by its labor.[24]

If Morison's and De Soto's premise were true that the state had no duty to help when a child was homeless or destitute, their conclusion that child labor was a necessity followed logically. In order to meet this objection in part, Lindsey sponsored an initiative proposal which was adopted the following year. The Mothers' Compensation Act of 1912 was one of the earliest aid-to-dependent-children laws in American history. Its basic aim was to provide means for mothers who were unable to keep their children solely because of financial need. Under existing laws their only option was to send them to the State Home for Dependent and Neglected Children. At the same time the Judge also launched a long-term campaign for a maternity law, finally enacted in 1923, which provided pre-natal and post-natal care for mother and child.

The opponents of such laws made the same dire predictions that were used in arguing against social security, "the welfare state," and various anti-poverty programs for the next half-century. Taxes would "skyrocket." The states would go bankrupt. Paupers from other parts of the country would descend on Colorado to get handouts. Sexual immorality would flourish, since the benefits of the "Lindsey bills" were not denied to the mothers of illegitimate children. Where were you going to stop?

Answering the critics, Lindsey characteristically combined folksy pleas based on common sense with conventional appeals based on high principle. The Judge had once visited a modern stock farm and had observed the great care given to colts and their mothers. *They* had pre-natal and post-natal care, but thousands of women and children did not. Did this make sense?

Lindsey instantly recognized that he had found a popular slogan for his campaign: "Horses' rights for women!" Using the more traditional rhetoric of the reformers of the day, he wrote in support of the Mothers' Compensation Act:

> The final provision of the act is . . . one of its best: "This act shall be liberally construed .for the protection of the child, the home, and the state, and in the interest of public morals, and the prevention of poverty and crime." It is a recognition by the state that the aid is rendered, not as a charity, but as a right—as justice due mothers whose work in their rearing is a work for the state as much as that of the soldier who is paid by the state for his services on the battlefield; it is a recognition for the first time by society that the state is responsible in a measure for the plight of the mother, and acknowledges its responsibility by sharing the burden of her poverty that is created largely by the conditions that the state permits to exist.[25]

Lindsey's most dramatic confrontation with the forces of reaction in Colorado, before the 1920's, occurred when he gave his support to the coal miners in one of the bitterest fights ever waged between labor and capital in the United States. In 1913, for the third time in twenty-one years, the miners tried to win union recognition and a promise from the operating companies to meet certain other demands regarded as essential to the workers' dignity as human beings. The matter of dignity was no mere rhetoric as far as the miners were concerned. Their resentment grew not merely out of dissatisfaction with wages and hours, bad as these were. The miners also chafed under the semi-feudal conditions existing in the company towns in which they and their families lived. The companies dominated their lives not only during working hours but off the job as well. The operators' influence in the incorporated villages in the vicinity of the mines gave them virtually unlimited power over school policies, elections, and law enforcement. Since post offices were usually located in company stores, privacy of the mails was often meaningless, and woe to the worker who was sent a union newspaper. Mine superintendents frequently doubled as mayors. The courts were also controlled by the operators, a fact that helped explain the rarity of a plaintiff's victory in any suit for damages, even though the death rate in Colorado mines was more than twice the national average. In September 1913 the United Mine Workers, clandestinely engaged in trying to organize the miners for more than two years, held a meeting in Trinidad, Colorado. They threatened a strike by the 23rd of the month unless the following demands were met:

1. Recognition of the union;
2. A ten per cent advance in wages on the tonnage rate, and a day scale practically in accord with the Wyoming day scale;
3. An eight-hour working day for all classes of labor in or around the coal lands and at the coke ovens;
4. Pay for our narrow and dead work, which includes brushing, timbering, removing flams, handling impurities, and so forth;
5. A check-weighman at all mines to be elected by the miners without any interference by company officials in said election;
6. The right to trade in any store we please, and the right to choose our own boarding place and our doctor;
7. The enforcement of the Colorado mining laws and the abolition of the notorious and criminal guard system which has prevailed in the mining camps of Colorado for many years.

The operators refused all offers of mediation, as they had done successfully in 1892 and 1903. Most of the miners were satisfied with the status quo, the operators asserted, and union spokesmen were outside agitators who did not speak for the men. Since more than four-fifths of the miners walked out on September 23, the operators' claims were not very convincing. Nevertheless, the miners' overwhelming support of the strike did not deter John D. Rockefeller, Jr., whose family controlled 40 per cent of the Colorado Fuel and Iron Company, from asserting, eight months later, that the operators were fighting for the principle of preserving the workers' right "to work for whom they please" without union dictation.

The operators reacted to the strike by bringing in scabs and enlisting large numbers of additional mine guards. Tension inevitably increased, and sporadic episodes of violence soon broke out. At the request of the operators, Democratic Governor Elias Ammons, whose election in 1912 Lindsey and other Colorado Progressives had regarded with little enthusiasm, sent the state militia into southern Colorado in late October "to maintain law and order." To the miners the militiamen were no better than strikebreakers, since the maintenance of "law and order" meant that the operators could continue indefinitely to run their mines while simultaneously refusing all proposals to mediate. The militia's presence also added fuel to the fire because of the bad repute state militias and state police forces had with organized labor throughout the country in an era when governmental intervention in labor disputes usually meant the use of force on behalf of the employers. Furthermore, miners' memories in Colorado did not have to be long to recall the cooperation between mine guards and the militia in crushing the coal strike of 1903. At that time guards and militiamen combined to round up several hundred strikers and lead them into two railway boxcars which were then taken to the state lines at Kansas and New Mexico respectively, where the workers were dumped with a warning never to return to Colorado. It should have come as no surprise, therefore, that the arrival of state troops in the new strike situation presaged more violence, not less.

On April 20, 1914, after several months of armed clashes between strikers and mine guards and militiamen, there occurred an episode which put the Colorado coal strike on the front page of every major newspaper in the country. To historians of the American labor movement, the event is known as the Ludlow Massacre. The scene for it was set when strikers and their families moved into tent colonies for the duration of the strike. The tents were purposely located at the entrances to the mines, and Governor Ammons charged, with some logic, that they amounted to a form of illegal picketing. Even before the Ludlow incident, the militia had begun the forced evacuation of the tent colonies. On April 19 they prepared to move against

Ludlow, mounting two cannon and several machine-guns on the hills above the tents. The question as to who fired the first shots may never be answered, but in view of what followed there can be no doubt that the militiamen responded hysterically at best, viciously at worst. The tents were indiscriminately sprayed with machine-gun bullets, then set afire, and in the aftermath eleven children, two young mothers, and seven strikers lay dead. One militiaman was killed in the process. Colorado was on the verge of civil war.[26]

Governor Ammons now appealed to President Wilson to send federal troops to Colorado. Wilson, a strong believer in states' rights, vainly hoped that a direct personal appeal to the elder John D. Rockefeller, asking that he accept federal mediation of the controversy, would make such a step unnecessary. John D. Rockefeller, Jr., who acted as his father's spokesman in the matter, rejected the appeal two days after it was made. On April 28, 1914, President Wilson sent federal troops to the strike zone, where they were to remain for the next nine months. The replacement of hostile mine guards and state militiamen by federal troops was an improvement from the miners' standpoint, but it still left the basic issue of the strike unresolved and the scabs still at work. New appeals by Wilson were again turned down by the Rockefellers, even when they were accompanied by an agreed concession on the part of the United Mine Workers in the matter of union recognition. Bolder steps appeared to be in order.[27]

On May 7, Upton Sinclair informed Judge Lindsey he intended to visit Colorado in a few days to write about the strike. Soon afterward the idea formed in Sinclair's mind of sending a delegation from Colorado, which would include some of the Ludlow victims, to urge President Wilson to shut down the mines. After his arrival in Denver, Sinclair became convinced that Lindsey would be the best person to head such a delegation. According to Sinclair, it was not easy to persuade the Judge to accept the assignment. Sinclair managed to enlist an interesting group of allies to work on him. They included John Reed, erstwhile Harvard radical who had briefly interrupted his journalistic stint in war-torn Mexico to come to Colorado; William Chenery, Chicago journalist now moved to Denver, and earnest supporter of liberal causes; Progressive stalwarts like Edward P. Costigan and James Randolph Walker; and several representatives of the United Mine Workers. On May 17, the day before he left for Washington, Judge Lindsey described his thoughts in a letter to Theodore Roosevelt's friend and supporter, George W. Perkins:

> My sole purpose and desire is to see the unfortunate distraction of my poor state brought to an end. I firmly believe that there will be a great loss of life and property unless Mr. Rockefeller will consent to a plan that I am going to propose to President Wilson. It is briefly this: That from military necessity and in the interest of peace and justice, because of a great crisis in the political and industrial affairs of our state; and because the present state administration has proven itself so impudent as to call for a rebuke from the President, that the President would be justified at least temporarily in closing down the coal mines of this state until the operators and the mine owners would consent to a fair and disinterested board of arbitration to be appointed by the President, hearing their debates and coming to a decision by which they should both abide or expect the condemnation of the public.[28]

The Lindsey party included the Judge's attractive young bride, the former Henrietta Brevoort of Detroit, whom he had married four months earlier, two wives of the strikers, one of whom brought along her two children, and a Ludlow mother, Mrs. Petrucci, whose three children had died in the Ludlow Massacre. Mrs. Edward P. Costigan, wife of the recent Progressive candidate for governor, also accompanied the group. After a brief stopover in Chicago, where Hull-House extended its hospitality to them, the group went on to Washington and made their headquarters at the New Willard Hotel, a short walk from the White House. On May 21 President Wilson's secretary,

Joseph Tumulty, sent a note to Lindsey confirming that the President would see his party the following day.

A few hours after meeting with the President, Lindsey wrote of his impressions to the publisher E. W. Scripps. He told how he had urged Wilson to order the army to prevent the strikebreakers from entering the mines. The Judge predicted that once the mines were closed down, it would "bring Mr. Rockefeller to his knees." The President was apparently very cordial in manner, even bouncing the two little children brought by the striker's wife on his knees during the course of the interview, while Lindsey asserted feelingly that "a real big issue of property rights as against human rights is on trial in this country." The visit may have fortified Wilson in his determination to keep the army in Colorado, but he remained unmoved by the appeal to use it to bring pressure on the owners and operators who, somewhat ironically, remained equally unmoved by Wilson's appeals to them. Thus the meeting failed to achieve its primary objective. A few weeks later Jane Addams attempted to console the Judge with the thought that the favorable publicity the meeting received made it worth the effort.[29]

Even before his meeting with Wilson, Lindsey had decided on one additional move in the East on behalf of the miners. He would go to New York City and ask to appear before the United States Commission on Industrial Relations, which was then conducting hearings on the Colorado situation. At the same time he would personally appeal to John D. Rockefeller, Jr., to meet with him and his delegation. Commission Chairman Frank P. Walsh cordially assented to hear the Judge and the women from Ludlow, but Rockefeller's office at 26 Broadway denounced as false all rumors that Rockefeller would meet Lindsey or his group either in lower Manhattan or at his Pocantico Hills estate outside Tarrytown. The *New York Times,* which editorially blasted Lindsey for his involvement in the strike and praised President Wilson for refusing to take over the mines, made an honest error in reporting that Lindsey had claimed that Rockefeller had agreed to a meeting, but its departure from its usual standard of journalistic accuracy was less pardonable when it subheadlined its story "Denver Socialist [sic] Said to Be at Pocantico Hills Discussing Colorado War."[30] Informed of Rockefeller's refusal to meet with him, Lindsey closed the matter with a statement to the press:

> My only direct personal interest comes from the fact that the mines in two of our counties alone have made seven hundred orphans in the last four years and these orphans come to me in the Juvenile Court in many instances.
> I pity Mr. Rockefeller with all my heart today. If any one should attempt violence against him, I would be one of the first to rush to his aid, for I do not believe in violence. But I know that the great majority of good people everywhere are coming to a realization that the relationship of property to life must be readjusted.[31]

Lindsey's parting shot at Rockefeller and the other mine owners came when he appeared before the Industrial Commission on May 28, 1914. The Judge congratulated the commission for hearing him and the miners' wives, and contrasted their "spirit of courtesy and consideration" to the arrogance shown by John D. Rockefeller, Jr. Obviously annoyed at the creation of a "Law and Order League" in Colorado which expressed sympathy with the owners, Lindsey expounded on his theme that although violence was wrong, "the attitude of such men is doing more to produce lawlessness and talk about confiscation and what they call anarchy than all the anarchists I know." Pressed by the commission for any remedies he might care to suggest, Lindsey candidly admitted the enormous complexity of the relations between capital and labor and proposed that the federal government might keep title to all remaining parts of the public domain where valuable natural resources existed. In this way the government could bring pressure on any party that refused to discuss a major issue of national concern, as the coal companies were contemptuously doing even in the face of an appeal by the President of the United States.[32]

In Lindsey's view his behavior in the coal strike episode had been quite moderate. After all, he had ignored suggestions that he picket the Rockefeller offices or escort his delegation to the Rockefeller estate. At a union-sponsored meeting in New York City, at Beethoven Hall, he was the only speaker who refrained from castigating President Wilson for being indifferent to the suffering of the miners. Finally, at the hearings of the Industrial Commission, he admitted the enormous complexity of industrial relations and stopped short of advocating federal acquisition of natural resources already in private hands.[33] For any doctrinaire radical the Judge's conduct was nothing more than that of a friendly gradualist. Yet, as Lindsey observed to Scripps, "I do not know of anything I ever did that provoked the 'Beast' so much as that trip to Washington and New York." Chambers of Commerce in Trinidad and other Colorado communities adopted resolutions condemning the strikers, then passed special resolutions condemning Lindsey. One apoplectic gentleman proposed that a committee be appointed to spit at the little Judge as he alighted from the train on his return. The Denver Chamber of Commerce charged that Lindsey did not represent public opinion in Colorado and made the trip east to feather his own political nest. Congressman George J. Kindel of Colorado asserted in the *Congressional Record* that Lindsey had "swept across the country with a troop [*sic*] of vaudeville artists with the purpose of adding luster to his peculiar fame by spreading denunciation and falsehood where it will best attract attention." The *Pueblo Chieftain* informed its readers that Lindsey was met on his return by his supporters from Market and Larimer Streets—a not too oblique reference to the red-light district in Denver. Lindsey told William Allen White of a whispering campaign about the moral character of the miners' wives who accompanied him to the East, and of anonymous letters intimating that he had been the impresario of a seraglio.[34]

Lindsey's role in the Colorado coal strike cannot be measured by its tangible accomplishments. Indeed, it might well be argued that the Judge's activities were a total failure, since the settlement of the strike did not occur for many months and ultimately involved more concessions from the miners than from the owners. But Lindsey's support did give the miners one advantage, at least outside Colorado. It gave their cause publicity that the support of no other person in Colorado could equal. For by 1914 Ben Lindsey was the one citizen of Colorado whose name was a household word throughout the United States.

4 / A National Figure

WILL ROGERS, REFERRING TO THE EFFORTS OF LINDSEY'S enemies in Denver to get rid of him, observed that outside Colorado nobody knew anything about Denver except that Judge Lindsey worked there. The remark was made in 1927 when Lindsey was having trouble with the Ku Klux Klan, but it would have been just as appropriate in the decade before the First World War. As early as 1905 the story was told in a national magazine of the Denver school inspector who sent a boy to the blackboard to write three proper names. "Of great men?" asked the boy. "If you like," said the inspector. And the boy wrote:

> George Washington
> Abraham Lincoln
> Ben B. Lindsey[1]

The Judge's fame rested, no doubt, on his solid contributions to the juvenile court movement. But, as he himself often pointed out, some of the principles and practices of juvenile court work were an outgrowth of a hundred years of beginnings and the contributions of a score of men and women. Why, then, was Lindsey regarded so universally as the embodiment of the movement?

A part of the answer was Lindsey's charismatic appeal as a speaker and his willingness to travel around the country publicizing his work in Denver. At the start of the Judge's career, motion pictures were scarcely in the nickelodeon stage, and chautauqua speakers provided one of the few living contacts with the great world for millions of rural citizens. Lindsey had many qualities that made him a prized speaker. Like William

Jennings Bryan, "the acknowledged king of the lecture trail," he could speak from experience, and his public career immediately gave him his credentials as a doer as well as a talker. His talent as a raconteur was formidable and was reflected in the numerous anecdotes that flowed so easily (and sometimes a little exaggeratedly) once he was on the platform. Like most good speakers, Lindsey was self-conscious about his style and techniques. He once wrote down his thoughts on how to be a successful orator. The key was preparation, the Judge emphasized, but preparation did not mean writing out the speech or committing it to memory. The essence of preparation was to steep yourself in the subject and then plunge into it "with great enthusiasm and without the slightest thought of having to follow a written page."[2] The method seemed to work. Lindsey's popularity as a lecturer led to an association with the Redpath Lyceum Bureau that lasted over twenty-five years and ended only when the talkies and the depression combined to make the chautauqua form a nostalgic relic of a simpler rural age.

The most pervasive theme in Lindsey's lectures on delinquents and pre-delinquents was the importance of environment in the child's development. Although the Judge sometimes oscillated between the premise that the child was innately good and the view that he (or she) was inherently amoral, he adhered consistently to the belief that the home and the community could manipulate the environment and create the best possible odds that the child would not go wrong.[3] Lindsey used the concept of environment in its broadest sense to include everything from the moral training given by church, home, and school to the institutional superstructure created by the economic and political system. In doing so, he was able ingeniously to combine the homilies one might expect from a Sunday school teacher with graphic illustrations of the hypocrisy of a society that preached morality but did not practice it.

Lindsey's advocacy of moral and religious training as an indispensable element in a good environment undoubtedly received a sympathetic hearing from audiences who thrilled to Bryan's talk on "The Prince of Peace" and enjoyed lectures of social significance flavored with a dash of familiar moral uplift. "Character is founded upon conscience, and conscience comes from the development of the human heart; therefore the necessity for moral and religious training, which is the very basis of all our principal education and the most important part of it," the Judge told a group of teachers. The home was, of course, the most important place for developing character, but sometimes, particularly in the case of children who were in trouble, it was not doing the job. He then described to his audience his own efforts in the Denver Juvenile and Family Court to fill the gap:

> I have found in our court work that nothing helps more than our little talks with the children. Sometimes these talks are better delivered in private; in fact, I should say in most cases; sometimes with the children all together. I should say it is more important to have frequent talks upon such subjects concerning morals than to teach grammar, arithmetic, or geography. . . . Now, among the subjects I would recommend would be these, which I have selected at random for the probationers in our court, who report every two weeks when we have report day, and it opens generally with a talk on a subject like this: "Our Duties to Each Other"; "The Absurdity of Hate"; "Truthfulness"; "About Quarreling"; "Usefulness, Gentleness and Kindness, Mercy and Charity"; "Money and Manhood"; "Evil Associations"; "Evil Thoughts"; "Evil Talk"; "Jealousy and Envy"; "I Forgot"; "What Is Success?"; "The Man Who Serves and the Man Who Makes Money"; "Public Service"; "A Pure Life."[4]

Many times the Judge warned against the habit of reading "dime novels," and pointed with pride to his practice of distributing to the probationers such magazines as *The American Boy, Men of Tomorrow,* and *Success.* At the time of the death of Elbert Hubbard, who was among the passengers on the

Lusitania, the Judge wrote to the author's son: "Like others, I have sent out thousands of copies of his *A Message to García.* His life was full of just such inspirational writings."[5]

Such remarks, taken out of context, might have led the listener to wonder if Lindsey were not merely another idealistic preacher. The thought would soon be dispelled by examples and anecdotes that showed the Judge to be neither naive nor sentimental. He never believed for a moment that "bad" boys could be reformed by moral suasion alone. Indeed, he liked to shock his audiences by assuring them from personal experience that the amount of lying, cheating, and stealing by "good" boys was far greater than they assumed. If any of his hearers responded defensively, the Judge went on to explain that a major cause of the phenomenon was that the children learned their lessons from the adult world.

These lessons were not the sermons preached in the churches, or the usual platitudes of commencement addresses, or the patriotic speeches delivered from the political stump. The lessons were the ways adults, especially some "successful" adults, behaved. Children were apt pupils, the Judge warned:

> They are the keenest observers in the world, and they have the keenest sense of justice, and the minute your example does not square with your precept your whole teaching becomes a farce; it is met with scorn by the child and he prefers to follow the ways of wickedness rather than righteousness, because he believes you lied to him. That, my friends, is one of the chief difficulties in training or in the instilling of morals into the children of this country. We do not go that way ourselves. We ought to.[6]

The impact of the Judge's personality on his audiences derived in large measure from his ability to weave into his addresses personal anecdotes that vividly drove home his points. A characteristic example was one he used to illustrate why it was not always easy for a judge to explain to young boys that stealing was wrong:

I recall very well a typical little gang from the Delgany district, down among the railroad tracks and bottoms, in Denver. The gang was made up of eight or ten boys, bubbling over with surplus energy, much misdirected; and finding it encroaching upon box-cars, and eventually the corner grocery, it had to be stopped. I remember a certain little fellow, the leader of this gang, who cross-examined the judge one day, somewhat to the judge's embarrassment. We were all seated around the table, talking in that chummy fashion that boys will talk in the alley when we can bring out their natural feelings and thought about things in general, and upon occasions like this I have been somewhat amazed and shocked at the observation of the child, and the impressions made upon his mind by the acts and conduct of men. Well, while we were sitting around the table chatting, little David, we will call him, suddenly said to me: "Judge, if old Britt, that runs the saloon down in our neighborhood, can keep open all day Sunday and stand in with the police, and the cop sits out on the beer keg and don't 'pinch' him, why can't the kids swipe then?"

I was so impressed with this unconscious indictment of the community by this boy that I called in Mr. Meyers, a stenographer in this city, and had him take down the question of the boy, but I must say it was very difficult for him to take down the answer of the judge.[7]

The Judge's concern with the moral tone of the whole society did not cause him to neglect the development of proposals for a community program of action to deal with the subject nearest his heart, juvenile delinquency. Among the key proposals, whose accomplishment the Judge had already achieved to a considerable degree in Denver, were close cooperation between the schools and juvenile courts, use of school buildings during vacation periods, development of vocational education programs, summer work projects, strict enforcement of all laws designed to protect children combined with rigorous prosecution of adults for violating them, and the substitution of detention homes for jails. The proposals, aside from the enforcement of the contributory laws, were not unique with Lindsey, but the Judge's ability to relate the need for such programs to the case histories of flesh-and-blood wayward children had a unique emotional impact on his readers and listeners. As young journalist Walter Lippmann observed in 1913, "By touching something deeply instinctive in millions of people, Judge Lindsey animated dull proposals with human interest."[8]

Lindsey never tired of explaining that the juvenile court system worked on the assumption that punishment, particularly incarceration, was almost always a confession of failure. It was wrong not only because children deserved to be treated with greater patience, but because it failed the pragmatic test. After all, the Judge argued, the only civilized rationale for punishment was that it acted as a deterrent. If the claim were true, he suggested, it was curious that there seemed to be no noticeable decline in the population of jails and prisons. One of the Judge's favorite and most memorable stories involved an eighteen-year-old, known to the Denver police as "The Daredevil Kid," who had a long record of arrests and confinements. Lindsey had only recently come to the bench when "the Kid" was brought before him just after he had succeeded in breaking out of the West Side jail. The Judge spent a considerable amount of time talking with him and decided that a first step in his rehabilitation would be to send him back to jail under the "Lindsey honor system." "The Daredevil Kid" kept his word, and Lindsey recounted what followed:

The next morning a captain of police came to see me.

"Judge," he said, "that was a very remarkable thing you did last night. The kid got back to jail all right. It was nearly midnight and when the night watch answered his call and saw him in the shadows he thought he was a ghost and nearly fell dead."

And the captain laughed.

"But," he continued, "don't take any more chances with that kid. His case is too notorious for you to fail—and believe me you will fail if you keep on taking chances with him."

"But why will I fail, Captain?" I asked.

"Don't you know," he shot back, "that kid has been in jail thirteen times?"

"Well, Captain," I said, "didn't it ever occur to you that the jail had failed thirteen times?"[9]

The activities of the "Kids' Judge" always made good newspaper copy. A month seldom went by in which some human interest angle involving Lindsey did not find its way into the Denver press, soon to be repeated as a filler or squib in some national magazine and in other newspapers throughout the country. The stories, which the Judge actively encouraged or even instigated, served a double purpose. They contributed to his favorable image in Denver, useful in the numerous campaigns he had to wage for his own re-election. And, since the Judge's personality was inseparable from the juvenile court movement, favorable press coverage helped the cause itself by giving Lindsey yet another forum for his message. Thus a story in the *Denver Post* in 1902, describing how he had celebrated his thirty-third birthday with "one of his boys," gave him an opportunity to insert a homily on rehabilitation:

> Do you know, when I first met that kid, he was one of the toughest ever? He had been to Golden and everybody said he ought to be sent back and kept there forever. But I gave him a chance and got him a new job and now you ought to see him. He saves some of his wages every week.[10]

In a similar vein, the Judge's encouragement of Denver newsboys to select an unofficial probation officer from their midst and his use of a temporary boy bailiff demonstrated his belief in encouraging self-help and group responsibility; but simultaneously it brought pressure on the legislature and County Commissioners to provide greater professional help for the court. Other human interest stories with a strong appeal and an obvious message included an interview in which the Judge poignantly described homes without fathers and pleaded with state legislatures to strengthen industrial accident legislation because "it is as important to stop the needless manufacture of orphans as it is to take care of orphans." Lindsey demonstrated this same knack for capsulizing a moral issue when he directed a query to some police officers who had been accused of using third-degree methods on juvenile suspects in order to discover the location of some stolen bicycles. "Which would you rather do," the Judge asked, "save five bicycles or save seven boys?"[11]

The Judge and his court inevitably aroused the interest of national magazines, whose reporters were soon flocking to Denver, observing the court and interviewing the Judge, and returning East "to write up Lindsey." During only the first half-decade of his judgeship, articles appeared in the *American Magazine, Arena, Charities, Independent, Ladies' Home Journal, Literary Digest, Outlook, Review of Reviews,* and *World Today.* In March 1906 Lincoln Steffens, anticipating a series of meetings with the Judge, wrote, "How glad I'll be to get out of here to the clear mountain air of the West. You may be anarchists, but you are not yet dead." Seven months later there appeared in *McClure's* the first of Steffens' three installments on "The Just Judge," the fullest treatment ever given to Lindsey and his court by any magazine. On reading a draft of the first article, S. S. McClure wrote to Lindsey that it would "create an immense interest in you all over the United States." Although "create" was not exactly the right word (five other national magazines had already carried glowing treatments óf the Judge), the length of the *McClure's* series and Steffens' special position among the muckrakers justified the publisher's exaggeration.[12]

During Lindsey's first decade on the court, his accomplishments in child welfare work and his identification with liberal causes generally were recognized at the national level by many appointments and elections to executive committees and advisory boards of such national organizations as the National Child Labor Committee, the Playground Association of America, the National Conference of Charities and Correction, the National Municipal League, the People's Lobby, and the American Prison Association. Through his attendance at regional and national meetings of these organizations, the Judge became acquainted with other nationally prominent persons such as Jane Addams, Florence Kelley, Julia Lathrop, Samuel McCune Lindsay, Paul U. Kellogg, Homer Folks, and Jacob Riis. The association with Riis, which went back to a National Conference of Charities and Correction meeting in 1903, was a warm and lasting one and was responsible for the most prestigious endorsement to date of the Judge's work.

Riis, a Danish emigrant who had personally known hardship and poverty in New York City, first achieved a degree of success as a police reporter for the *New York Tribune*. In 1890, with the publication of *How the Other Half Lives,* a study of the slums of Manhattan, he became an author as well as a journalist. The book came to the attention of Theodore Roosevelt, who served as New York Police Commissioner from 1893 to 1895. Roosevelt arranged an interview with Riis and was as impressed by the man as he had been by the book. For two years the nightly wanderings of the "two brothers in Mulberry Street," as they were called, ferreting out vice and police corruption, became legendary. Their strong friendship continued as Roosevelt moved up the political ladder to become President of the United States in 1901.

In the spring of 1904 Riis arranged a White House meeting between Roosevelt and Lindsey. As Riis guessed, the two relatively young men (Roosevelt forty-five, Lindsey thirty-four) responded favorably to each other, and the meeting led to a genuine and long-term friendship as well as a relationship of mutual political support on several occasions. At Lindsey's request, and with Riis's support, President Roosevelt in his 1904 Annual Message endorsed the basic principles of the juvenile court movement and recommended that Congress consider developing a juvenile code for the capital city. In their deliberations, he proposed, they should make a careful study "of what has been accomplished in such States as Illinois and Colorado by the juvenile courts." The Judge wrote his thanks for the "boost" in separate letters to Riis and the President, and informed

Roosevelt that it was often his practice to quote both of them in his speeches.[13]

Undoubtedly Lindsey's greatest accomplishment as chief crusader for the burgeoning juvenile court movement lay in the role he played in encouraging laws to create or strengthen existing systems all over the country. The Denver court became a national clearing house in the field as legislators, judges, and private associations wrote to the Judge, asking his advice and support in their efforts to establish juvenile courts and enact other legislation to improve child welfare. Often they showed their awareness of Lindsey's forceful personality, as well as his expertise, by pleading with him to appear in person before their legislatures or legislative committees to explain the need for the new laws.

The Judge helped in numerous ways. He sent out hundreds of copies of his two-hundred-page booklet *The Problem of the Children and How the State of Colorado Cares for Them* (1904), which was strikingly effective as propaganda because it offered something to all levels of its audience. Legislators could find in it the principles and major provisions of all the laws which the Judge had drafted and had successfully fought for in Colorado. Judges and probation officers found in a section on "The Administrative Work" a description of the practical operation of the laws, with facsimiles of forms, charts, and records that the Judge found useful in his own court. Charitable and religious groups, struggling to have legislation enacted in their own states and communities, were given ammunition to counter the arguments of hostile legislators that the program would cost too much. In sections called "The Expense" and "Facts and Figures," the Judge amassed statistics on the old system to demonstrate that the maintenance of the jails, the operation of the fee system, the red tape of the criminal courts, and, finally and conclusively, the high rates of recidivism among the juvenile victims actually cost far more, even in the short run, than did the new system with its reliance on methods that were more effective as well as more humane. Sending a copy of the booklet was usually the Judge's first step when he received a general inquiry about the Colorado system. Supplementary commentaries were published as new "Lindsey bills" were enacted. When specific questions were asked, the Judge would often dictate a lengthy personal reply to the writer.

The Judge also accepted invitations to appear personally on behalf of pending legislation whenever he could fit an appearance into his schedule. In 1908 he estimated that he had appeared before at least fifteen legislatures or legislative committees during the past five years. Two letters from widely separate parts of the country illustrate the direct influence of the Judge's support. A. E. Winship, editor of the *Journal of Education*, wrote from Boston to Lindsey, "You did the trick for us," and E. A. Fredenhagen, general superintendent of the Kansas Society for the Friendless, commented on the Judge's visit, "I know you helped us in a manner no one else could, and our law stands as a monument thereof." Other states in which Lindsey played a major role in drafting legislation or seeing it through to enactment, either by extensive correspondence or personal appearance and endorsement, were Illinois, Indiana, Kentucky, Nebraska, New Jersey, New York, Ohio, Pennsylvania, and Washington.[14]

Lindsey took great pride in the part he played in creating a climate of public opinion that helped pave the way for the acceptance of such laws. Even more tangible was the influence he had on the laws themselves. The very language of the statutes was sometimes taken verbatim from Lindsey's Colorado laws. The theory that the child offender should be regarded not as a criminal but as a delinquent, "as misdirected and misguided and needing aid, encouragement, help and assistance," as stated in one of the 1903 Lindsey bills, was incorporated intact in statutes of Tennessee and Missouri in 1905 and 1909. But the greatest satisfaction of all, as far as the Judge was concerned, lay in the success he achieved in having the Colorado Adult Delinquency Law adopted in many parts of the country. This law, with its principle that all adults who contributed to the delinquency of a child could be criminally prosecuted, was the judge's most original contribution to juvenile legislation. A Russell Sage Foundation study of delinquent children, published in 1912, called it the most significant legislation on the statute books for the prevention of delinquency among children. The Judge was untiring in lobbying for it. Within three years of its adoption in Colorado it was adopted in Illinois, Kentucky, Nebraska, Massachusetts, Indiana, New Jersey, and Wisconsin. On Lindsey's recommendation it was also included in the law creating a juvenile court in the District of Columbia. By 1920 forty states had so-called contributory laws making adults criminally liable for contributing to a child's dependency or delinquency.[15]

Although national interest in the Judge focused on his position in the juvenile court movement, his interest in other liberal causes and his constant willingness to give them his public support broadened his appeal among reform groups nationally and thus played an important part in the growth of his national reputation. The jurisdiction of Lindsey's two judgeships, first in Denver and later in Los Angeles, never extended beyond the lines of a single county, but his energetic involvement in liberal causes, nationally and internationally, characterized his entire public career.

If frequency of endorsement is the yardstick of enthusiasm, the woman suffrage movement was second only to children's causes in the Judge's heart during the Progressive era. The issue was already settled in Colorado, one of the first states to give full suffrage to women (in 1893), but the Judge's support was still useful in other parts of the country, and he was always willing to supply a public letter in support of the suffragettes. On two major occasions he spoke in the East on behalf of the cause. At Carnegie Hall in April 1910 he received "a storm of applause" as he addressed a large audience at a gathering sponsored by the League for Political Education. A year later the President of the Cambridge, Massachusetts, Political Equality Association credited him with attracting "the biggest and finest meeting" the group ever had.[16]

Lindsey's participation in the woman suffrage movement occurred at a time when its ideology was changing. An historian has recently suggested that the great shift in the rationale of woman suffrage in the early twentieth century was from justice to expediency. The classic argument from justice asserted simply that since women were equal in humanity, they should also be equal in political rights. The newer argument from expediency was more complex. The claim that women voters would support such measures as child labor laws, pure food standards, and the abolition of the saloon undoubtedly appealed to some male Progressives who were more concerned with these matters than with the equality of women. But the argument from expediency could also have its illiberal side when some suffragists suggested that votes for women would hasten immigration restriction and improve the chances for "clean government" in the "foreign-dominated" corrupt cities.[17]

Although Lindsey never explored all the ramifications of the two positions, he did make it very clear that his own view was based on the argument from justice. His rejection of the argument from expediency did not grow out of a doctrinaire approach, however. The Judge was always quick to point to the practical results of a good moral position. His reason for rejecting the newer approach was that he thought the claims made for it were demonstrably false. He would become quite annoyed when suffrage enthusiasts outside Colorado, without his consent, pointed to his own record of legislative accomplishments as an example of the results to be expected in an equal-suffrage state. On one occasion, when he was asked for a quotable statement about the help he received from women in his campaigns, he replied:

> I do not like to answer questions categorically like those you sent me. I can say generally that I regard women's suffrage as a success because I believe they are entitled to suffrage as a matter of

justice. Many of them did help me in our fights with the politicians for the children and the home, as many of them opposed me, just like men. Women, in my judgment, are just the same as men in politics, subject to the same strength and weakness, and I am one of those who believe that such questions as the uplifting of morals and purifying of politics are entirely immaterial to the right of women to vote.

In a similar vein the Judge wrote to Ida Tarbell that his experiences in Denver convinced him that the supporters of equal suffrage erred in asserting that it would produce such "rosy" results. He advised another correspondent that he was "fed up" with all the talk about the effects of woman suffrage, but reasserted that he would continue to support it enthusiastically because he believed in self-government. Lindsey adhered to this stand and showed his concern not to hurt the cause in a personal letter to his close friend George Creel. After making some blistering remarks about the fatuous activities of certain women's clubs, the Judge added that he would never make such comments publicly for fear they would be exploited by "unscrupulous anti-suffragists."[18]

A number of nationwide reform groups with strong moral orientation eagerly and successfully sought the Judge's endorsement. Lindsey's early experiences with youthful offenders and some of their parents convinced him that excessive drinking was often interwoven with the poverty, broken homes, and instances of nonsupport that contributed to juvenile delinquency. His early crusade against the "wine rooms" of Denver always caused him to look on saloon-keepers and breweries as particularly sinister examples of corrupt vested interests in "the system." The Judge welcomed the opportunity to join forces with others in attacking them. "No one appreciates more than I do," he wrote to Mrs. Frances P. Parks, "the glorious work you are doing. God bless the W.C.T.U. It means so much to the little children of this nation." Such endorsements were reciprocated as the Prohibition party and the Anti-Saloon League became two of the Judge's most reliable supporters at election times. In 1917 he authorized the national chairman of the Prohibition party to use his name on behalf of immediate national prohibition, a policy he later came to regard as a mistake.[19]

Lindsey's widely publicized accounts of his chalk talks to the children on such topics as gambling, smoking, and reading dime novels soon brought his name to the attention of other moral reformers. It is singularly ironic that the Judge, who came to be regarded in the 1920's as the chief advocate of the sexual revolution and who was then frequently denounced by clergymen as the nation's leading corrupter of youth, once served as second vice-president of an organization that had Anthony Comstock on its advisory board. The organization was the National Purity League, and its self-proclaimed mission was to devote itself to "social purity and the suppression of vice and the white slave traffic by educational and religious methods." The Judge, who did not smoke and rarely drank, was always a dependable speaker for the American Anti-Cigarette League and for several years allowed his name to be used on its letterheads as one of its vice-presidents. His election to the National Council of the Boy Scouts of America no doubt was a tribute to his well-known moral soundness as well as his reputation as a juvenile court judge.[20]

An unusual feature of Lindsey's personality and one that made him attractive to widely divergent types was his ability to combine a sensitivity to the dominant values and popular culture of the times with a responsiveness to ideas and people who were considered dangerous, or at best offbeat, by conventional middle-class Americans. In the Progressive period, especially, the first trait was more in evidence, though the latter quality was not wholly absent, particularly in the Judge's private correspondence. The two sides of Lindsey were often complementary rather than contradictory, but the more private side sometimes revealed a greater subtlety than was found in his public statements.

Historian Henry May has called a belief in the reality and eternity of moral values "the first and central article of faith in the national credo." Lindsey constantly and sincerely appealed to such values in his writings and speeches and coupled his affirmation with a firm declaration of his belief in their inevitable triumph. Asked by a young student for help in a debate on the subject of progress, the Judge wrote:

> Personally, I heartily support the idea that the world is getting better. I cannot see it another way. I am naturally an optimist. I couldn't be Judge of the Juvenile Court if I were not. . . . There ought not be any question from any source as to the truth of the affirmative of your proposition that the world is getting better. Christianity—everything would be a failure if it were not so, and we would all be involved in chaos.[21]

Lindsey's belief in the ultimate triumph of the good in society was closely related to his view that "bad" boys were almost entirely a product of a bad society. "I never saw but few children criminals," he wrote to the editor of a Colorado newspaper, "and I doubt if even they could be classed as such." For many years, when newspapers or school children asked him for his favorite quotation, he would send them the lines of James Whitcomb Riley:

> I believe all chillun's good
> Ef they're only understood;
> Even the bad ones, 'pears to me
> Es just as good as they kin be.[22]

The Judge's dominant belief in the goodness of children was transferred, within limits, to adults. At any rate, Lindsey *wanted* to believe in the good motives of those who were active in the good causes of the times. He felt uneasy, therefore, when his friend and ally E. W. Scripps confessed that he and Clarence Darrow were motivated more by hatred and contempt for the upper class than by any altruistic concern for its victims. Replying to the publishing magnate, the Judge admitted that he sometimes wondered if it were not true of all reformers, yet in the final analysis he could not bring himself to accept it, and wrote:

> I do believe there is such a thing as real love of right and justice and a real, unselfish interest in the sufferings and misfortunes of the oppressed. It may be, as I grow older, and my enthusiasm cools with age, and I can make a more perfect analysis, I may change, but, truly, I do not think you and Darrow should hold any such notions. In any event, I shall not—not yet.[23]

One intellectual paradox which Lindsey never fully resolved was brought out strikingly in his relationship with Lincoln Steffens, one of his three or four closest lifelong friends. The issue was the logical implication of Lindsey's environmentalism when it came to passing moral judgments on bad *men*—or, more broadly, bad adults. After all, it was not so difficult to forgive the youthful and the immature. But Lindsey's style characteristically invoked as harsh a condemnation of "the Beast" as it eloquently pleaded for a compassionate attitude toward children. Even though the Judge made the Beast an abstraction, its tools were very real human beings whose transgressions he treated in a manner scarcely calculated to make them lovable or even forgivable. Yet if children went wrong only on account of a bad environment or, in the rare instance, a pathological condition, and if adults were merely children grown large, was it not both uncharitable and unjust to denounce or punish them for their crimes?

Lindsey's friend Steffens thought that it was, and used a parable to make his point. One of Steffens' favorite stories was his account of a confrontation he claimed to have had with a bishop, which led to a discussion of the problem of the origin of evil. The journalist used the biblical version of the Garden of Eden as the background for his lesson. After describing the events, he asked if the responsibility were Adam's because he ate the forbidden fruit? Or was it Eve's because she tempted Adam? Or was the explanation the one so dearly loved by the clergy—that it was the serpent (Satan) who tempted Eve? No, Steffens would say, as he warmed up to his punch line: the problem was the apple! Steffens applied this moral to American society in 1908 in an article entitled "An Apology for Graft," in which he argued that since "the system" was at fault because it offered the best "apples" to the strongest men, reformers should concentrate on abolishing "the system" and "let the crooks go, who would confess and tell us the truth."[24]

Some liberals found the article upsetting, and Francis Heney, erstwhile prosecutor of political corruption in California and a friend of both Lindsey and Steffens, asked the Judge to write to the "wavering" muckraker and "make an effort to set him right." Lindsey diplomatically wrote, in a "Dear Stef" note:

> I am afraid your article . . . is being misunderstood. I think people sometimes confuse sympathy and justification, and it seems to me your article was an expression of sympathy for the underdog, rather than an offer of excuse for his crime. Christ sympathized with the sinner, but I believe he threatened all kinds of punishment to those who persisted in evil. I have myself, I think, made the mistake of letting my sympathy for the underdog run away with my judgment at times when I perhaps seemed to do what some people are inferring you have done. We will have to have the criminal courts and fearless prosecutors to prosecute grafters and thieves for a long time yet. Where I get off the trolley, I think, is this: I see the little fellows getting all the jail sentences and prosecutions, while the big fellows under our commercialized system of politics and general corruption of public morals are allowed to go free. . . .[25]

No reply to this letter has been found, but it is fair to assume that the Judge was in Steffens' thoughts twenty-three years later when he reflected, "The only reaction I got from this article was the wonder of good citizens and liberals whether I had sold out and gone back on reform!" The Judge's very gentle reproof had no adverse effect on the friendship of the two men and may even have made Steffens the more determined to convert Lindsey. That the debate was still on two years after Lindsey wrote is illustrated in a remarkable letter describing a meeting at Steffens' home in Connecticut, where Lindsey and Heney had come "for a jaw" after one of the Judge's speaking engagements in New York City. Steffens was describing with relish, though not maliciously, to Brand Whitlock, reform mayor of Toledo, how Heney had shifted his position to join him in "educating" the Judge:

> The best thing we did was to yank Lindsey along about a mile beyond where he had ever gone before. He had delivered a great address . . . Friday night; we all had heard it. Heney had spoken there too. But Lindsey wound up his hour and a half with an appeal for righteousness, and we jumped on him. He started it. He asked me what I thought of his speech. Persuaded that he really wanted to know, I told him. That let Record* loose, and he was awful. It was as if he had thrown the little judge down on the floor and beat him black and blue. Ben hollered for help,—once; he appealed to Heney. Hadn't Heney prosecuted bad men? And didn't that mean that he believed in bad men and good men? And Heney used to, you know; and he still habitually acts from that theory. But when he is thinking, Heney is as clear as the next one. So we went back on the judge.
>
> And that ended it. When Heney showed that he believed "something made bad men" and that good men were no good, little Ben gave up. He promised not to preach righteousness any more as a cure for evil, but to declare that we must abolish principles.[26]

Either Steffens overstated his triumph or the Judge had a change of heart, for he never publicly or privately declared in favor of the "abolition of principles." Even if he had been inclined to do so, it would have been risky for an elective official to make such a vaguely dangerous statement. Also, as a public figure with numerous political enemies, it would not have been easy for Lindsey to indulge in the luxury of refraining from attacking individuals, and the Judge's combative style of campaigning did not abate over the years. Nevertheless, Lindsey did repeatedly acknowledge his intellectual indebtedness to Steffens, and the journalist's views doubtless reinforced the Judge's in-

* George L. Record, lawyer and active leader in New Jersey Progressive politics.

clination to be compassionate toward adults, at least those adults who were not trying to do him out of his job. As a judge Lindsey continued to believe that confinement was sometimes necessary, but he stressed increasingly that its purpose was always to cure, not to "punish, hurt, or degrade." Even those whom society regarded as the most vicious criminals should be treated with altruism and compassion, since the world was barely out of the Dark Ages in its understanding of human motivation. Consistent with this view, the Judge wholeheartedly lent the prestige of his name, in 1914, when he served alongside Edwin Markham, Jack London, Helen Keller, and Clarence Darrow on the advisory board of the Anti–Capital Punishment Society of America.[27]

Steffens should have recognized, and probably a part of him did, that any relinquishing of moral tone by the Judge would not only have been inexpedient but, more important, would have run counter to Lindsey's whole personality. It was, for example, singularly appropriate for the Judge to describe one of his early lecture tours in the East by saying that he had just spent six weeks "preaching the gospel." The expression was not ironic. The Judge's temperament always moved him to appeal for reform in terms of moral duty. A strong national influence in the Progressive era which he found thoroughly congenial was the Social Gospel movement. Among the books he frequently recommended to young correspondents were Charles Sheldon's *In His Steps,* Walter Rauschenbusch's *Christianity and the Social Crisis,* and Bouck White's *The Call of the Carpenter.* The Social Gospel suited Lindsey partly because he liked to use such biblical language as "devourers of widows' houses" in his jeremiads against "the interests." It also had the advantage of providing an ethical-religious context devoid of any narrowly sectarian overtones, since the movement was not confined to any particular brand of Protestantism and had its analogues in Catholicism and Judaism. Its imagery could thus be invoked successfully with liberal elements in all major faiths and still be acceptable to others, like Lindsey, who had little or no interest in organized religion but who did have a strong moral orientation.[28]

Much of Lindsey's national appeal was based on his ability to observe and articulate what was familiar to large numbers of people. Brand Whitlock expressed the thought of many of Lindsey's readers when he wrote of the serialized version of *The Beast*:

> That story of yours in *Everybody's* is doing a lot of good. I wonder if you saw the comment I made on it and sent to Cosgrave.* I thought at first of indulging in some grim, sardonic humor and saying that to anyone who understood conditions the story was monotonous because it was the same everywhere, but I did not yield to that temptation for fear I would be misunderstood, but I said instead that the story of Denver was the story of every other city, and that if each reader would just look about him in his own town he could see it gradually being unfolded there.

Other readers did "look about" and see it elsewhere. "It is a great story you are telling in *Everybody's Magazine,*" Jacob Riis assured Lindsey, "and the East is following it with even sharper attention than your western country, for it is typical of the fight that goes on all over." Senator Robert M. La Follette of Wisconsin, on a speaking tour in Denver, shared with the Judge a letter from his wife in which she told of reading the Lindsey articles to the La Follette children. An associate justice of the Supreme Court of Colorado feelingly confided to the Judge his sorrow over rarely meeting an honest man in his public life and concluded: "Your audience is now the entire country. You have the faith and confidence of a vast majority of people. Be true to them and your future is assured. The Beast can't hurt you." For another decade and a half, at least, the prediction was correct.[29]

The empathy Lindsey projected in his anecdotal writing brought him more than the usual share of letters which any celebrity must expect from admirers, petitioners, cranks, and

* John O'Hara Cosgrave, editor of *Everybody's Magazine*.

persons simply suffering from an acute sense of anomie. Although the annual volume of such letters did not reach into the thousands until the 1920's, when Lindsey began to emphasize sexual themes in his writings, there was sufficient variety to his concerns in the pre-war years to arouse an urge in hundreds of ordinary citizens to write to him. Lindsey's small staff of assistants struggled valiantly to send every coherent writer at least a short answer, even when there was nothing to be done but to suggest that the party consult a lawyer, a clergyman, a physician, or, in the expressive terminology of the times, an alienist. If the writer lived in Denver it was occasionally possible to give a specific referral, but many of the letters were from outsiders with domestic relations problems (desertion and nonsupport ranked high) that could not be responsibly settled from afar.

The tedium of handling this correspondence was sometimes relieved by unusual letters. Some fell into a very clear-cut category which was aptly characterized in red pencil, "Nut." Sometimes a correspondent would show unintended humor, as in the case of a boy who elaborately praised the Judge's principles and methods but went on to inform him, in chatty style, that he was planning to "look up" a former teacher who, he alleged, had punished him unjustly—menacingly adding, "now that I am about his size." In a similar spirit, the Mutual Improvement League, an organization operating from within the confines of Arizona State Prison, was moved to write to the Judge: "Your [election] victory has a wholesome influence, especially upon us, because of our desire to see 'the higher-ups' get theirs and because you are our friend." On the gentler side a little girl in Mount Gilead, Ohio, gave the Judge some advice in 1909 on how to conduct his court:

> I saw your picture in the magazine and was anxious to write and tell you how much I love you for your kindness to the children. Little girls are very sensitive and feel delicate about telling any man the naughty things they have done. This is the reason

you do not get the whole truth from them, as you do from boys. I think they should be allowed to make their confessions to your wife, and she could tell you what they said.

Although the advice was premature, since Lindsey was four years away from first meeting his future wife, the little girl came remarkably close to describing a working arrangement that Lindsey later found useful with delinquent girls.[30]

Lindsey's eclectic interests, his intense curiosity, and his driving energy kept him in close touch with the changing mood of his times. Although the Judge was no revolutionary, he always had a friendly feeling for radicals and doubters. The same Lindsey who had a genuine friendship with Theodore Roosevelt and professed admiration for the aphorisms of Elbert Hubbard could also write to Max Eastman of his hope that *The Masses* would survive "the usual financial difficulties and embarrassments that come to such a publication." And he could assure Alexander Berkman, editor of *The Blast* in San Francisco, of his sympathy and support for Berkman's paramour, Emma Goldman, in her difficulties with the police over her public advocacy of birth control. The Judge's willingness to question the conventional wisdom and his concern that social institutions adapt themselves to changing times were evident in his attitudes toward the churches and the schools. He doubted that the church would ever regain the confidence of the people, "which it was fast losing," unless it became involved "in subjects that are rather economic . . . as distinguished from moral issues." In the field of education he frequently charged that the schools lost many pupils because they failed to interest the young. The school curriculum was often irrelevant to the needs of the children, Lindsey maintained, and the school regimen often bore a strong resemblance to that of a prison. Lindsey was responsive to John Dewey's call for a greater emphasis on social morality and democratic values in the public schools. He was interested, too, in methodology as well as content, and was intrigued with the new Montessori Method and its stress on teaching materials, games, and freedom of expression in the learning process. In 1913 the Judge joined John Dewey and other educators in an evening visit to Thomas A. Edison's laboratory in West Orange, New Jersey, where the inventor demonstrated the uses to which he hoped motion pictures could be put in revolutionizing the elementary school curriculum.[31]

Although Lindsey did not systematically explore most of the subjects that interested him, and rarely made any comments on his reading aside from a brief word of praise for some author he especially liked, his broad interests and mental receptivity made him an interesting person to intellectuals as well as to politicians and the general public. Nor was the interest confined to nonacademic intellectuals such as Steffens, Lippmann, and Scripps. Edward Thorndike, pioneer educational psychologist at Columbia, in an unsolicited personal letter, declared that "mental and moral education" would be much easier if others had the same insights as the Judge. G. Stanley Hall, philosopher-psychologist, invited the Judge to speak at Clark University, where Hall doubled as teacher and president. Stanford University invited the Judge, whom economic circumstances had forced to be a high school dropout, to give its annual Phi Beta Kappa address. That undergraduates as well as faculty appreciated Lindsey was apparent in an account of a visit to the East which the Judge wrote to his friend Scripps. It revealed Lindsey's unusual capacity to combine an empathy for youth with an almost conservative faith in the ultimate triumph of political democracy:

> During my visit East, I think the most enthusiastic audience I had anywhere was at Harvard University; the next, perhaps, was Yale. At lecture hall in Harvard—the largest hall in Cambridge—the place was packed and jammed, and I think there were nearly as many turned away as were able to get in. I was amazed to find one of the most radical groups of students I ever encountered. During the past few years, I have visited many large universities in America—and the most radical leaders of these groups are such men as the grandson of former President Elliot of Harvard

and the grandson of Henry W. Longfellow. I found similar radicalism among the professors, especially at Harvard and at Columbia University where I had lunch with some of the faculty.
Nothing could have been more sympathetic, enthusiastic, and
genuine than the reception given me at these great universities.
Indeed, I have been almost compelled to promise to return to
Harvard next year and deliver a series of lectures at the invitation
of some of the radical groups and before the professors and the
students.

I should say that it is perhaps the most hopeful and significant
thing I have encountered in all my travels over the nation. From
the many letters and invitations I have received from Leland Stanford University I have an idea that there is a similar spirit in that
institution. Truly, I was somewhat startled at the radicalism of
some of the Harvard men—men from the very first families of
America—families of wealth and intelligence where we might
expect to find everything that is reactionary. If anything, I rather
gasped at what seemed to be their extremes, but no doubt that is
due to the exuberance of youth and their devotion to ideals is the
sort of exaggeration that will eventually be balanced by that sound
judgment that will make them average up about right as tremen-
dous powers for good in the fight ahead.[32]

Perhaps the person who best described Lindsey's growing
reputation and appeal throughout the country was the daughter
of Senator La Follette. Writing to thank the Judge for the
prestigious support he had given the cause of woman suffrage
by allowing his name to be associated with it, she concluded:

I don't suppose you're conscious of the deep personal feeling
that people have for you all over the country, whether in little out
of the town villages or in the poor congested quarters of the big
cities, or the leisurely homes of the more well-to-do. No name that
I ever mention in speaking gets the same quick, warm response.
And no one that I quote from carries the same finality of conviction.[33]

It was not the first time that the Judge's name had been used
to bolster a national cause, but the pace of his participation was
soon to be quickened as he became deeply involved, in 1911–
1912, in the national Progressive movement.

5 / The Bull Mouse and Colorado Progressivism

INDSEY'S EMERGENCE AS A MAJOR LEADER OF THE PROGRESSIVE
movement in Colorado was a logical outcome of his
involvement in municipal, state, and national politics for
almost a decade. As early as 1905 the Judge, convinced that it
was pointless to talk about controlling the public utilities companies as long as their agents controlled the machinery of government, had prepared a Voters Registration Act to prevent the
padding of election rolls that had notoriously characterized elections in Denver and several other Colorado communities for
years. Although the legislature added some weakening amendments to the bill, its passage was hailed by the *Denver Post* as an
important first step in giving some control of government to
"the people." As Lindsey put it, if the legislature could be persuaded to add a direct primary law and a headless-ballot amendment to its achievements, it might become possible "to hear
Lincoln's Gettysburg address read aloud in Colorado without
turning pale."[1]

As the Judge's remark implied, there was still a great deal
to be done before "direct democracy" came to Colorado. A few
months after the passage of the Voters Registration Act, Lindsey
joined a group of progressive businessmen to form the State
Voters League. The Judge was chosen its first president. The
League adopted the slogan, "A Square Deal for Every Voter,"
openly professed its nonpartisanship (its vice-president was a
Republican), and proclaimed as its first specific goals the enactment of an efficient primary law and the adoption of legislation

to protect bank depositors through adequate regulation and supervision. Although even these modest aims were not to be attained for several years, the State Voters League was an important milestone in Lindsey's career because it brought him into contact with three of the men who were later to play important roles in the Colorado Progressive movement.[2]

The first of these was Edward P. Costigan, whom Lindsey had known briefly in his boyhood when they had spent two years together at Notre Dame. Costigan had gone on to graduate from Harvard. Subsequently he read law and was admitted to the bar in Utah, and began a law practice in Denver at the turn of the century. He soon became identified with the liberal faction of the Republican party and was helpful in winning the first, and last, Republican nomination for Lindsey in 1904. The Judge and Costigan became political collaborators for more than a decade and remained friends until Costigan's death in 1939. Two other officers in the State Voters League with whom Lindsey sometimes worked closely were James H. Causey, an investment broker who later became state treasurer of the Colorado Progressive party, and James S. Temple, manager of the Denver branch of the Western Newspaper Union and later candidate for the office of State Treasurer on the Progressive ticket in 1912. Although Lindsey's relationship with Causey and Temple was always peripheral in contrast to his association with Costigan, it was indirectly responsible for a rather close association, a few years later, with E. W. Scripps. Causey was instrumental in persuading Scripps in 1906 to establish the *Denver Express* as a counterweight to the partisan *Republican* and *Rocky Mountain News* and the erratically reformist *Denver Post*.[3]

In spite of his frequent and friendly associations with liberal Republicans, Lindsey continued to consider himself basically a Democrat. In 1906 a number of the Judge's friends urged him to run for governor on the Democratic ticket. By this time he had acquired a national reputation as the "Kids' Judge," and his attacks on the varieties of chicanery that characterized Colorado politics had marked him as a reformer who was not a one-issue candidate. A scandalous situation that had followed in the aftermath of the last gubernatorial election seemed to make 1906 a promising year for the Democratic candidate. In 1904 it had appeared that the Democratic candidate, Alva Adams, had won the governorship. Accusations of large-scale fraud were soon made, however, and the state legislature, dominated by Republicans, had the task of deciding certain contested election results. The legislature made a curious compromise. Alva Adams' Republican opponent, James Peabody, was declared the winner but only on condition that he resign immediately in favor of his Republican Lieutenant-Governor, Jesse McDonald. The 1906 election would give the voters their first chance to react to the charge that Adams had been cheated out of the governorship. Some observers thought that any Democrat would have a good chance of winning on the "vindication issue." By early summer, however, it was still not clear who the Democratic candidate would be.

In July 1906 Lindsey wrote privately to Adams (who had served two previous terms as governor) and asked about his intentions regarding the 1906 campaign. Lindsey pledged his support to the former governor if he ran. Adams' personal reply did not differ from his public statements on the subject. He mentioned his earlier service, declared that there were other fine candidates among the Democrats, and expressed the hope that he would not be asked to run. A few cynics surmised that he may have left out an additional consideration—an ambition to become a United States Senator. In any event, one thing was crystal clear to any moderately astute political observer: Alva Adams had not closed the door on the Democratic nomination for the governorship.[4]

At the same time that Adams was professing his desire not to run, the *Denver Post* introduced a new element into the political scene when it announced its support of a "draft Lindsey" movement. The *Post's* motives were not entirely clear, but some observers believed that the move was an effort to steal the thunder from Senator Thomas W. Patterson, Democratic king-maker and owner of the *Post's* journalistic rival, the *Rocky Mountain News*. A few days after the announcement in the *Post,* Lindsey declared that he would accept the nomination if it were offered to him at the forthcoming Democratic convention. Alva Adams now got off the fence and paid a visit to Senator Patterson in Denver. After their meeting Adams announced his candidacy for the governorship. The *Rocky Mountain News* immediately came out in support of Adams, and a month later the Democratic convention gave him the nomination.[5]

There can be little doubt that Lindsey's wisest course at this point would have been to withdraw from the race. By mid-September it was clear that his only important support came from the *Denver Post*. When the Judge refused to support a slate of candidates for the legislature backed by the *Post* and, in some instances, by Senator Patterson's rival for influence in the Demo-cratic party, Mayor Speer of Denver, the *Post* withdrew its sup-port of Lindsey and eventually endorsed the Republican candi-date for the governorship. As the Judge correctly surmised, there was no longer the faintest chance for his candidacy. The Repub-licans shrewdly nominated a clean-government type, the Rev-erend Henry Augustus Buchtel, a Methodist minister and chan-cellor of the University of Denver. The election results in November were:

> Henry A. Buchtel, Republican 92,602
> Alva Adams, Democrat 74,416
> Ben Lindsey, Independent 18,014
> William Haywood, Socialist 16,015
> F. C. Chamberlain, Prohibitionist 2,087

The returns shed an interesting light on one aspect of the Judge's original decision to enter the race. In August Lindsey had confided to Lincoln Steffens that he had just talked with

Clarence Darrow, who was in Denver, about Adams' possible candidacy. Darrow had urged him to run, Lindsey told Steffens, on the ground that Socialists and "laboring people" would have little enthusiasm for Adams but would strongly support the Judge. After the election Lindsey always maintained that if Patterson had backed him rather than Adams at the state convention the entire Democratic ticket would have won in November 1906, and even Alva Adams could have been elected United States Senator a few months later by a new Democratic legislature. If Lindsey's premise that Adams' vote could have been transferred to him more or less intact is correct, and if even a small number of Socialists would have defected in the Judge's favor, the assertion that Lindsey could have won the governorship has considerable plausibility.⁶

Although Lindsey never became a candidate for national office, his interest in the national scene went back almost as far as his involvement in state and local politics. It grew out of several considerations which may be roughly classified as ideological, political, and personal. On the ideological or policy level, Lindsey's prevailing view that crime was basically a result of economic and social injustice logically led him to encourage and support national leaders who also advocated giving "the people" a more direct voice in government through such measures as the initiative, the referendum, the recall, and the direct primary. These measures, the Judge always insisted, must be supported not merely as ends in themselves. "Direct democracy," as he reminded his readers in *The Beast,* would be the entering wedge whereby substantive measures such as the eight-hour law, employers' liability legislation, strengthened public utilities commissions, and improved child labor laws throughout the nation could be attained. Given his Progressive beliefs, Lindsey logically supported and worked with leaders outside Colorado on the same bipartisan basis that caused him to associate with Progressive Republicans at home. As early as 1904 he congratulated Republican Robert La Follette on his re-election as governor of Wisconsin (two months later La Follette was to be chosen by the legislature to go to the United States Senate). On the same day the Judge sent a victory message to reform Democrat Joseph W. Folk, who had just won the governorship of Missouri, and added, "I am for you for President in 1908." As political events rolled on toward the Progressive campaign of 1912, Lindsey's widely publicized speeches and articles placed him in the vanguard of nationally known political figures whose sympathies were consistently on the side of Progressive leaders and causes.[7]

On the political level Lindsey's involvement in emergent national progressivism was reflected in the endorsements he exchanged with candidates from one end of the country to the other. Pre-eminent among them was Theodore Roosevelt, whose political association with the Judge lasted from 1904 to 1916 and whose friendship was apparently never marred by a single incident. On numerous occasions Lindsey visited Roosevelt in the East, and each gave the other political support. What could have been the one serious test of their friendship occurred in 1916 when the Judge supported Woodrow Wilson's successful bid for a second term in the White House. Roosevelt and the remnants of the Progressive party supported the Republican candidate, Charles Evans Hughes. Lindsey knew that Roosevelt personally detested Wilson and clearly felt a certain diffidence about asking him if he could quote some favorable comments about himself that Roosevelt had made in earlier years. The Judge was in the midst of his usual quadrennial battle to stay on the Juvenile Court, and every endorsement helped. Roosevelt rose to the occasion in a very warm reply to the Judge in which he expressed his regrets that Lindsey could not see his way clear to support Hughes but reaffirmed his admiration for his record in Colorado and authorized him to repeat his earlier endorsements.[8]

In addition to Roosevelt, Lindsey exchanged political endorsements with Brand Whitlock, reform mayor of Toledo, whose novel *The Turn of the Balance* (1907), written while he was in office, appealed to the Judge for its humanitarian concern with prison reform; with Tom Johnson, former conservative businessman whose legend held that he saw the inequities of the capitalist system only after a streetcar conductor persuaded him to read Henry George's *Progress and Poverty* and who went on to become reform mayor of Cleveland; and with Hiram Johnson, who completed the prosecution of the notorious Abe Ruef machine in San Francisco after his predecessor, Francis J. Heney, was shot in open court, and who subsequently became governor of California and Progressive candidate for Vice-President of the United States. By 1910 it may be fairly said that there was a national progressive (still small p) network burgeoning and that Lindsey was one of those in the center of it. When Senator La Follette's future career seemed in jeopardy in the 1910 Wisconsin primaries, out-of-state progressive stalwarts such as Albert Cummins of Iowa, George Norris of Nebraska, and Francis Heney of California (whose gunshot wound had not proved fatal) descended on Wisconsin to support him. Among the most effective speakers in the visiting delegation was Ben Lindsey. Two weeks after his victory, La Follette wrote to the Judge:

> Had it not been for the campaign which you and other friends made in behalf of our cause, I feel certain that the money of the opposition and its close organization would have prevailed to the extent of rendering the legislature doubtful, if not giving it control.[9]

Since Lindsey never became a candidate for national office, the question arises why he spent so much time and energy on national politics. Aside from reasons of principle and practical political advantage, Lindsey's national prestige as a juvenile court judge and his travels throughout the country put him in contact with the leading political figures of his time, and the Judge understandably took an almost boyish delight in being on the inside track of political trends. The pleasure must have been multiplied when he reflected on the hard years of his youth and how far he had come. Although Lindsey never lost the common touch, he now "walked with kings," or at least with their American equivalents. At times his ebullience over the distinguished company in which he found himself almost overflowed. In a letter to "the Bunch," as he called a small group of his liberal Colorado friends, he wrote:

> I had a *great* visit with T. R. He is *just* great, great! Never saw him in better, fitter shape for the fight, and *radical*—just as radical as we want him. Had a private conference with him and his manager, Mr. [Medill] McCormick last night at Sagamore Hill. *Just a few friends,* Anne Morgan [the daughter of J. P. Morgan] among them. The invitation was to spend the afternoon and night at his home. We had a great time. . . . Lordy, Lordy, around the fireplace last night it seemed like a meeting of our Bunch.[10]

Perhaps Lindsey's infectious enthusiasm was part of the explanation for Theodore Roosevelt's abiding affection for him. After all, it was part of the Roosevelt legend that the newly elevated President had once exclaimed, at one of his first White House dinners, "Isn't this fun!"

Lindsey's national prominence as a representative of progressivism grew with his political victories in Colorado. His defeat in the 1906 gubernatorial race was soon forgotten as he went on to win re-election to the Juvenile Court two years later in a campaign that attracted national attention. Failing to win the nomination of either the Democratic or Republican parties in 1908, the Judge confounded political professionals by winning a landslide victory as an independent candidate. Only E. W. Scripps' *Denver Express* had strongly supported Lindsey's candidacy from the beginning, but the support of liberal clergymen and "working people," as the Judge wrote to Lincoln Steffens, clinched the victory. Endorsements from William Allen White, Brand Whitlock, Francis Heney, and La Follette also reminded Denver voters of the Judge's national reputation.

A year later a national audience read Lindsey's story of the campaign as his "The Beast and the Jungle" began its serial appearance in *Everybody's Magazine*.[11]

In the next four years Colorado progressivism reached the zenith of its success. Lindsey was a key figure in every phase of the movement at the state and local levels as well as on the national scene. The stage was set for a series of victories when liberal Democrat John Franklin Shafroth was elected governor at the same time Lindsey won his own re-election as an independent. When the new legislature met in January 1909 the governor's recommendations, in his inaugural address, included the adoption of a direct primary law, the initiative and referendum, a new banking law, a strengthened public utilities commission, the direct election of United States Senators (soon to be achieved by federal constitutional amendment), and the adoption of the headless ballot. Although most of these measures became bogged down in the legislature for some time, there was compensation for Lindsey in the Denver election of May 1910, which represented one of the greatest Progressive victories in the country on the municipal government front.

In that election the voters of Denver approved the initiative, referendum, and recall amendments to the city charter and voted to create a public utilities corporation that would assume municipal ownership of the city water supply. The Denver Union Water Company, which hoped for renewal of its existing franchise, and Mayor Robert W. Speer, who campaigned for "a business settlement of the water question," went down to defeat. The victors were the Municipal Ownership League, the Denver Christian Citizenship Union, the Denver Citizens' party, and some segments of the Denver press. The result was a victory for many forces, but Lindsey could justifiably claim that he played a major role in the achievement. He was actively involved with all the groups that helped bring about the victories, and he was a member of the executive committee of the

Citizens' party which drafted the amendments to the city charter. Perhaps most important of all, his articles in *Everybody's Magazine,* which appeared while the municipal election campaign was at its peak, strongly advocated "direct democracy" and portrayed the Denver Union Water Company as the living embodiment of "the Beast" and Mayor Speer as one of its principal tools. Not surprisingly, the Judge wrote exultantly to William Allen White in the aftermath of the election:

> We won a glorious victory at the Spring elections over the combined opposition of the Democratic and Republican machine. . . . Our proposed charter amendments for the initiative, referendum, and recall for the city of Denver won out against the bitter opposition of both party machines, the Democratic Mayor, the police department and all the public service corporations, with a campaign fund that was almost unbelievable to outsiders—we had about $1,400 and the sentiment of the community, with the *News* and *Times* and the Denver *Express* putting up a splendid fight for us.[12]

In 1911 the Judge continued his active participation in municipal politics, pressing strongly for the commission form of government, a Progressive panacea that eventually came to Denver for a brief period (1913–1916), only to die even more quickly than it did in every other major city where it was tried. George Creel, a fellow enthusiast for commission government, was a relative newcomer on the Denver scene. Lindsey affectionately described him to Brand Whitlock as an "editorial writer on the *News* and reformer-in-chief of the greatest aggregation of anarchists and insane people (the compliments of the enemy) ever gathered under one tent." Creel was a high-strung, articulate intellectual entrepreneur who would spend a lifetime alternating careers in public service and journalism. A Democrat, he soon became a member of that remarkable group, "the Bunch," which included Edward P. Costigan; Boyd Gurley, editor of Scripps's *Express;* former Senator Patterson of the *Rocky Moun-*

tain News; and Josephine Roche, Progressive daughter of a wealthy mine owner who served in various capacities on the Denver Juvenile Court and in later years became treasurer of the United Mine Workers. Lindsey and Creel became lifelong friends even though the young journalist's career in Denver was destined to be relatively short.[13]

Although Lindsey also found time in 1911 to play an active role in supporting the passage of several items of child welfare legislation he had drafted through the Colorado legislature, his mind was turning increasingly in the latter part of the year to the question of whose candidacy for the presidency he would support in 1912. The Judge had returned to the Democratic fold after his defeat in the 1906 race for the governorship, and had thoroughly mended his fences with the liberal Democratic element represented by Governor Shafroth and former Senator Patterson. In the fall of 1911 Lindsey played a major role in organizing a Woodrow Wilson Democratic Club in Denver. Lindsey knew the New Jersey governor slightly as a result of their mutual involvement in the Short Ballot Association, a national Progressive organization that also counted William U'Ren of Oregon and William Allen White among its prominent members. Joining with the Judge in the formation of the pro-Wilson Denver group were George Creel, Boyd Gurley, and Edward Keating, managing editor of the *Denver Express* who later became well known nationally as co-author of the first federal child labor law, the ill-fated Keating-Owen Act of 1916. In addition to his brief organizational role, Lindsey also helped the Wilson campaign in its early stages by helping William F. McCombs, Wilson's campaign manager, to make contacts with important Colorado Democrats, notably George Hosmer of Denver.[14]

The Judge's correspondence with national Progressive leaders, as well as his activities in Denver, made it perfectly clear that his support of Wilson did not guarantee that he was irrevocably committed for 1912 to the Democrats, or even to

Woodrow Wilson. Lindsey stated his position clearly to Senator La Follette in late October 1911:

> I am, as you know, while nominally a Democrat, just as much interested in the Progressive La Follette organization here as I am in the Progressive Democratic Wilson organization, and I have taken an active part recently in helping to establish both, feeling quite assured that neither of you will be opposed to each other in 1912. . . . If you should be nominated as a Progressive Republican against a Reactionary Democrat, it would be the joy of my life to get out and support you.[15]

Although the Judge did not explain why he felt assured that La Follette and Wilson would not "be opposed to each other in 1912," it was clear that Lindsey planned to make his own final decision by assessing the prospects for national progressivism in the light of rapidly changing developments. In October 1911 the nature of things to come was still very unclear. Perhaps the biggest question mark in regard to the coming campaign was the role that would be played by the Judge's closest friend among the potential candidates, Theodore Roosevelt.

There can be little doubt that Roosevelt was always Lindsey's favorite candidate. Although some of the Judge's close friends, such as E. W. Scripps and Lincoln Steffens, were skeptical about the former President's ability to "see the Beast," as Steffens put it, Lindsey always maintained that Roosevelt would ultimately take the "radical" stands that all of them would like to see a national leader assume. Undoubtedly Lindsey's assurances to his friends were partly motivated by deep feelings of affection and gratitude toward Roosevelt. On numerous occasions Roosevelt had given him strong support in his magazine, *The Outlook*. In August 1910 Roosevelt had visited Denver to give a public speech. A reception committee, hostile to Lindsey, had failed to invite the Judge to appear with Roosevelt on the platform, notwithstanding their well-known association and friendship. As Roosevelt spotted Lindsey in the audience (perhaps by prearrangement), he turned to several members of the committee who were escorting him and said, "Here is the man I have been demanding to see all day," and proceeded to invite the Judge to accompany him to the platform. The episode attracted national attention, Upton Sinclair wiring to Lindsey from New York, "Great about Roosevelt and you." It was a gesture Lindsey was not likely to forget.[16]

In November the Judge wrote to Roosevelt and asked about his intentions. He hoped that Roosevelt would not issue any Sherman-like "I would not run if nominated" statement to the press, because he felt that an unequivocal withdrawal from the race would comfort "the interests" too much. He realized that Roosevelt probably did not wish to be a candidate in 1912, but he wanted him to know that if Wilson were the Democratic candidate and Roosevelt the Republican, then he, Lindsey, would support Roosevelt. In early December Lindsey received a warm confidential reply from the former President. That Roosevelt's emphasis on the confidential nature of the letter was neither insincere nor merely flattering is indicated by the fact that parts of it would have been harmful to his own interest if they had appeared in the press at this time. Roosevelt asserted that Taft and other leading Republicans, such as Senator Aldrich and Speaker of the House Joseph Cannon, had so "burdened" the Republican party that any presidential candidate put forward by it in 1912 would be defeated. Nevertheless, Roosevelt declared, he was not prepared to state that he would "not accept the nomination under any circumstances." In the first place, such a statement would be too pleasing to "the special champions of Mr. Taft, and the special representatives of privilege and special interest," a point substantially the same as the one that Lindsey had made in his own letter of inquiry. Furthermore, Roosevelt added, there was at least one circumstance in which a Republican victory might be won—if a nomination clearly came from "the people" in spite of "any kind of wish or ambition" on his part. He added, however: "I do not think there will be any such demand." Perhaps this sentence was the least candid one in his letter. By January Roosevelt had moved significantly closer to entering the race. In mid-February he announced that his hat was in the ring.[17]

The person with whom Lindsey most fully shared his thoughts about the coming election, at least by correspondence, was E. W. Scripps. Although Scripps had gone into semi-retirement in 1908, he continued to maintain editorial control over his national chain of newspapers for several years. Meanwhile he advised his managers and editors to be guided by three principles: make a profit, observe the Ten Commandments, and serve the cause of the laboring man. After 1908 Scripps spent much of his time at his baronial estate Miramar, just north of San Diego, writing lengthy disquisitions on politics and economics which he shared with a number of Progressive leaders. As Scripps's directive to his editors suggested, he was an individualist whose ideas did not allow easy labels. He professed a strong sympathy for socialism, declared that the masses were constantly deceived and betrayed by a small elite that made all the important decisions for society, and made "God damn the rich!" one of his favorite private slogans. On the other hand, Scripps was often an autocrat in his own business and personal relations, had a strong belief in the survival of the fittest, and thought that most political reformers were frauds. A conspicuous exception to the last generalization, in his judgment, was Ben Lindsey. Lindsey's very character, the publisher once wrote to Lincoln Steffens, "is medicine to a sick soul."[18]

In January 1912 Scripps, in a letter to the Judge, offered his view on the relative merits of the potential candidates in the forthcoming presidential race:

> I am not only out of the party fold, but all of my newspapers are out of the party fold. Here is our choice. La Follette rather than any other Republican, Wilson rather than any other Democrat. Roosevelt rather than any other Republican than La Follette. Wilson rather than any Democrat or Republican except La Follette. La Follette sooner than any other Republican or Democrat, except

Wilson. Any Democrat rather than Taft. Roosevelt rather than any Democrat other than Wilson. Personally, I would rather support a Socialist than either Taft or Harmon,* if both Taft and Harmon lead their parties. If La Follette were nominated for the presidency, and Hiram Johnson for the vice presidency, I would rather support this ticket than Wilson and Lindsey.[19]

The La Follette candidacy presented an agonizing dilemma to many Progressive leaders in January. Scripps's letter to the Judge arrived just as a Roosevelt-La Follette crisis was approaching. Roosevelt was now in the process of deciding when and how to announce his candidacy. Already some Progressive leaders, such as Gifford and Amos Pinchot and Medill McCormick, while still nominally supporting the Wisconsin Progressive, were urging Roosevelt to declare himself. La Follette's staunchest supporters felt that Roosevelt's entry into the campaign at this late date would be an act of treachery against their candidate, who had fought against the conservative Republican national administration for years and had earned, in their opinion, the right to be considered the first choice for the nomination among Progressive Republicans. It was evident that Roosevelt's pending announcement was awaited with mixed feelings even by those who preferred him to La Follette. In February 1912 an incident occurred that enabled Ben Lindsey and other former supporters of La Follette to announce their shift to Roosevelt a few weeks later with a minimum loss of face.

On February 2, 1912, Senator La Follette delivered a disastrous speech before a publishers' dinner in Philadelphia. Although the content of the address has been described as impolitic (especially his attack on the press), the manner of delivery was the real tragedy of the evening. The Senator, affected perhaps by physical illness or mental exhaustion or both, delivered a rambling, repetitious, and almost incoherent address. Shortly afterward his office announced that he was canceling his speaking engagements for the next two weeks on account of ill-

* Judson Harmon, conservative Democratic governor of Ohio.

ness. The word was rapidly spread that La Follette was a nervous wreck and that his candidacy in 1912 was out of the question. Four days after the Philadelphia fiasco, Edward P. Costigan, now the recognized leader of Progressive Colorado Republicans and a sincere supporter of La Follette to this time, wrote from Washington, D.C., to fellow Progressive Republican leaders in Denver that he was convinced that the mantle of leadership had now inevitably fallen upon Theodore Roosevelt.[20]

For Lindsey the move to Roosevelt was hardly a shift at all, since he had never made a final commitment to La Follette. Given his relations with his own party, however, he felt it appropriate to write to Woodrow Wilson following Roosevelt's announcement of his candidacy. The Judge advised Wilson, in a private letter, that he had informed William McCombs in November that if Roosevelt became a candidate he felt he would have to support him for "personal reasons." Wilson wrote a courteous reply and said that he understood. Lindsey now began an all-out effort in Colorado on behalf of Roosevelt.[21]

The Judge surmised correctly that La Follette was still Scripps's first choice. Although Scripps did not dislike Roosevelt, he always believed that La Follette was the better man, both in terms of personal character and social perception. Scripps was troubled by what he regarded as the undue haste with which some of La Follette's Progressive supporters had deserted him for Roosevelt. Lindsey, in a letter to Hiram Johnson, suggested that Scripps may also have felt aggrieved that some of them had not consulted the publisher before announcing their shift of allegiance. Although Lindsey had never suggested to anyone that he would have supported La Follette over Roosevelt, he may have felt a certain diffidence about explaining his position to Scripps. Earlier he had written highly laudatory letters about La Follette to Scripps and had even come close to saying that La Follette was a man of greater depth than Roosevelt, as Scripps clearly felt. Now Lindsey tried to strike a responsive chord in the publisher by assuring him that Roosevelt had grown more radical. "I remember," Lindsey wrote to Scripps, "that one of [Roosevelt's] criticisms, a year ago, of our story, "The Beast and the Jungle," was that our story was all against the rich and that we did not point out the crookedness among the so-called criminal poor. He doesn't talk that way now." Despite Lindsey's efforts to make a case for Roosevelt, Scripps never seemed to recover his enthusiasm for the presidential race after the La Follette-Roosevelt rupture. In the final election he went along with most of his editors who decided to support Wilson against Taft and Roosevelt.[22]

After Roosevelt's formal entry into the presidential race, Progressive Republicans in Colorado began a campaign to send a delegation committed to him to the Republican convention scheduled to meet in Chicago in June. Lindsey was active in the effort, corresponding with Roosevelt, Medill McCormick, and Gifford Pinchot about the situation in Colorado and arranging meetings between Pinchot, Roosevelt, and Costigan while the latter was in the East. In many ways, however, the situation in the Colorado Republican party reflected the circumstances of the party in other states where there were no required presidential primaries. In spite of considerable grass-roots support for Roosevelt, the pro-Taft wing of the party dominated the machinery of the state Republican convention. Progressive Republicans argued that the state convention vote of 656 for Taft to 242 for Roosevelt ought to be recognized by splitting the Colorado delegation and giving Roosevelt's supporters at least some minority representation, but the argument got them nowhere. Faced with defeat, they decided to send a protesting delegation to Chicago. Its purpose was to strengthen Roosevelt's contention that he was the most popular Republican candidate despite Taft's majority among convention delegates. The two dominant personalities in the protesting Colorado delegation were Costigan and Lindsey. Two weeks after the convention nominated Taft and proceeded to adjourn, Costigan observed that the Colorado protesters received the same "federal officeholders'

'steamroller' " treatment that had made other Progressive pro-
tests over the running of the convention an exercise in futility.
With Taft's nomination official, the moment of truth for Colorado Progressives—and for Theodore Roosevelt—was at hand.
The answer was not long in coming. Before the week was out
Roosevelt announced that he would accept a third-party nomination. Costigan and Lindsey now returned home to help organize the Progressive party of Colorado. As the first national Progressive convention prepared to assemble in Chicago two months
later, Roosevelt asked Lindsey to second his nomination.[23]

On several occasions there had been newspaper speculation
that Lindsey might become a candidate for Vice-President.
Despite a comment by the Judge to Scripps in December 1911
that he knew enough about politics "to know that such a thing
would be quite impossible," the notion was not unreasonable.
Lindsey had a national reputation as a fighter for Progressive
principles, and the fact that he was a Westerner would give
geographical balance to the Progressive ticket. Lindsey's comment to Scripps had been made in regard to rumors of a Democratic nomination, usually in association with Woodrow Wilson.
Given the organization of the Democratic party in Colorado at
the time, the Judge was probably right that any support for a
Democratic nomination from his own state delegation was most
unlikely. His prospects as a Progressive aspirant might be more
promising.[24]

The closest approach to an official endorsement for the vice-
presidency that Lindsey ever received was a motion by the protesting delegation of Progressive Colorado Republicans that
attended the Republican National Convention in June. Under
the chairmanship of Costigan they declared in favor of a Roosevelt-Lindsey ticket. The motion meant little, however, since the
delegation claimed no official status (it called itself a "protestant" rather than a contesting delegation), and the task of organizing the Progressive party of Colorado still lay ahead. While
it is doubtful that the prospect of such a nomination played the

major role in Lindsey's original support of Roosevelt's candidacy, he was sufficiently intrigued by the idea to write to Gilson Gardner, an important member of the Scripps organization and a close confidante of Roosevelt, that he believed Scripps would be enthusiastic about a national Roosevelt-Lindsey ticket. There is no evidence that Lindsey ever directly approached Roosevelt on the matter. Although the Judge played an active role in organizing the Colorado Progressive State Convention that met on August 1 in Denver, and was chosen as a delegate to the National Progressive Convention where he seconded Roosevelt's nomination, nothing further was done about a Roosevelt-Lindsey ticket. For his running mate Roosevelt chose Governor Hiram Johnson of California.[25]

On one level the ensuing 1912 Progressive campaign in Colorado was a disaster. The Democrats won the November election in a landslide. The recognized leader of the Colorado Progressives, Edward P. Costigan, was defeated in the race for the governorship by Elias Ammons, whose reputation as a liberal Democrat was soon to be tarnished by his role in the great coal strike of 1914. Not a single statewide candidate of the Progressive party was elected. Lindsey was able to take some consolation in his own re-election to his judgeship, though he did not win the race as a candidate of the Progressive party.

Nevertheless, 1912 may be fairly called the greatest year of Progressive achievements in the history of Colorado. In May a combination of Progressive Republicans and Democrats brought to a temporary end the career of Robert W. Speer as mayor of Denver. In November, despite the defeat of Progressive candidates, the voters of Colorado exercised their recently won initiative to approve several major reforms advocated in the Colorado Progressive platform, including a number of measures that Lindsey had personally drafted. Notable among them were the mothers' compensation act, a women's eight-hour law, the headless ballot, a strengthened civil service law, legislation restricting the power of judges to punish for contempt of court, and a unique measure drafted by Lindsey that provided for the recall of judicial decisions. The election of Democrat John W. Shafroth to the United States Senate was also a victory for progressivism, if not for Colorado Progressives. By contrast with the rather meager record of the next few years, the period 1910–1912 would appear in retrospect as the heroic period of Colorado progressivism.[26]

Lindsey retained his connection with the Colorado and national Progressive movement for two more years, serving on the Legislative Reference Bureau of the national Progressive Service and acting briefly as a national committeeman. At the same time he continued his own personal campaign for a wide variety of reform measures, including a state constitutional amendment to allow women to sit on juries, a law to provide for the appointment of a woman as assistant judge in handling the cases of girl delinquents in the larger counties, a general codification of the laws of Colorado relating to women and children, an improved adult probation law, and a law restricting newspaper publicity in juvenile cases. Only the last of these measures was enacted in 1913. The following year saw the state torn asunder by the coal strike controversy. In November 1914 Costigan ran again as Progressive candidate for governor and was again defeated, this time by a Republican opponent, George A. Carlson. At the beginning of 1915 the Judge confided to Hiram Johnson that he saw little prospect for the future of the Progressive party in Colorado. By 1916 both Lindsey and Costigan were ready to support Woodrow Wilson and permanently identify themselves with the Democrats. For Costigan it was the beginning of a national career, starting with an appointment to the federal Tariff Commission and culminating in the 1930's in a United States senatorship and a role of legislative leadership under the New Deal. For Lindsey there were still many political battles to be fought in Colorado. Meanwhile, events in Europe were laying the groundwork for two unexpected interruptions in the Judge's career.[27]

6 / Over There

IN 1914 FEW AMERICANS WERE INTELLECTUALLY OR EMOTION-
ally ready to cope with the outbreak of a general war in
Europe. In later years it became a popular pastime among
collectors of human foibles to discover quotable pre-1914 statements by popular journalists and respected statesmen assuring
their audiences that general wars were a thing of the past. The
"Hague System" for the arbitration of international disputes, the
fear among the ruling classes that war would bring revolution
and socialism, and a generalized notion that modern man had
outgrown war were cited by those who counseled optimism.
The confidence that peace was inevitable undoubtedly contributed to a certain lack of American interest in world affairs.
Complacency was sometimes reflected at the highest level.
When Woodrow Wilson gave his first inaugural address on
March 4, 1913, his sole reference to foreign affairs was a peripheral comment that the nation's high tariff policy was having an
adverse effect on the volume of American exports.

Like most of his contemporaries, Ben Lindsey gave little
sustained thought to what was happening in foreign countries.
He did, of course, take pride in the interest that his court elicited
abroad, and he was pleased by the visits of foreign social workers
and judges who came to Denver to study his methods. A reformer had more than enough tasks to keep himself busy at
home, however, and the Judge usually confined his involvement
in matters outside the country to giving a few words of encouragement and advice to those who were advancing children's
causes abroad. Lindsey's humanitarian sympathies did move
him to take stands in two other areas that had international

ramifications. He spoke out sharply against the pogroms in Russia and lent his name in 1907 to the executive committee of the Friends of Russian Freedom, which denounced czarist political repression and the persecution of the Jews.[1] Another subject which aroused the Judge's liberal and humanitarian sympathies was the peace movement. He frequently professed his admiration for Tolstoy, calling the Russian advocate of nonviolence "the man with the greatest vision that has found any expression on this small planet." Conversely he abhorred militarism, both for the regimentation of the spirit that it encouraged and for its social waste. When David Starr Jordan of Stanford University sent him a copy of his book *The Unseen Empire* (1912), with its scathing indictment of the cost of armaments, Lindsey congratulated the author, endorsed the book, and expressed his interest in "spreading and boosting this sort of thing."[2]

As the world holocaust entered its second year in the summer of 1915, at least one American felt a growing compulsion to do something personally to halt the slaughter of hundreds of thousands of young men. In August Henry Ford announced he was ready to make any sacrifice to bring peace to suffering humanity. Ford's declaration attracted the attention of a strong-willed Hungarian woman by the name of Rosika Schwimmer. Madame Schwimmer, as she was invariably called, was on a lecture tour in the United States and was trying to arouse support for mediation of the war by the neutral countries. She had impressive credentials. Madame Schwimmer was a recognized leader in both the equal suffrage and peace movements in Europe and had a cordial relationship in the United States with Jane Addams, also a strong believer in mediation. In November 1915 Madame Schwimmer managed to obtain an interview with Ford. With the help of Louis P. Lochner* she persuaded Ford

* Lochner's name was most widely known to the general public a generation later when he served as a foreign correspondent in Berlin and won a Pulitzer prize for his reporting in 1939.

to advance $10,000 to lobby for "continuous mediation." The idea at this stage was to bring pressure on President Wilson to establish a formal commission for mediation with all the prestige of the most powerful neutral nation behind it.

Ford and Lochner left for New York City and set up a meeting at the McAlpin Hotel on November 21 with Jane Addams, Dean George W. Kirchwey of Columbia University Law School, Paul Kellogg, editor of *Survey,* the leading journal in the social welfare field, and Madame Schwimmer. Two important decisions were made at the meeting. First it was agreed that Ford and Lochner would go immediately to Washington and ask President Wilson to appoint a commission whose expenses would be underwritten by Ford. Also, it was decided to charter a ship to take the commission to Europe. This was the result of a remark by Lochner, perhaps facetious, that appealed to Ford's imagination. Despite a protest from Jane Addams that Lochner's proposal was flamboyant, Ford authorized Madame Schwimmer to conclude a deal with a neutral shipping company. Within twenty-four hours she chartered the Scandinavian-American liner *Oscar II,* soon to be dubbed the "Ford Peace Ship."

On November 22 Ford and Lochner met with President Wilson. The meeting began cordially. If the President found Ford's dangling one leg over the arm of his chair during the interview offensive, he concealed any resentment at the implication that this was a negotiation between equals. After Ford and Lochner stated their case, Wilson said he was most sympathetic but was in no position to commit himself to any specific mediation proposal. To Ford, who had just expressed his willingness to finance a commission if the President would appoint one, the President's remarks were most unsatisfactory. "He's a small man," Ford observed to Lochner after the meeting. But the project was not dead. On November 24 Ford held a press conference in New York City and revealed that he had chartered a ship which would carry an expeditionary force of peacemakers to Europe on December 4. In words that he probably regretted later, he announced, "We are going to try to get the boys out of their trenches and back to their homes by Christmas Day." At Madame Schwimmer's suggestion, an invitation was sent to Judge Ben B. Lindsey to join the expedition. She urged that the Judge's international reputation, both as a defender of children's causes and a supporter of woman suffrage, made him an obvious choice. If her memory can be relied on twenty-seven years afterward, Lindsey's was the first name that occurred to her.[3]

Lindsey's reaction to the invitation, which came in Ford's name, was mixed. The Judge was sympathetic with the motives behind the expedition but skeptical about its practicality. The very endorsements it was receiving from peace societies and clergymen reinforced Lindsey's doubts. His own belief in the irrationality of war had not led him to absolute pacifism. While it was true that the "continuous mediation" proposal did not logically require its adherents to be pacifists, Lindsey was concerned that his friends understand that he was a supporter of preparedness at the same time he advocated peace.[4] Leaving aside questions of principle, there were immediate personal considerations to take into account. He would not want to make the trip without his wife. It would also be necessary to make financial arrangements to compensate a judge who would serve during his leave of absence from the court. If these matters could be worked out to his satisfaction, the Judge advised Ford, he was ready to join the peace expedition. Characteristically, he asked the advice of a few friends in regard to a decision already made. Theodore Roosevelt, who understood him, suggested that he go. Although Roosevelt was utterly contemptuous of what he liked to call the "flapdoodle" pacifist mentality, he advised Lindsey that his presence might accomplish some good in what was doubtless a worthless venture. After a further exchange of telegrams with Ford, the Judge and Mrs. Lindsey agreed to join the delegates who would sail on December 4 from Hoboken for Norway.[5]

There is no reason to believe the Judge ever had any real faith in the "continuous mediation" proposal. A few days before the *Oscar II* sailed he commented to J. P. Morgan's daughter, Anne, whom he knew slightly through her interest in social welfare projects and their mutual friendship with Roosevelt, that "the most important thing that can come from such an effort is the proof of its futility, if that should be the way it turns out." The remark may have reflected a certain diffidence about participating in a venture that was being described in the press alternately as "pro-German" or "crackpot," but it is more likely that it simply represented Lindsey's recognition that peace was not to be won by sending a motley group of well-intentioned voyagers to Europe on little more than a week's notice. To Charles A. Beard he wrote, "I am very much afraid it is a hopeless undertaking, but it may be we will go."[6] The question inevitably arises, why *did* he go?

Lindsey's reasons, though they were perhaps not entirely clear in his own mind, probably grew out of a general restlessness and lack of direction which had been troubling him for some time. Ford's invitation, which arrived on the eve of the Judge's forty-sixth birthday, came at a time when he was at the peak of his fame as a juvenile court judge. Yet the court alone had never entirely satisfied his eclectic interests and restless spirit. Even the peripheral work associated with the judgeship, notably his numerous legislative campaigns for child welfare, absorbed only a part of his fantastic energy. He had a constant need to be where the action was, politically and culturally, and in spite of his deep involvement in Colorado politics he cultivated his association with such men as Riis, Steffens, Roosevelt, and Scripps not only for the political help they could sometimes give him but also for their wide range of ideas and for the vicarious feeling they gave him of being at the window of the great world in which he wished to play a role. When the first announcement about the Ford Peace Ship was made, there were rumors that William Jennings Bryan, Thomas A. Edison, and

Jane Addams would be among the passengers.* If the rumors were true, it would be the kind of company Ben Lindsey would find congenial. In any event, the trip would certainly give him an opportunity to meet Henry Ford!

The situation in Denver in 1915 may also have made an opportunity for escape very welcome. For several years the Judge had carried on a feud with Dr. Mary Elizabeth Bates, one-time chairman of the Board of County Visitors for Denver, and E. K. Whitehead, secretary of the State Bureau of Child and Animal Protection.† The feud originally concerned a disagreement, which became public, about the adequacy of existing child labor laws in Colorado and a jurisdictional conflict between the Juvenile Court and the Board of County Visitors respecting dependent children. After the publication of *The Beast,* Whitehead's organization escalated its attacks on Lindsey in a small journal called *Clay's Review.* The Judge replied that this was what he would expect from an agency of "the interests." Undoubtedly Lindsey's growing habit of referring to Whitehead as "Spitehead" did nothing to appease the situation. In 1912 Whitehead and Dr. Bates formed an organization they called the Women's Protective League. Its chief aim was to bring about a recall of Lindsey by convincing the voters that the Judge was consistently lenient with sex offenders. In crude propaganda circulars distributed by the league, alleged black rapists were singled out as the beneficiaries of the Judge's softness. The campaign reached its low point when an investigator for the league claimed that the Judge had once sexually molested two boys in his court chambers. A grand jury investigation was launched which culminated on April 12, 1915, in a public censure of Bates and Whitehead and an indictment of the investigator for criminal libel. On the same day the grand jury made its report,

---

* All three were invited. Ford's press agents in New York erroneously announced that Addams and Edison had accepted. Bryan eventually came to the pier and saw the party off, as did Edison.

† The latter organization, despite its title, was merely a private agency that received a partial public subsidy.

Governor George A. Carlson announced that he would veto two bills recently passed by Judge Lindsey's enemies to abolish the Juvenile Court. A month later the governor also vetoed a bill to continue public subsidy of the Bureau of Child and Animal Protection. It was a moment of unique triumph for the Judge.[7]

In spite of the resounding vindication, the bitter struggle took its physical and psychological toll on Lindsey. Toward the end of it the Judge began seriously to consider the possibility of leaving Denver and devoting all his time to public lectures. Upton Sinclair and Lincoln Steffens encouraged him to do so, Sinclair commenting that it was hopeless to engage in such petty fights "as long as the capitalist system exists." Charles and Mary Beard concurred and summarized their reasons:

> First, we think you have had enough of that atmosphere out there and that to live in so much bitterness and nagging is not good for your spirit. Second, we agree with you that you have done your big work on the bench there so far as working out the details and principles of the juvenile court and that further service cannot add to your experience or knowledge of the problems involved. Third, we are inclined to hold that you have had enough of the actual contact with the unwholesome things that naturally come up in a juvenile court and would find relief from it welcome. Fourth, judging from the splendid lecture we heard you give here in New Milford, you could find all the platform work you wanted for an indefinite period and could help immensely not only the juvenile movement but the whole progressive movement as well. Fifth, we do not see how your enemies can make any capital out of your going because you have just won a big battle and you have come out of all the mess with a clean bill of health.

The Redpath Lyceum Bureau, asked by the Judge to let him know "the very best proposition" they could make, offered him a renewable contract for thirty-eight weeks at $15,000, more than three times his judicial salary. Whatever his reasons, the Judge ultimately decided against the move and even gave reports of his offer to the press, but his continuing exploration of other opportunities suggests that his search was genuine and not merely an election maneuver. Indeed, the potential prospects afforded by the Ford invitation at the end of the year may have been Lindscy's main reason for accepting it.[8]

The departure of the Ford Peace Ship took on a carnival-like atmosphere which the press exploited to the hilt. In all fairness, circumstances played into their hands. Ford helped by inviting more than fifty newspaper reporters and about two dozen college students to come along on the trip. Roger W. Babson wanted to join the party, wiring unsuccessfully to Lochner, "In the interest of peace, I beseech you to decide in favor of the Paramount Pictures Company." A band appeared to serenade the peace pilgrims as they prepared to leave, and one of the reporters accompanying the expedition decided to marry his fiancée at dockside. The ceremony was performed by one of the better-known delegates, the Reverend Jenkin Lloyd Jones, a minister who had won a degree of fame—or notoriety—throughout the Midwest and whose flowing white beard somehow added a bizarre note to the festivities. Ford generously gave the newlyweds a "bridal suite" aboard the *Oscar II*. He offered Thomas Edison a million dollars, as the two men stood on deck just before sailing time, if the near-deaf inventor would join the expedition, but Edison appeared not to understand. In the general confusion two stowaways successfully concealed themselves and made the trip across the Atlantic. Several anonymous wags sent caged squirrels to the vessel to accompany the "nuts." As the *Oscar II* steamed southward down the Hudson into Upper New York Bay, a publicity-seeker calling himself Mr. Zero swam after the ship but did not join the expedition. The whole scene was a cartoonists' paradise.[9]

After a brief flurry of excitement following the discovery of the stowaways, the voyage seemed to be settling down to a rather placid routine. Aside from reading, talking, and playing games of leap-frog, the only special feature of the daily regimen was a series of lectures by the delegates on their various specialties. The Judge gave several talks on juvenile court matters, appropriately stressing that the approach of such courts was a viable alternative to violence. On the fourth day out an event occurred in Washington that was destined to break the calm on the *Oscar II*. On that day President Wilson delivered his Annual Message to Congress and made a forceful plea for preparedness, coupling it with specific proposals for increasing the size of the Army and adding new ships to the Navy. Aboard ship, Henry Ford authorized the appointment of a committee to draft a preparedness resolution. Since the committee, with Ford's approval, was dominated by the pacifist element on board, it predictably drafted what could be accurately called an anti-preparedness resolution. Ford indicated that it would be available for the signatures of those delegates who wished to sign until the following Monday, when he proposed to send it to the President. Judge Lindsey's earlier concern that participation in the expedition might become equated with an anti-preparedness stance was prophetic.

There was immediate resentment among some of the passengers against the resolution, both for its content and the circumstances of its presentation. Louis Lochner, a member of the committee, reminisced years later that it had been a mistake to present the delegates with a finished document they had never had an opportunity to discuss. Undoubtedly the secret deliberations of the self-appointed group did create a mood of distrust, and rumors soon arose that a cabal was running the expedition and was planning to punish nonsigners, perhaps by sending them all home from the first port the ship reached. As a matter of fact, Lochner, Madame Schwimmer, and some others were in favor of doing just that, but Henry Ford was unwilling to take so drastic and unpopular a step.

Opposition to the resolution came also from those who believed that to support mediation did not logically compel one to oppose Wilson on preparedness. At least a dozen delegates indicated that they were not willing to sign the resolution, and their decision was immediately telegraphed by the reporters aboard to their newspapers and wire services. Unfortunately for the anti-preparedness advocates, the opponents of the preparedness resolution included Judge Lindsey and S. S. McClure, undoubtedly the two names next to Ford's among the passengers that were most widely known by the general public, and Louis B. Hanna of North Dakota, who was not widely known but who compensated for it by being the only governor aboard the Peace Ship.

The aftermath of the whole affair was somewhat anticlimactic. Ford wrote a round-robin to all the passengers in which he expressed his regrets for any "misunderstandings" that had arisen and assured them that "all invited guests will still be my invited guests to the end of the trip." A stubborn and somewhat devious man, Ford attempted to explain the absence of vote or discussion on the resolution by asserting that if a vote had been taken, "the action of the majority would have been binding on the minority." The bulk of his letter was devoted to asserting contentiously that since an announced purpose of "the Mission" was to prevent future wars "through the abolition of competitive armaments," the "best interests" of the expedition required an expression of "solemn opposition" to preparedness. Although there is no reason to believe that Ford's letter won any converts, its assurances that no delegates would be sent home prematurely apparently appeased the worst fears of the opposition, and the remainder of the voyage was comparatively calm. At least some of the delegates were able to poke fun at themselves. Years later Elmer Davis,* who was at the time a young reporter for the *New York Times,* recalled a mock trial aboard ship of S. S. McClure, who was "indicted" for trying to convert some of the young college students to "seditious pacifism." Judge Lindsey served as prosecuting attorney and Mrs. Lindsey played the role of a "sob sister" for one of the New York newspapers. The trial—or perhaps it would be more ac-

---

* Davis later became a nationally prominent radio broadcaster and served as director of the Office of War Information during World War II.

curate to call it the party—was evidently a fairly exuberant one. Davis reported that it ended when the jury finally returned with an announcement that "The bar is closed."[10]

In the public mind the final disaster beset the peace expedition on December 23 when Henry Ford, pleading illness, left the group shortly after its arrival in Norway and returned to the United States. For those whose understanding of the expedition came exclusively from the newspapers, which alternately ridiculed the voyage or emphasized the squabbles among the "peace delegates" over the preparedness resolution, Ford's action seemed to represent the inevitable vote of no confidence in the delegates and in the expedition itself by a practical man who had at last regained his senses. Perhaps the verdict was correct, though Ford always insisted that his stated reason for leaving should be taken at face value and that his personal presence was not essential to the success of the expedition. In any event, most of the delegates stayed on with Ford's support, met with peace groups in Sweden and Denmark as well as Norway, and were permitted to cross Germany and make similar contacts in Holland. Eventually, in February 1916, their efforts led to the creation of a six-nation Neutral Conference for Continuous Mediation, to which Ford gave financial support until the final severance of diplomatic relations between Germany and the United States following the German decision to begin unrestricted submarine warfare on February 1, 1917.

Lindsey's association with the expedition was largely peripheral after Ford's departure, though he did serve briefly on a committee created for the dual purpose of managing the affairs of the expedition and bypassing Madame Schwimmer. The committee was authorized by Ford, who had become convinced that the Hungarian lady was an intolerably divisive force because of her tendency to be secretive and domineering. Lindsey was also elected as an alternate delegate to the Neutral Conference that later met in Stockholm and The Hague, but he never actually served. He and Mrs. Lindsey left the peace party in The Hague on January 19, 1916, and returned home after making a brief trip through Germany.

The entire episode had a rather unpleasant aftermath for the Judge. During the initial voyage across the Atlantic Lindsey had had several discussions with Ford. In the course of their talks the Judge urged him to consider the possibility of forming an organization to feed and clothe war orphans and find permanent homes for them after the war. Apparently Ford expressed some interest in the idea, even to the extent of agreeing to underwrite Lindsey's subsequent excursion to Germany in late January for the purpose of gaining some impressions of conditions affecting children in the war zones. When the Judge returned from Europe he was eager to work at such a project and told Ford that he was even willing to abandon the court to devote all of his time to it. By March 1916 it was clear that Ford either had second thoughts on the matter or that Lindsey had ascribed too much importance to Ford's seemingly cordial reception of the original suggestion. Relations between the two men cooled decidedly from this time, and the Judge's subsequent contacts with Ford were through Ford's hard-nosed private secretary, E. G. Liebold, who was well known for his ability to keep people at a distance from his employer. Later in 1916 Ford refused several requests for financial help in the Judge's campaign for re-election, though he did relent to the extent of helping the Lindseys meet a mortgage payment on their home. It was the last act of their relationship.[11]

As the slaughter in Europe continued relentlessly, the Judge's attitude became dominated by an emphatic hope that America would keep out of it. He publicly expressed his conviction that the country would not be endangered even by a German victory, asserting at the same time that all of the belligerents would be ruined if they did not soon come to their senses and end their irresponsible squandering of lives and property. On the relative merits of the belligerents' causes, Lindsey professed complete neutrality. He continued to support

Wilson on the issue of preparedness, but he was critical of the President for acquiescing in Allied violations of international law while holding Germany to a standard of strict accountability. On humanitarian grounds the Judge was appalled at the effects of the British blockade on the food needs of babies and young children in Central Europe, and felt that it was hypocritical to express moral outrage at the inhumanity of German submarine warfare while remaining silent about the blockade. When the British published a blacklist of American firms allegedly giving indirect aid to Germany and forbade British subjects to have any dealings with them, Lindsey joined in the wide resentment against this interference with American "rights," forgetting that the British government was not prohibited by any principle of international law from making any rules it wished to regulate the conduct of its own subjects. The Judge suggested to George Creel that it would be fitting for President Wilson to use the blacklist episode "to bring the Allies to their senses," but Wilson continued to reject all suggestions that the United States make any demands on the Allies that could not be gracefully compromised.[12]

When war finally came to the United States in April 1917 the Judge did not let his past views interfere with his support of it. He found solace and justification in reminding Scripps that liberals of unimpeachable credentials, such as Justice Louis Brandeis and Clarence Darrow, had come around to the same position. On the large issues of the war and the peace settlement that would follow, Lindsey found them "so full of perplexities" and "so inscrutable" that he was unwilling to condemn those who continued to adhere to some of his own former views. When Scripps supported Socialist Max Eastman, the editor of *The Masses* who had run afoul of the loosely worded Espionage Act, the Judge wrote to Scripps:

I am highly pleased to know the attitude you took with reference to Max Eastman. We certainly need men like that, especially when the reconstruction period comes. I am hoping to the good Lord we can all be together then for the real constructive work in turning civilization right side up after it has been turned upside down. I have long felt that the whole thing was a conspiracy against nature, against justice, and against everything else that ought to be; and the consolation I am getting from the whole miserable mess is that we will see this with clearer vision when the storm is passed.[13]

The excitement of wartime aroused the old restlessness of the Judge again, and perhaps of Mrs. Lindsey as well. By October 1917 he was asking George Creel, who had become chairman of the Committee on Public Information, the official propaganda agency of the United States, what he might do to help in the war effort. Creel set up interviews with President Wilson and Secretary of War Newton D. Baker, and after a second meeting with Creel it was agreed that the Lindseys would visit Britain, France, and Italy, where the Judge would address American soldiers and Allied audiences. The Creel Committee paid the Lindseys' expenses, and the British Bureau of Information in New York City eventually gave the Judge a $1,320 stipend for some lectures he gave on Anglo-American friendship after his return to the United States.[14]

The Lindseys were lionized overseas, especially in England where they were house guests of the Duchess of Marlborough, the former Consuelo Vanderbilt, as well as Sir Robert Baden-Powell, founder of the Boy Scouts, and American-born Lady Astor. At intervals during the social whirl the Judge spoke about his experiences in the Juvenile Court to diverse audiences of war workers, Oxford scholars, and settlement volunteers. In France he briefly left Mrs. Lindsey to visit the war front, and in Italy he spoke to a select group of jurists on the juvenile court movement. For years afterward the Lindseys remembered the interlude as one of the most exciting in their lives. It was their second and last trip abroad.

The trip produced only one tangible result: on his return to the United States the Judge prepared a series of articles on the impressions he gained from the trip. His old literary collaborator Harvey O'Higgins, whom George Creel had brought to Washington as vice-chairman of the Committee on Public Information, again did the actual writing of the articles, which first appeared in *Collier's* in 1919 and were published in book form a year later under the title *The Doughboy's Religion and Other Aspects of Our Day.* The two men followed the same pattern that characterized the writing of all of Lindsey's five major books. The Judge initially spoke at length about his experiences and impressions while his collaborator took copious notes. O'Higgins then wrote a first draft and submitted it to the Judge. Lindsey was always fortunate in finding collaborators who "got him" immediately, as he put it, and it was never necessary to make major changes in the manuscripts that came to him. The literary collaborators all had sufficient stature to be listed as co-authors, though all of the books used the autobiographical form.

The *Doughboy's Religion* was essentially an opening shot for the national Democratic campaign of 1920. O'Higgins, in a preface, billed Lindsey as "the advance agent of the New Freedom," and Lindsey went on from there to contrast the domestic reforms of the first Wilson administration to the "Junkerism" of American reactionaries who were presumably to be found chiefly in the Republican party. The Judge tried to place his theme in an international context by asserting that the essence of "the Junker faith" was the same everywhere in the world. It invariably assumed that an elite would rule in every country, and it never failed to accuse its natural enemies, reformers and labor leaders, of "socialism, bolshevism, disloyalty, pro-Germanism." Given the civil liberties record of the wartime Wilson administration, it was not a little ironic that its defenders would raise such an issue, but the theme was at least consistent with Lindsey's earlier view that "the Beast" was always lying in wait to block every move toward a more democratic society.[15]

In contrast to "the Junker faith" Lindsey placed "the dough-

boy's religion." Its essence was "service," not the kind that Warren Harding and George F. Babbitt were soon to preach, but
service to mankind through economic and social reforms. The
doughboy acquired this faith, said Lindsey, in the trenches, where
bravery, loyalty, and *collective* effort were the chief virtues. He
was determined not to return to a society in which a laissez-
faire, devil-take-the-hindmost philosophy prevailed. On the international level the doughboy's religion would require cooperation through Mr. Wilson's League of Nations, which Lindsey
now urged the country to embrace. As a piece of campaign
propaganda the Lindsey-O'Higgins effort, in spite of its simplistic history and occasional Committee on Public Information
clichés, was not bad. But the country, and especially the Senate,
was not ready to listen.

Those who read *The Doughboy's Religion* carefully may
have been less interested in its comments on political and economic questions than they were in another aspect of the book.
At several points the Judge emphasized the insignificant role
that the doughboys assigned to sexual immorality as a vice. On
one occasion the YMCA conducted an informal poll among the
troops to discover what they considered to be the worst sins. The
poll revealed that to the soldiers in the trenches the major sins
were cowardice and selfishness. When a distressed YMCA official asked the boys if they did not wish to include sexual
immorality, "they just gave him the horse-laugh," Lindsey
recalled.[16] Perhaps, the Judge concluded, there was too much
concern in America, especially in the churches and among the
older generation, about one kind of morality. Perhaps, also, this
neurotic concern was institutionalized in a wide range of laws
and attitudes that made for a great deal of ignorance and suffering. Lindsey's elaboration on these themes in the next decade
was to give him his reputation, on the popular culture level, as
the chief spokesman in America of the sexual revolution of the
1920's.

7 / Prophet of the Jazz Age

L INDSEY'S ROLE AS SPOKESMAN FOR THE "FLAMING YOUTH" OF
the twenties was a logical outcome of his courtroom experiences, his social and intellectual attitudes, and his
strongly felt need to be in the center of the action.[1] Given his
background and temperament, it would be hard to think of a
more likely candidate to serve as the leading popularizer of the
revolution in manners and morals that was being hailed in
novels and popular magazines and in the rapidly rising "cathe-
drals of the cinema," as the pretentious adolescent movie industry was describing its new theaters.[2]

As early as 1907 the Judge drew on his courtroom experiences to write a one-page article for the *Ladies' Home Journal*
on the subject "Why Girls Go Wrong." Lindsey expressed
himself in a Victorian manner that was appropriate to his audience and probably, at that time, to his own personal style as well.
Thus a girl never became a prostitute. Rather "she fell to the
very depths." Similarly, certain books were not merely obscene
but were "the most improper literature that the fiendish mind
of man could invent." But the article also contained ideas which
were later refined and expanded to become major themes of the
Judge's writings in the twenties. The main point of his message
to women was that his courtroom observations of adults as well
as children convinced him that sexual ignorance was the major
cause of "broken homes, desertions, sorrow . . . and the great
mass of social ills which infest society." The Judge blamed the
ignorance of foolish parents, whose "mock modesty" made
them too embarrassed to discuss sexual matters with their children, especially if the children were daughters. In 1907 Lindsey

was satisfied to stress the need for parental guidance as the means of filling the sexual knowledge gap. In later years he decided this was not enough. Parents would have to be educated first.[3]

The Judge's total personality was ideally suited to his role as popular spokesman for the sexual revolution of the twenties. His chief qualifications were a highly developed sense of compassion, a rational and humane approach to ethical questions, and a vigorous skepticism toward organized religion, especially when it sought to impose its dogmas or moral standards on a secular society. In addition to these traits Lindsey had a strong, though not unlimited, faith in science as a provider of answers to the problems of mankind. Above all, he had an open-mindedness toward avant-gardism in all fields that was wide enough to encompass an enthusiasm for the psychological mysticism of a Maeterlinck and the ponderous scientific prose of a G. Stanley Hall.

With all these qualities the Judge had a great sensitivity to the intellectual currents of his time. As historian Henry May has pointed out, the sexual revolution of the twenties actually had its origins in the pre-war years, and at least two of its representatives had an impact on the Judge.[4] The first was Havelock Ellis, who combined a rational and humane approach to sex with a singularly felicitous literary style which gave his writings a wider popular appeal than some of the more difficult and specialized works of the emerging Freudians, many of whose writings were not yet available in English. In 1910 Ellis' *Sex in Relation to Society* was first published in the United States. Lindsey had earlier purchased Ellis' *The Criminal.* He may well have been impressed by the English author's sharp criticisms of the prisons for their failure to rehabilitate the inmates and by his awareness of social factors as causes of crime, two themes already very close to Lindsey's heart. If the Judge was already favorably predisposed toward Ellis, his feeling must have been reinforced as he read *Sex in Relation to Society,* which carried a markedly favorable notice of his own article in the *Ladies' Home Journal*. Lindsey gave the new book a warm endorsement in a note to Ellis' American publishers.[5]

Havelock Ellis' book, the third volume in his seven-volume *Studies in the Psychology of Sex,* may have helped the Judge to formulate some of the ideas he later did so much to propagate in the twenties. Of course these ideas were not unique to Ellis, and the Judge undoubtedly derived some of them from many other available sources. But there is a remarkable parallelism between the views advanced in *Sex in Relation to Society* and those of Lindsey in his two popular books *The Revolt of Modern Youth* (1925) and *The Companionate Marriage* (1927). Among the outstanding similarities are the emphasis on the need for sexual education of the young, the awareness of the growing influence of economic independence on the sexual freedom of "the new woman," and the ardent hope that birth control could contribute to marriages that were healthily child-centered. Ellis, in language that doubtless appealed to a juvenile court judge, looked forward to the day when universal knowledge of contraception would make it possible for all children to be wanted children. Finally, and perhaps most significantly, throughout Ellis' work was a pervasive plea for the acceptance of a variety of sexual standards to meet different personal needs, a call for an end to excessive governmental interference in matters of private sexual conduct, and an advocacy of "free marriage" and "free divorce" that had many of the same elements and much the same rationale as Lindsey's "radical" proposals a decade and a half later.[6]

A second author who influenced Lindsey was Walter Lippmann. In 1913 Lippmann, then only twenty-four years old, wrote his first book, *A Preface to Politics.* The young author acknowledged his debt to Sigmund Freud and his disciples for the main theme of the book—that a truly progressive society would come into being only when men of vision and understanding discovered and channeled the unconscious and hidden sources of human motivation. In a memorable chapter called "Well Meaning But Unmeaning: The Chicago Vice Report," Lippmann pointed out the fundamental inconsistency of two sets of statements in the vice commission's report. On the one hand, it declared:

> So long as there is lust in the hearts of men, it will seek out some method of expression. Until the hearts of men are changed, we can hope for no absolute annihilation of the Social Evil.

But at the beginning of the report the same commissioners who wrote these words also proclaimed:

> Constant and persistent repression of prostitution the immediate method; absolute annihilation the ultimate ideal.

The first statement, Lippmann felt, suggested an enlightened attitude, despite the pejorative "lust," because it seemed to recognize the need to redirect the universal sexual impulse in socially desirable ways. The second statement, on the other hand, seemed to reflect the traditional punitive approach and evaded the central problem. Undoubtedly the Chicago authorities would fall back on the latter policy, with the usual results, for, as Lippmann observed, that was the way with "routine minds."[7]

Lindsey was very much taken with Lippmann's book. No doubt the Judge was pleased by Lippmann's compliments to himself, expressed in the book, for the great gains he had made for children's legislation by acting upon his intuitive recognition of the importance of appealing to the deep human instinct to protect the young. Indeed, as Lindsey correctly surmised, he and Theodore Roosevelt were really the heroes of the book, for both of them, in Lippmann's view, had the statesmanlike wisdom to underplay abstract issues and hit for the heart. But Lindsey's attention was also attracted by another feature of *A Preface to Politics*—an emphasis on the importance of sexual instincts which was uncommon in political treatises of the time. In November 1913 the Judge wrote Lippmann a more than cursory thank-you note. In a six-page letter in which he congratulated the young journalist for his "suggestive, profound, fundamental, and thought-compelling book," Lindsey elaborated on some of the absurdities of the criminal law regarding sexual conduct, especially its treatment of statutory rape. Finally he asked Lippmann what he would think of his writing a book that might be called *Sex and Sin,* with concrete examples from his own experiences in juvenile court work to support his conclusions. Lippmann, in a handwritten reply to the Judge's letter, urged him to write the book and further assured him that when he was writing *A Preface to Politics* Lindsey's activities in Denver were constantly in the back of his mind. Despite Lippmann's encouragement to write *Sex and Sin,* the Judge put the idea in limbo for several years as his energies were diverted by two trips to Europe and continuing political squabbles in Denver. But the role he was eventually to play in the sexual revolution was clearly anticipated more than a decade before the publication of the books and articles that have usually caused this phase of Lindsey's career to be associated exclusively with the twenties.[8]

Lindsey's friendship with Harvey O'Higgins probably gave additional impetus to his new direction. O'Higgins, a volatile Irishman, and his Zelda-like wife Anna, represented to Lindsey the glamour the Judge always associated with New York City. When he was not out in the territory muckraking the Mormons or serving as a public relations counsel of sorts to the government as a Committee on Public Information official, O'Higgins was writing plays that made minor splashes and operating on the fringes of the New York literary and theatrical scene. Whenever the Judge visited New York he attended the theater with the O'Higginses. They were the first friends to whom he introduced his young wife, and they reciprocated the compliment by letting the newlyweds have the use of a farmhouse they owned in Martinsville, New Jersey, for their honeymoon.

Like Lindsey, O'Higgins was an ex-Catholic. He shared the Judge's agnosticism as well as his belief that the churches were too inclined to side with the wealthy and the powerful and to forget their duty to the poor. O'Higgins had also become infatuated with the Freudian theories that were beginning to circulate in New York literary salons in the pre-war years, and he may have been as responsible as Lindsey for the attacks in *The Doughboy's Religion* on the excessive concern of the churches with sexual morality. In 1924 O'Higgins, in collaboration with a psychiatrist, wrote *The American Mind in Action,* which abounded in Freudianisms. It took up the cudgels against American "Puritanism," which O'Higgins, in language typical of contemporary popularizers of Freud, viewed as the chief blight on American civilization.[9]

A journalist who knew both Lindsey and O'Higgins felt that O'Higgins was a kind of grey eminence and deserved to be condemned for encouraging Lindsey to become involved in controversial matters that were certain to lead to serious political difficulties for him. It is likely, however, that O'Higgins served more as a catalyst to latent inclinations in the Judge. Lindsey was, after all, an independent character and shrewd enough to realize what a storm his writings in the twenties would raise. Even when he appeared to be mindlessly following the fads of the day, Lindsey always stopped short of total commitment to any intellectual system. A close friend of O'Higgins and Lindsey recalled that the Judge showed exasperation on several occasions with how far overboard "poor Harvey" had gone for the current Freudian jargon.[10]

The early twenties were a propitious time for the Judge to act on the idea he had been toying with as far back as his correspondence with Lippmann in 1913. On the level of popular culture, middlebrows who had never read a line by Freud were glibly talking about repressions, complexes, the *ego,* and the *id.* Popular women's journals, particularly confession and movie magazines, were celebrating or deploring (or celebrating while seemingly deploring) the current trends among youth and calling them a revolution in morals. The universal interest in human behavior, and in sex particularly, was enhanced by a feeling that a new mood was abroad in the land that was changing attitudes and conduct in many areas, especially among young people. The feeling seemed to be epitomized in two popular book titles of 1922, F. Scott Fitzgerald's *Tales of the Jazz Age* and Warner Fabian's *Flaming Youth.*

The new climate was not entirely a myth created by the media. National Prohibition *was* new, after all, and it did produce the largest number of lawbreakers among the "respectable" classes in American history. Skirts *were* shorter than ever. The automobile, though it was not new, first became a middle-class necessity and a common working-class luxury in the twenties, and also symbolized the morals revolution for several reasons. The new term "joy rides" suggested illegal drinking, sexual liaisons, high speed, and orgiastic parties in distant roadhouses. The movies, in those days before the Hays Code, were making their contribution to the new mood by advertising the sexual revolution with such film titles as *Foolish Wives, Forbidden Fruit, Give Her Anything,* and *The Way Women Love.* Theda Bara, Pola Negri, Clara Bow (the "It" Girl), and a host of public relations experts were happily helping the process along.

In January 1924 Judge Lindsey paid a visit to New York City and, at the suggestion of George Creel and Harvey O'Higgins, contacted Bernarr Macfadden about the possibility of writing a series of articles on the current generation, emphasizing its sexual conduct and attitudes as they came to the attention of a juvenile court judge. Macfadden, head of a publishing empire which included magazines such as *True Story, True Romances, Dream World,* and *Muscle Builder,* was a good choice from the standpoint of appealing to a wide, if not very select, audience. On the other hand, he was considered somewhat disreputable in more established publishing circles, both for his health faddism and the sensationalism of some of his publications, which included the notorious *New York Evening*

Graphic. After talking with Lindsey, Macfadden arranged a meeting between the Judge and his supervising editor, Fulton Oursler. At Oursler's suggestion they were later joined by Wainwright Evans, a professional writer currently under contract to Macfadden. Evans was Oursler's first choice as a collaborator for the Judge. After several meetings an agreement was worked out. Evans would set up a lengthy series of interviews with the Judge and prepare a series of articles for Macfadden's *Physical Culture Magazine* under the title "The Revolt of Youth." He would give full time to the project and would be listed as junior author. The Judge was to receive $500 for each article. In the event the articles were published later as a book, Lindsey and Evans would share equally in the royalties.[11]

Oursler guessed that Lindsey and Evans would find each other congenial, and he was right. A graduate of Princeton and the son of an Episcopal minister, Wainwright Evans had a deceptively stern appearance that masked a sense of humor and a deeply compassionate nature. He was strongly sympathetic with the Judge and his ideas. Evans was happily married to a charming woman who shared his intellectual interests. They were the parents of a boy and a girl of high school age. The Lindseys were now a family, too. After a series of miscarriages by Mrs. Lindsey, they had adopted a baby girl and called her Benetta, a composite of their first names. In terms of Lindsey's and Evans' personal backgrounds, it was hard to imagine a more unlikely pair to symbolize a flamboyant revolution in morals than these two respectable family men in early and late middle age. Evans made two extended trips to Denver in 1924, and by the end of the year he had a series of articles ready to print. In late 1925 they were published as a book by the avant-garde house of Boni and Liveright under the title *The Revolt of Modern Youth.** Within a year the book was translated into German, Dutch, Danish, Swedish, and Japanese, and was separately printed in London for distribution in the British Empire.

* Cited hereafter as *The Revolt.*

For better or worse the Judge's international reputation as the leading American spokesman for the sexual revolution was made.

The Revolt consisted of a series of stories based on case histories from the Judge's experience, chiefly involving young women between their early teens and early twenties. They were, as the Judge was proud to remind his readers constantly, "case histories" in a sense analogous to those of a physician rather than a judge, since many of his "patients" came to him voluntarily and not because they were in trouble with the law. The episodes, which were almost entirely sexual in content, were freely interspersed with the Judge's opinions and interpretations.[12] Although *The Revolt* occasionally suffered from a certain amount of digression—one of the Judge's intellectual traits —it dealt basically with three themes: the nature of "the revolt of youth," the inadequate response to it from parents and society, and the need for constructive action.

Lindsey explained the revolt chiefly in terms of the considerable affluence of many of the younger generation in the twenties in contrast to the economic hardships of earlier times. Commenting on a certain lack of courtesy or even tolerance in the younger generation toward their elders, Lindsey observed:

> These things are symptoms. Symptoms of what? Why, symptoms of a state of mind which is saying to the whole adult world, "So you think you are so much wiser than we, do you! We are just to take your words for things, are we! You must have one line of behavior and we another! You are old and wise while we are young, foolish, and ignorant. All right; show us! Produce the truth if you've got it. Meantime, we go our way!"
>
> Thirty, forty years ago, youth couldn't have flung such a challenge with the least hope of success. Today, the day of the automobile, the telephone, speed, good wages, and an unheard of degree of economic independence for everybody, it can.

The Revolt was not unique, in 1925, in declaring that the experiences of the war, the greater economic independence of

women, the automobile, and the movies were profoundly in-
fluencing moral standards and attitudes. What distinguished
The Revolt from other contemporary efforts to discuss the new
trends in manners and morals was Lindsey's unabashed exuberance and optimism about the younger generation and the future,
at a time when so many people in his age group were wringing
their hands and wondering where it would all end. Here was a
middle-aged man, the best-known juvenile court judge in the
country or, for that matter, in the world, who was willing to say:

> Youth is at least trying to think straight. It is trying because
> of the contagion of science; for science is an impersonal thing, and
> no respecter of traditions; and science is freeing the world. Modern
> youth is growing up under the wing of science; and since that is
> so, we shall see what we shall see. Coming? It is coming like a
> tidal wave.[13]

The key phrase was "trying to think straight." Much of the
banality and mischief of the younger generation, which the
Judge did not deny were sometimes present, represented an
emotional reaction against the failure of the older generation to
provide a workable and, above all, a credible set of values for
coping with youth's physical and emotional needs. The indictment of parents and social institutions that followed, buttressed
as it was by tragic firsthand examples of the cruelties inflicted
on the young by the old, was probably for the average reader the
most memorable part of the book.

Lindsey's chief villains were clergymen, sadistic or vindictive school authorities, and all others who wished to "terrorize
people into being good." Their chief sins were cruelty, ignorance, and smugness. A typical episode containing some of these
elements involved a high school girl who had become sexually
involved with a boy. Unlike some of the girls in the episodes
Lindsey discussed, this one was fortunate enough to end the
affair without becoming pregnant. Nevertheless, her upbringing caused her to be conscience-stricken about her conduct, and
she felt the need to confide in an older person. The Judge's de-

scription of what followed conveys the spirit of *The Revolt*. It carries a forceful statement of Lindsey's attitudes and illustrates why he was regarded by so many young people as their most effective spokesman and even their idol:

> So she went to one of her teachers, an old maid, who would have been a far better and wiser and more charitable person if during her own girlhood she had been guilty of the same misstep this child had made.
>
> This woman immediately took the girl's story to another old maid, who spread the news. The school authorities got hold of it, called the girl up on the carpet, grilled her, smacked their lips solemnly over the details of her story, and then expelled her as a moral menace to other students. She was bad; she was contaminated; she was impure.
>
> Unfortunately, she believed their judgment, and the effect on her own psychology was devastating. I had a big job on my hands later making her see that she was not ruined, that she had simply made a mistake, that she could come back, and that her judges were a gang of savages wearing too many clothes.
>
> But she never really held her head up again. The weight of social disapproval was too much for her. She finally solved the problem by getting out of Denver.
>
> And yet she was a very fine girl, with a moral sense about her that placed her infinitely above the two she-cats who dragged her down, and above the purblind pedagogues who, finding her on the edge of the cliff, kicked her over into the abyss. Those two women are active workers in one of our large Denver churches. They go to service every Sunday, and are socially well known. They deserve to be in the penitentiary.[14]

The radicalism of *The Revolt* was not confined to an occasional sardonic remark, such as the one about the "old maid" with its supposedly Freudian insight that repression makes people mean. Pervasive throughout the book was Lindsey's rejection of the notion that his judicial office obligated him to use threats or coercion, or even to censure, when young people or adults confided in him concerning "immoral"—and sometimes even illegal—activities. Two case histories in *The Revolt* exemplified an attitude that seemed particularly radical because it was expressed by a judge. In the first episode a young career woman of twenty-two visits Judge Lindsey on her own initiative and freely admits that she is having sexual relations regularly with a young man named Bill. (The Judge used fictitious names in all episodes but vouched for the accuracy of all other details.) Lindsey suggests to "Mary" that it would probably be a better arrangement to marry Bill. Mary, an able career girl, refuses on the ground that she is making more money than Bill. The Judge decides not to press the issue any further and reflects on the changing standards that are the consequence of young women's growing economic independence. But the story is not finished. Later Bill comes to see the Judge, complaining that Mary has left him for another man with whom she is now living. Bill wishes to marry her and hopes to enlist Lindsey's support in persuading her to come back to him. In an aside the Judge comments ironically to the reader on the "reverse twist" of the classic Victorian situation in which the male cad deserted the "fallen woman" who became "damaged goods" once she ceased to be a virgin. When Lindsey discovers that Mary's new lover has an ample income, he decides that it will probably be impossible to do anything for Bill. The Judge concludes the episode by speculating that Mary will probably marry the second man and implies that the marriage will be successful, another subtheme of *The Revolt*—that illicit sexual liaisons may be unwise, but they are tragic only when a girl becomes pregnant, becomes venereally infected, "gets caught," or, in some ways the most important, *believes* that they are tragic.[15]

A second episode in *The Revolt* revealed elements of Lindsey's social philosophy that must have been even more upsetting to conventional people. The parents of a seventeen-year-old girl oppose her marrying until she is much older. She is in love with a man of twenty-two and is determined to marry him. Since the only way she can obtain her parents' consent to the marriage is by having them discover that she has had sexual intercourse with the young man, something she has not in fact done, she now sets out to do so. She confides her plan to the Judge, who warns her against it. She nevertheless carries it out and comes back to the Judge for help in persuading her parents to permit the marriage. Lindsey agrees because he believes that the girl's father is quite unrealistic in expecting her to go East to college and not marry until she is at least twenty-five. The parents ultimately consent after the Judge has interceded on the girl's behalf, and in Lindsey's words, "[The young couple] had a big church wedding, and today she is a happy wife and mother, and one of the leaders of Denver society, a young matron above reproach." Again, as in Mary's case, loss of virginity does not lead to disaster. From the standpoint of rigid moralists, however, at least two other aspects of the episode must have been even more disturbing than Lindsey's apparent failure to censure the girl for her actions. First, since the girl was seventeen years old, her plan involved statutory rape on the young man's part, even though she made the amorous overture. Yet there was no indication in the Judge's account that he made any mention of this fact in his warning to her. Second, Lindsey quite deliberately described the young woman as "a good girl" in spite of her having plotted a deliberate seduction of the young man and having admitted that she had committed at least one earlier act of premarital intercourse with another man.[16]

Lindsey was far too alert to people's feelings to be unaware of the questions such episodes would raise in their minds about the propriety of his silence, especially in view of his judicial position. To those who would listen he offered a practical defense of his methods. As far as giving the young people a verbal "roasting" was concerned, he commented in regard to the young career woman's case:

> What could I say? Reprimand her? Impossible. A reprimand wouldn't have changed her view and would merely have deprived me of what hold I had on her.[17]

The failure of many parents, teachers, and clergymen to recognize that censure based on notions of sinfulness was an outmoded approach accounted, in Lindsey's opinion, for much of the failure in communication between generations. The Judge's refusal to reprimand was based on a rationale that applied even more strongly to any suggestion that he ought to use coercion or threaten to apply criminal sanctions. To the extent that many young people confided in him voluntarily, such a response on his part would have been tantamount to betrayal. But there was an equally compelling principle that prevented the Judge from invoking the criminal law in matters of sexual conduct. As he clearly indicated throughout *The Revolt,* he had become convinced, particularly by what he had learned in the privacy of his chambers, that such matters were not properly subjects for criminal sanctions at all, except in such noncontroversial areas as child molesting and actual physical assault. The point was not that moral codes were unimportant, but rather that the resort to fear and coercion, by the state or anybody, was wrong. If a society were truly enlightened, Lindsey insisted, the ethics of private sexual conduct must be self-imposed. The proper role of the state should be confined to education. In an atmosphere of freedom, strengthened by such education, the Judge had faith that most young people would behave in a civilized manner. As he expressed it in *The Revolt:*

> Sex is simply a biological fact. It is as much so as the appetite for food. Like the appetite for food, it is neither legal nor illegal, moral nor immoral. To bring Sex under the jurisdiction of law and authority is as impossible as to bring food hunger under such jurisdiction. That is why, when the law and the prescribed custom run counter to desires which are in themselves natural and normal, people refuse to recognize the authority of law and custom, and secretly give their often ill-considered desires the right of way. This they will continue to do until Sex can be presented to them in another light, with law and authority as completely eliminated as it is in the case, say, of gluttony.[18]

The Judge was at his best in *The Revolt* at the anecdotal

level, when he was reciting case histories that had the ring of authenticity while expressing his righteous wrath at the cruelty and stupidity of parents, clergymen, and teachers. When he turned to the more difficult task of providing a theoretical framework for reform, or of indicating the exact method and content of the sex education that would be presented "in another light," his results were sometimes sketchy and rather vague. An outstanding popularizer of contemporary social and intellectual trends, Lindsey often displayed a characteristic weakness of popularizers—a superficiality which reflected either a limited knowledge or a limited understanding of some of the subjects he discussed.

The Judge himself occasionally seemed to recognize the dilemma. Early in *The Revolt* he announced, "I am not attempting to offer solutions. I have no panacea." Despite the disclaimer, Lindsey was too much the activist reformer to resist offering solutions. His catch-all answer seemed to be "education," but he insisted that it was not necessary to be too specific about the goals. All that was needed for the "State of Tomorrow" was

that by means of a right system of education, we lay upon the hearts of our young people the conviction that they have a solemn duty to be good and productive citizens of the world; that we plant in their minds the suggestion, the faith; that it is their normal desire to be such; that we make it possible for the Good Will and the spontaneous Idealism, which are Youth's natural gift from God, to grow unhampered, as grow the flowers of the field; that we protect them from Fear and from the acceptance of second-hand, standardized, cut-to-pattern thought as from a plague; that we give them a background of essential knowledge which withholds no Fact on the ground that there are things which must not be known or discussed; and, finally, that we teach them the Art of Living, and permit them a philosophy of effort which will carry them through, and keep them headed wondering, yet fearless, toward the far horizons to which they naturally aspire.[19]

Given such hazy guidelines it is not surprising that Lindsey was more effective when he argued from experience on behalf of a few limited, specific reforms. The twin dangers of sexual misconduct that the Judge encountered in his work with juveniles were venereal disease and unwanted pregnancies, and it logically followed that the proposal he advocated most strenuously in *The Revolt* was the inclusion of information about birth control and venereal infection in any educational program for teen-agers. In a decade when birth-control clinics were still subject to police harassment, Lindsey boldly advocated the repeal of all federal and state laws that restricted or prohibited the dissemination of information about contraceptives.

Lindsey's rationale for advocating birth control was not based solely on his belief in the desirability of reducing illegitimate births. It also included a reduction of illegal abortions, the greater emancipation of women (married as well as unmarried), and the ultimate achievement of Havelock Ellis' ideal of a society in which all children would be "wanted children." Also scattered throughout *The Revolt,* as a justification for birth control, were references to the need for educating youth in its "eugenic duty." Several reviewers noted Lindsey's aphorism that "an illegitimate baby is one conceived by parents who are biologically unfit," but they failed to point out that Lindsey's notion of what constituted unfitness in a biological sense was never made very clear. Although there was a considerable controversy between eugenists and anti-eugenists on the biological and social causes of "inferiority," *The Revolt* failed to refer to any of the vast literature on the subject. Instead Lindsey discussed the issue on the level of Good ("scientific" and favorable to eugenics) versus Evil ("unscientific" and therefore unfavorable). The Judge also made some rather vague references to a "dominant racial strain" that hopefully could be developed in the United States, and cited "the puritan strain that settled New England" as a kindred type. It would be unfair to impute a belief in racism or intolerant nationalism to Lindsey, especially in view of his vigorous attacks against the Ku Klux Klan and other self-appointed "patriots" of the twenties; but his loose allusions to "the thousands of unfit and decadent bipeds who now swarm over the country like noxious insects" and to "hordes of morons, who are at present spawning, unchecked, like herring in the sea" did little to raise the level of sophistication of the general audience to whom the book was addressed.[20]

A major issue of the sexual revolution of the twenties, on which Lindsey had not yet formulated a position, was the future of the institution of marriage. Several case histories in *The Revolt* involved unhappy marriages, and the Judge frequently referred to the dilemma of youngsters, as well as young adults, who were biologically ready and eager for sexual activity but psychologically and economically unready for conventional marriage. He also mentioned several instances in which young unmarried couples lived together, apparently quite satisfactorily, in what were being widely described as "trial marriages." Perhaps, Lindsey suggested, such arrangements afforded a solution to the problem. Where love and mutual respect existed, he believed, such "marriages" were ethically superior to the many loveless marriages that were held together only by economic necessity. Lindsey was not yet prepared, however, to commit himself fully to trial marriage, which was, of course, legally not marriage at all, though his treatment of this arrangement in *The Revolt* was decidedly sympathetic. It would take more time and thought to formulate his ideas on the future of marriage. In the summer of 1926 Karl Harriman, editor of the *Red Book Magazine,* provided the necessary spur when he arranged a meeting between Lindsey and Wainwright Evans in Chicago. Harriman proposed that Evans write a series of articles on modern marriage based on Lindsey's anecdotes and observations. The three men quickly reached an agreement and work began immediately. Since Lindsey was on his way to give a series of lectures in the East, they arranged for a stateroom on the Twentieth Century Limited and the Judge began tentatively outlining some themes. In New York City Evans and Lindsey went to the Algonquin Hotel, where the Judge invariably stayed on his lecture tours, hired a public stenographer, and worked for another day. The rest of the work was carried on by correspondence, with Evans forwarding drafts of the articles to Lindsey for comment as he completed them. By the end of 1926 Evans had finished the first articles. The Judge sent offprints to friends and correspondents. From England Bertrand Russell, perhaps thinking this was some radical American publication, cordially thanked Lindsey for sending copies of the articles in *"The Red Magazine."* Once again the articles —this time in slightly expanded form—were published separately as a book by Boni and Liveright. Its title was to be the public's chief association with Lindsey's name for the rest of his life. It was called *The Companionate Marriage*.[21]

8 / Companionate Marriage: Image and Reality

IN NOVEMBER 1927 THE LARGE FLOODLIGHTED SIGN ON THE southeast corner of Fifth Avenue and 42nd Street in midtown Manhattan that had advertised Emil Ludwig's best-selling *Napoleon* was replaced by Boni and Liveright with their newest attraction, *The Companionate Marriage*. The term soon came to mean all things to all men. To many it signified legalized promiscuity. To others, who read the book less carefully or not at all, it meant random cohabitation without benefit of judge or clergy. For the Boston chapter of the Daughters of the American Revolution it was the name of a book to be blacklisted in the same way as *Elmer Gantry* and *An American Tragedy*. For at least one member of the House of Representatives it was an offense that ought to be added to the federal criminal code if practiced in the District of Columbia. The congressman may have scored some points with his strait-laced constituents by proposing a law to that effect, but the bill never saw the light of day after it went to committee. A few months after *The Companionate Marriage* was published a major Hollywood studio saw possibilities in the title and it became the basis—typically the very remote basis—for a popular movie of 1928 starring Betty Bronson and Richard Walling. "Companionate marriage" had traveled a long and glamorous road from its unpretentious academic origins four years earlier.[1]

The first use of the word "companionate" to describe a type of marriage different from the kind officially sanctioned by church and state was made in 1924 by Melvin M. Knight, a social scientist on the faculty of Barnard College. A man of wide-ranging interests, Knight had originally won his doctorate in genetics at Clark University and went on to publish numerous books and articles in the fields of sociology, economics, and history. In a short article in a sociological journal in 1924 Knight described what he regarded as a major change in the family as an institution. The traditional family, he asserted, was an arrangement for regulating reproduction, providing a rudimentary education for children, and determining the inheritance of property. In the simpler agrarian societies of the past the family was held together by economic forces, since each person had a contribution to make.

Two developments were steadily eroding the traditional family, according to Knight. The first was the industrial revolution, with its encouragement of rapid urbanization. The other was a growing knowledge and wider practice of birth control. Together these trends were responsible for "an unobserved division of an historical institution." Now at least two kinds of family existed: the traditional family, and a new institution (really not a family at all) which Knight labeled "the companionate."

Knight defined the companionate as "the state of lawful wedlock, entered into solely for companionship, and not contributing children to society." As a social scientist he was mainly concerned with pointing out the cultural lag in the legal system because it failed to recognize the division of the historic family and treated the companionate as if it were the same institution. Although Knight did not offer a detailed program for regulating the companionate, he did illustrate his argument with some existing anachronisms which he felt grew out of treating the companionate as a family. One was the divorce and alimony system which, in theory at least, treated the dissolution of a companionate and a family in the same way. According to law, what was sufficient legal cause for the divorce of a childless couple was equally valid for the divorce of a couple with five children. Conversely, the absence of a valid "cause" was as much of a barrier to the divorce of a childless couple as it was to the breakup of a genuine family. For Knight there was all the difference in the world between the two cases. As a general rule he saw no compelling social interest in preserving a companionate which either party wished to end, and no justification for alimony where the woman was healthy and able to work. His only reservation about "instant divorce" for childless couples was that there should be a brief interlocutory period of a few months to make certain that a very human error had not already transformed a companionate into a family.

On a larger scale Knight was concerned that the existing economic and legal system was discouraging reproduction by the ambitious and well-educated. Intelligent people recognized that the traditional family, though it might be a boon to society, was often a crushing financial liability for parents. Despite the social approval and esteem in which it was supposedly held, the traditional family was now formed in circumstances that were often not very attractive. The wife, as soon as she became pregnant, was expected (and often required) to give up her job, if she had not done so already, and live on her husband's earnings. The husband was now expected to support three people, as a starter, with no assurance that his earnings would be any greater than they had been when he was a bachelor. In an industrial society, there were no farm chores to do, and a man's children were increasingly protected by child labor laws from contributing to the family income. Worst of all from the social standpoint, Knight suggested, tax benefits could even favor the companionate by giving an economically comfortable but childless couple a "family" exemption for the wife even though she was neither making a contribution to society as a productive worker nor making a real family by reproducing. As Professor Knight liked to observe sardonically to his students, "Some get all the prosperity and the others get the posterity."[2]

Wainwright Evans first heard of Knight's article shortly

after he began writing the new series for the *Red Book Magazine*. It occurred to him that Knight's term, changed to an adjective and combined with "marriage," would be a catchy phrase to describe a proposal that seemed to be emerging from his correspondence with Lindsey. He began inserting it in the articles and soon was convinced that it was the best of several possible titles for the forthcoming book. After considering some other possibilities such as *Modern Marriage,* which they rejected as too bland, and *Love, Marriage and Divorce,* which Evans disliked as "a shot-gun type of title," the two collaborators settled upon a consideration of the relative merits of *Marriage on Trial* and *The Companionate Marriage.* Although Lindsey found both titles appealing, he had some reservations about "companionate marriage" on the ground of vagueness. But the enthusiasm of the Boni and Liveright editorial staff in New York combined with Evans' belief that the title would make the book "sell like hell" carried the day. *The Companionate Marriage* it would be.[3]

Although *The Companionate Marriage* was as important for its nuances and digressions as it was for Lindsey's specific program, a brief consideration of his proposals is necessary since the Judge invariably fell back on them as his first line of defense when his numerous critics attacked him. He began with a definition of his title. "Companionate marriage," he stated, "is legal marriage, with legalized birth control, and with the right to divorce by mutual consent for childless couples, usually without payment of alimony."[4]

The first point that Lindsey insistently made in his numerous debates with clergymen and others throughout the country was that companionate marriage was not trial marriage. Confusion arose occasionally because trial marriage was itself a term with at least two definitions. On the one hand it might refer to the relationship of a couple who lived together but were not married. It was in this sense that Lindsey himself had earlier used the term in *The Revolt.* Clearly, this kind of trial marriage should not have been confused with the companionate since Lindsey stated unequivocally that the latter involved legal marriage. There was a second meaning to trial marriage, however, which was rather more difficult to distinguish from the companionate. In this usage trial marriage referred to a legal marriage that the partners entered with "a candid recognition that it will probably be a temporary episode." Lindsey maintained that the difference between this kind of arrangement and companionate marriage was that such marriages put the primary emphasis on the tentative and experimental nature of the union whereas his concept of the companionate, even though it could be dissolved by mutual consent, was that it would be permanent, though at least temporarily childless. Although many of Lindsey's critics believed that this was a distinction without a difference, the Judge insisted that it was of profound psychological importance and that it also exposed the falsehood of the charge that he was hostile to permanent monogamous marriage.[5]

Lindsey's companionate marriage proposal necessarily implied some important changes in the status quo. While it was true that the basic elements of companionate marriage were already being practiced in the United States, especially by the more prosperous and the more enlightened, they often had to do so by the same methods that were used to circumvent Prohibition—by "bootleg" methods, as Lindsey indignantly declared. Furthermore, he pointed out, the less affluent and the less knowledgeable, to their sorrow, sometimes never even discovered these bootleg methods. Certain features of American society—particularly its laws and religion-based prejudices—still operated as a serious deterrent to the pursuit of happiness, which Lindsey maintained was the only legitimate goal of all social arrangements. Among the resulting injustices produced by this system of law and prejudice were the sexual entrapment of young people into early marriages, the barriers that stood in the way of getting the best information available about birth control, the strict divorce laws of some states, and the unfair alimony arrangements sometimes sanctioned by the courts.

The first two problems were simply reverse sides of the same coin. Young couples often had more children than they could afford simply because they did not have access to reliable information about contraception. The result was not the happy, comfortable, middle-class family scenes pictured in magazine advertisement stereotypes, but families of tired, frustrated, overworked parents, old before their time, and large numbers of children whose educational, clothing, and even nutritional needs could not be met by the father's wages. Lindsey thought the psychological and spiritual deprivation to be found in such homes, for the parents as well as the children, was often as bad as their material condition.

In *The Companionate Marriage,* as in *The Revolt,* the Judge again called for the repeal of all federal and state laws which forbade the use of the mails to disseminate information about birth control or prohibited the medical prescription of the diaphragm, then regarded as the most effective contraceptive device available. Beyond these negative recommendations for the repeal of existing laws, the Judge proposed positive legislation to require the public schools to include information about birth control in required sex-education courses.

One of the more radical aspects of Lindsey's proposals regarding birth control was his forthright advocacy of giving contraceptive devices to all persons who wanted them, regardless of whether they were married. In an era when, despite all the talk about the sexual revolution, there was still a great reluctance to discuss publicly such subjects as birth control or venereal disease with explicitness, Lindsey's uncompromising stand on the matter seemed daring and dangerous. The Judge was as candid in giving reasons for his proposal as he was blunt in stating it. Aside from venereal disease, unwanted pregnancies were the most common tragedy resulting from pre-marital relations. The presence of these two blights, in undiminished statistical vigor, demonstrated that keeping people in ignorance had not kept them from engaging in illicit sexual acts. Since a certain amount of such activity was inevitable, the only civilized and humane social policy was to do everything possible to avert the tragedy of illegitimacy or its alternative, abortion.[6]

The other major part of Lindsey's program which required some changes in law and attitudes was that dealing with divorce and alimony. In the Judge's opinion it was the supreme anomaly of the law of divorce in most states that the one legally unmentionable ground for divorce was the best reason for getting one —namely, the fact that two adults no longer wanted to stay married. When the couple was childless and had made an honest but unsuccessful effort to save their marriage, the Judge could see no justification for denying them a divorce. For the existing law Lindsey found two explanations, which he stated with characteristic outrage. One was the "superstition" that divorce was contrary to the law of God. The other was the alleged financial interest of the legal profession in the "divorce racket." The lawyers, according to Lindsey, did not wish to make divorce impossible, but they certainly wanted it to remain a complicated adversary proceeding which would put money into their pockets indefinitely. Lindsey, like Professor Knight, also believed that alimony payments, especially in the case of childless marriages or marriages of relatively short duration, were unfair and even contrary to the interests of society when they made it difficult for a man to remarry and support a family. Ever the pragmatist, the Judge refused to lay down a flat rule for alimony awards but reminded his readers that it was contrary to the temper of the times to regard women as economically subservient to men, even if alimony was a form of subservience that some of them welcomed. In an era of greater equality of rights, reflected by the recent adoption of woman suffrage, there was little excuse for alimony when the divorcée was young, childless, and able to work.[7]

The Judge's proposals, as far as changing the law went, were easy enough to put down and justify in a few paragraphs, but the significance of *The Companionate Marriage* went far beyond the definition of the term and the statement of the program. As with all of Lindsey's writings the book's main impact came from the anecdotes the Judge told from his own experiences. In a way they were even more shocking than the episodes in *The Revolt*, which dealt mostly with adolescents or very young adults. In *The Companionate Marriage* the Judge was announcing that the officially sanctioned moral code was a flop for many established and respectable middle-aged people as well.

The Judge's evidence was drawn from cases that came before the domestic relations department of his court and from the confidences of persons who knew of his reputation for not passing judgment on people even when he believed they were behaving unwisely. The episodes Lindsey described covered a variety of marital and extra-marital problems, but quite a few of them contained the same lesson, which was virtually the main theme of the book. The lesson was that jealousy and possessiveness were the two principal enemies of happiness in human relationships. A rigid belief in monogamy often made problems worse because it encouraged people to think that husband and wife had a property right to each other, body and soul. In Lindsey's view this belief was contrary to human nature and was becoming increasingly unacceptable to large numbers of people in the fast-moving and skeptical climate of the 1920's. Perhaps the most extraordinary example of what Lindsey called "The Revolt of Middle Age" is as interesting for Lindsey's own reaction to it as it is for the facts themselves.

The story of Mr. and Mrs. Frederick Blank, as he called them, typified what the Judge considered a far more common arrangement in American society, at least at the upper levels, than was generally realized. The Blanks were an attractive, economically comfortable couple, probably in their thirties. Mrs. Blank had arranged an appointment with the Judge to discuss the adoption of an illegitimate child whose mother was a young friend of hers. She was not planning to adopt the child herself, nor was her young friend's problem in any way related to her own revelations which followed later. After the Judge promised to help arrange an adoption, his conversation with Mrs. Blank drifted to the implications of the girl's conduct. Mrs. Blank seemed to be anxious to talk about herself and informed Lindsey that both she and her husband occasionally had discreet affairs with persons they liked. The "bombshell" was yet to come, however.

> "Does your husband know it?" I asked. "Of course," she said placidly. "We agree on these things. We love each other, but we enjoy these outside experiences; so why not take them? I think we care more for each other on account of them."

According to the Judge, his reaction to Mrs. Blank's revelations was hardly blasé:

> It isn't often that I get paralysis of the tongue, but I got it then. I simply sat and looked at her. I had suspected this kind of thing was going on, but here was the evidence. Here was a new one. Sex scrapes were old stuff; collusion for obtaining a divorce was as old as the divorce laws; statutory rape was an item of my daily routine; and unbelievable coincidences in human lives were the kind of thing I expected as a matter of course. But here was collusion in adultery on the part of people who were as far from gross vulgarity as any you would be likely to find in a day's run.

After a few moments the Judge recovered his usual aplomb and began to question Mrs. Blank. His manner was that of a social researcher rather than a judge or moralist. How did Mrs. Blank arrive at such unorthodox views? It began, she said, when she discovered that her husband was having an affair. She responded traditionally by announcing that she was going home to mother. Mr. Blank, after several hours of pleading, persuaded her to stay, arguing that his liking for the girl had never affected his love for her. He also promised to discontinue the relationship. To this point the Blanks' marital problem seemed to have reached a thoroughly conventional ending.

But the ending did not prove satisfactory. After a few months Mr. Blank became increasingly irritable and preoccupied. His wife suspected that he was either having another affair or seething over the restrictions she had forced him to impose on himself. When she asked him if he were "going out" with someone, the rage of his denial persuaded her that he was telling the truth. It also led to Mrs. Blank's moment of truth. "I've been thinking things over," she said to her husband.

> The present arrangement won't do. Telling people they mustn't do things makes them want to do them. I've made that mistake with you. Suppose we arrange it this way—that I'm to give you full liberty—and that you are to give me the same.

At first Mr. Blank reacted with typical male chauvinism to his wife's offer that she accept his occasional infidelities in return for letting her have a few of her own. His defense of the double standard was hard to maintain, however, particularly when she used the same argument he had used with her—that an occasional brief and enjoyable affair need not destroy true love. Perhaps a more compelling argument was her adamant refusal to accept a double standard. Given the alternatives, Mr. Blank chose the single standard with discreet liaisons allowed to both parties and no questions asked.

Mrs. Blank's replies to the Judge's relentless probing indicated that she was neither a wild-eyed crusader nor a person who thought she knew all the answers. Did she really accept the new arrangement in her heart? She conceded that it was still difficult to reject the values of a lifetime, but asserted that it was better and more honest than pretending to adhere to monogamy, which did not work for many people and led to frustration or hypocrisy, or accepting the double standard, which was unfair to women. Would she recommend such arrangements for everybody? Ideally she would recommend them for everyone who wanted them, but she believed that it would be psychologically very difficult for most couples to take the first step of having a frank conversation on the subject. Did she believe there were any special circumstances that made her case different from others? She replied that her husband's wealth and leisure made it possible for him to carry on an occasional affair without in any way depriving her of material needs. Admittedly it would be harder for a wife who was completely dependent on her husband's small earnings to accept the fact that he was spending money on another woman. Finally, the care of children would be a problem, especially for a mother who wished to exercise her extra-marital rights. If she and Mr. Blank had children, their ability to employ nurses and governesses would still give her free time for occasional dalliance. Clearly Mrs. Blank had covered all the bases.

As their talk neared its end, Mrs. Blank turned the tables and asked her interlocutor a very human question: What did he think of her? Lindsey's reply and conclusion must have been as comforting to her as they were disconcerting to some of the Judge's readers:

> "I think you're rich but honest," I said. "You would like to have me tell you that I think you are doing right. In like manner most conventional persons would reproach me bitterly for not telling you that you are an impure woman and a highly immoral person. But I could not do the work I am engaged in if I permitted my mind to form fixed judgments on human behavior. You must excuse me, therefore, from taking sides. It is part of my job not to take sides. I simply note the facts; and I find them interesting because they are among the indications that some sort of a social change is on the way.
>
> "That there are people in the world with your convictions seems to me significant and not necessarily alarming. There are some persons who regard as alarming every aberration of social conduct with which they don't happen to agree; but I am not of their number. I am greatly obliged to you for the truth. I hope you will keep me informed of future developments in your way of life if there are any."

I have not talked with Mrs. Blank since that interview; but so far as I know, she and her husband continue with apparent success in their individualistic scheme of living.[8]

The title of the Judge's book soon became a shorthand expression for all the ideas and attitudes implied by the words "sexual revolution." In vain did Lindsey protest that his actual proposals were downright conservative. In vain did he point to repeated statements in the book that in describing unconventional conduct he was not necessarily approving it. The Judge's proposals were largely ignored or forgotten as *The Companionate Marriage* came to be regarded as a challenge flung in the face of American puritanism. In spite of the Judge's disclaimers, the characterization was not altogether unfair.

The Companionate Marriage became the leading literary symbol of the American sexual revolution of the twenties for several reasons. Above all, it was so because Lindsey's exuberance in living in an era when old values were being questioned and discarded fairly breathed on every page. If he did not specifically endorse the unconventional conduct of his cast of characters, it was nevertheless true that the experimenters he described were almost invariably honest, attractive, and strong while those who adhered rigidly to the old standards were usually dullards or psychological misfits. The very format of the book strengthened the impression that it could serve as the bible of the liberators. On the front of the dust jacket were endorsements by Havelock Ellis and Floyd Dell. Inside, a descriptive table of contents provided a detailed guide to the book. A partial breakdown of a chapter entitled "Chastity: What It Is Not" implied an awareness of Freudian ideas, a rejection of puritanical values, and a firsthand knowledge of the New York theatrical scene. It promised to discuss "The popular virtue: White, Blonde, Nordic, Protestant, and Feminine: Conventional chastity a hotbed for the growth of sex obsessions. A 'God-fearing home': The Fall of Rome, an old chestnut among 'purity' fanatics. . . . 'Rain': The end of a missionary who dreamed of 'mountains in

Nebraska.' "* Obviously the Judge was thoroughly enjoying his joust with the Philistines.

The media contributed in important ways to the book's symbolic role. Popular magazines and Sunday supplements found the temptation to ballyhoo companionate marriage irresistible. To achieve the desired prurient effect they alternately dubbed it "pal marriage," "contract marriage," "jazz marriage," "free love," and, most frequently, "trial marriage." When two music teachers in Seattle proclaimed that theirs was a companionate marriage, the *Los Angeles Examiner* carried a photograph of them having coffee in their apartment. The caption accompanying the photograph declared, with total irrelevance, that the young couple was enjoying some domesticity, *"Judge Ben Lindsey notwithstanding,* when [they] were through teaching for the day." The clear implication of the newspaper was that the Judge's concept of companionate marriage was entirely sexual, and that couples who practiced it would somehow not carry on the same normal domestic activities that other couples did. Readers of the *St. Louis Star* were informed, "Lindsey's Trial Marriage Idea Bolshevistic, Says Divorce Judge." One newspaper cartoon showed black and white children marching in pairs out of a foundling asylum, presumably implying that any program as subversive as companionate marriage probably carried implications of miscegenation as well. Each child in the cartoon bore a tag with the name Lindsey on it. The caption was "Companionate." Perhaps Will Rogers was right when he punned, "Judge Lindsey and I went up together [in a Goodyear blimp] and discussed companionate marriage—which was over the heads of most people."[9]

It was hardly surprising that Lindsey's chief public critics were religious spokesmen, especially those who were prominent nationally and did not object to sharing the front page with the

* W. Somerset Maugham's *Rain* currently starred the popular Jeanne Eagels in the role of Sadie Thompson, a prostitute converted to Christianity until the fanatic and sexually repressed missionary who "saved" her makes a sexual advance toward her.

Judge. Aimee Semple McPherson, the flamboyant West Coast evangelist, announced, "I believe only in permanent monogamous marriage." The Judge had met Aimee once and liked her, and so chose not to become involved in a public argument with her. He privately confided to Wainwright Evans, "She is very human, well-meaning, and one of the most frightfully oversexed women I have ever met." When Billy Sunday called the Judge's proposals "nothing but free love" and "barnyard marriage," Lindsey publicly responded, "He would be burning witches and heretics if he had his way." A minister in Seattle indignantly told a local Lions Club, "If Lindsey or any other moral degenerate made such a proposition to a daughter or sister of mine, I'd wring his dirty neck." Scores of ordinary clergymen attacked Lindsey in their sermons and received notices, at least in their local newspapers.[10]

Privately Lindsey received hundreds of letters after the publication of *The Revolt,* and the numbers reached into the thousands after the appearance of *The Companionate Marriage.* The letters that were antagonistic followed a fairly predictable pattern. They accused the Judge of regarding people as animals and took him to task for defying God's commandments, especially the ones that forbade adultery and the coveting of one's neighbor's wife. A typical message came on a postcard from Denver: "You may have had an abundance of experience and your plan may seem logical but 'He is one who is greater than thou' and it seems more reasonable to adopt His plan."[11] Two other recurrent charges were that Lindsey was betraying his judicial trust by encouraging youth in lawlessness and immorality, and that he must be a "Bolshevik." A letter from an angry young woman in Georgia showed how some readers felt their entire way of life was threatened by the implications of Lindsey's writings:

Dear Sir:
    I have read your articles in the last three issues of The Red Book. Just such articles are helping the young generation down the

road to destruction. I sincerely hope your ideas will never become laws.

In regard to the "well known Denver man who, in his profession, is nationally known," I certainly trust that his daughter has more depth of character than he has. However, I agree with him when he says that the way to protect our young folk against themselves is to keep them busy. That will take care of the *entire problem!* If this well-known Denver man has enough sense to realize that, how can he say: "If my daughter were to remain unmarried, I should consider it a capital misfortune if she should let that interfere with her right, as a woman, to live out her sex life"? How base and low; uncultured—Oh! almost uncivilized! That's the animal showing up. If she should never marry, she should never "mate" as the swine do. And if she did, she should have the same respect as the swine do.

Why are the young folk so obsessed with sex? For the simple reason that they get sex at every turn. Everybody's talking sex. Every play or movie they see is 100% "sex appeal." They go home and "Mother" is using every beauty aid and dressing like a sixteen year old in order to attract Mrs. Jones' young husband and get his admiration, if she can't get him. In every magazine and paper they pick up "sex appeal" is being discussed by some "nationally known" person. How in the world can they think of anything else? Some of these "nationally known" people should be nationally ostracized when they try to advocate such standards for a civilized Christian nation.

Judge Lindsey, by the time you've gotten this far in my letter, I suppose you'll say, "Oh, this is some old maid about sixty years old trying to express her views," but you were never so wrong (except in your opinion of morals). I am twenty-two years of age and am told by many that I am beautiful and attractive. I am a college student and very popular with boys and men. I have been out quite a bit with this much discussed young generation. . . . I have had girls confide in me, and I've had lots of boys talk seriously with me about the kind of girl they admire, respect and want for a wife. So you see, I have a tiny right to know a bit about the young people, too.

I have yet my first time to know of illicit love bringing happiness. Happiness isn't secured except in a righteous way. When divorce is made as easy as you say it should be, then we will be on the same plain [*sic*] as our colored servants. Men and women will be exchanging husbands and wives like tagging one another on the Ball room floor. Your law may be suitable for the "wild west," but not for "our dear old Georgia" and the South.

Yours for a cleaner nation. . . .[12]

Critics of *The Companionate Marriage* were not found exclusively in the ranks of the socially conservative and the religiously orthodox. Among the temperate critics of Lindsey's proposals were some persons well regarded in liberal circles. They usually went out of their way to dissociate themselves from the reactionaries and publicity-seekers who were constantly denouncing the Judge as the leading contributor to the decline in American morals. Thus Bernard De Voto, reviewing Lindsey's book in the *Saturday Review of Literature,* castigated the Judge's critics, declaring that the Judge was "altogether on the side of the angels, and against his opponents all righteous men must be of one voice." At the same time, however, De Voto was skeptical about the role that sex education or the conscious guidance of the state could play in resolving "the sexual agony." In a similar vein Walter Lippmann agreed with the condemnation of the occasional cruelties of the "official morality" and the absurdities of existing divorce laws made by Lindsey and others, but had some reservations about companionate marriage as a social panacea. Lippmann found the core of the program—the period of time in which the childless couple would decide whether they were "compatible"—deficient because it failed to define that elusive concept, and because it implied that compatibility was a kind of wonderful accident grounded chiefly in physical attraction. Lippmann went on to accuse the Judge and other exponents of the sexual revolution of being excessively romantic. They failed to recognize, he argued, that "love cannot be isolated from the business of living, which is the enduring wisdom of the institution of marriage." Lippmann doubted that many couples could "live successfully by the conception that the

primary and secondary functions of sex are in separate compart-
ments of the soul," or that marriages would prove enduring
without the conviction that the relationship was permanent.[13]

Undoubtedly some of Lindsey's opponents feared that companionate marriages would be formed, especially by young men,
without a sincere intention of making them last. Jane Addams,
while publicly commending Lindsey's humanitarian record, expressed concern that the Judge's program "would tear down
what women have been fighting for over uncounted generations
—legal responsibility for parenthood and some protection for
the woman." Even Miss Addams seemed to be confusing the
issue a bit on this occasion, for though her point might be valid
that conventional marriage was more in women's interest than
companionate marriage, it was hard to see how Lindsey's proposals weakened "legal responsibility for parenthood." As the
Judge liked to point out, he was sometimes a stronger supporter
of the responsibility for parenthood than were advocates of the
status quo. For example, state divorce laws commonly allowed
a marriage to be dissolved if a single act of adultery could be
proved. Lindsey argued that the state had a moral obligation
at least to try to preserve all marriages, companionate or traditional, and even questioned the wisdom of allowing divorce for
a single act of adultery if the couple had children. The Judge's
distaste for coercion was such that he never went so far as to
maintain that *any* marriage should be continued indefinitely
against the wishes of either partner, but he was quite insistent
that a mandatory *effort* be made to resolve differences. Since no
state required such counseling as a condition for divorce,
Lindsey's claim that his program in one respect made divorce
less easy than it was under existing laws was accurate.[14]

The largest number of letters the Judge received after publication of *The Companionate Marriage* fell into the "Dear
Abby" category. Thousands of ordinary people demonstrated
the truth of Lindsey's assertions about the practical unavailabil-
ity of reliable birth-control information when they wrote to ask

his advice, particularly about "that most effective method." A poignant and typical inquiry came from a farmer's wife in Wisconsin:

> Dear Sir:
>
> I turn to you as a friend in need, I am a young mother with one baby after another and so on with no one to turn to for advice, could you tell me when a conception is possible and when not, I was told once there was some time after menstruation when and when not but do not know which. I love my family dearly and also my husband and do not want to drive him astray or ruin my health through some things or other. We have both decided our family is large enough if there was some way to solve our problems. Could you advice me to some books on this delicate subject. I would be very thankful to you beyond expression. Please do not make my name public, I speak to you as if you were my Father with such confidence cause I feel so lost and alone with all what faces me.
>
> Yours very truly.[15]

Lindsey had prepared a more or less standard reply which he used to answer such inquiries. On this occasion he simply added an introductory sentence:

> I think one of the greatest injustices that women have to contend with is the law against their having proper information on the subject you refer to. Federal statutes absolutely prohibit any information being sent through the mail. Here in Denver it can be given by the specialists who work in connection with our Maternity Clinic, but that is through some loophole they find in the law. You might write the American Birth Control League,* 104 Fifth Avenue, New York City, and they might be able to tell you of some doctor in your city who could give you proper advice.[16]

Although most of the letters seeking birth-control information came from the poor and barely articulate, occasionally a letter from an educated correspondent revealed that a lack of information, or misinformation, was not a monopoly of the

---

* The American Birth Control League was a forerunner of the Planned Parenthood Association.

underprivileged. A professor in a western agricultural college confided to Lindsey:

> Because we did not have reliable information on the subject, my wife gave birth to two children too soon after a serious major operation. This greatly impaired her health and resulted in the loss of both children. We are now practicing birth control according to advice given us by the pastor of our church who violated the laws of the land in rendering a most Christian service.[17]

The professor was not completely accurate in saying that it was a violation of "the laws of the land" to give information about birth-control techniques. State laws were not uniformly rigid on the subject, nor were they always enforced. By 1930 at least a few states permitted the operation of birth-control clinics. Yet there was more than a grain of truth in the professor's assertion. Federal laws were still used, sometimes unpredictably, to keep birth-control information out of the mails and to ban at the customs house books from abroad that dealt with the subject. As late as 1929 Mary Ware Dennett, a pioneer figure in the birth-control movement, was indicted and convicted for mailing a copy of her pamphlet *The Sex Side of Life: An Explanation for Young People*. On the private level of economic coercion, even professors of sociology sometimes discovered the perils of using questionnaires that touched on such topics. In describing the continued vitality of repressive elements in American society, Lindsey wrote to Upton Sinclair:

> Of course, I can imagine what you think of the recent conviction of Mary Ware Dennett. There was also recently a raid on the Birth Control League in New York City, and professors from several universities have been expelled because of a questionnaire on family relations that called for replies on certain matters relating to sex. I suppose you have read how, when it was proposed to admit girls to physiology classes in the high schools, the eminent clergy rose up on their hind footsies and protested against girls having any information on physiology lest it corrupt their morals. This, I might say, happened in your "favorite city" of Boston.[18]

In addition to the requests for information about birth control, many writers wanted Lindsey's advice about their own
sexual problems. The Judge followed the same routine with
these letters that he had used earlier when people had written
to him about juvenile delinquency and dependency. Since an
even greater share of his correspondence now demanded psychological counseling if it were to be handled adequately, the
Judge frequently sent only a cordial acknowledgment accompanied by a suggestion to seek help in other quarters. When
married persons asked for advice about sexual techniques, the
Judge frequently recommended that they purchase Harland
William Long's *Sane Sex Life and Sane Sex Living,* a popular
liberal sex manual first published in 1919. When relatively
simple problems were presented to him, Lindsey sometimes attempted to give commonsense answers. In spite of the Judge's
identification with the "sexual revolution," his replies often carried the same advice that would have been given by any moderately liberal clergyman. A year after publication of *The Companionate Marriage,* when a young man asked his views
concerning a contemplated pre-marital living arrangement with
his girl friend, the Judge sent a typical Lindsey reply:

> I do not favor the relationships you refer to for young people
> except in marriage. Due to the fact that I have a great deal of
> charity for those who do not live up to this rule, and whom I have
> always been willing to help in their difficulties, a false impression
> has perhaps gone out as to my real views. I think it would be much
> better if you would try to avoid anything of the kind. It would
> seem to me that if you confide in your parents on both sides they
> might help you in an early marriage, in which you could refrain
> from having children until you were ready and able to take care
> of them.

A few months later the Judge warned a teen-ager:

> A girl cannot take the risk that boys take. . . . If either one of
> the boys in question had the real love for you that he ought to have,
> then you should get married; in the meantime, as to the thing you
> ask me about, my advice is, *don't.*[19]

Perhaps the two most gratifying letters that reached Lindsey concerning *The Companionate Marriage* came from Havelock Ellis and Bertrand Russell. By the time they wrote to him the Judge had come under a barrage of criticism and his position on the Denver court was in jeopardy. Both Englishmen had harsh words for Lindsey's enemies, Ellis calling them "the unfortunate elements of savagery in your community." Both also expressed a minority, though accurate, view when they wrote that Lindsey's companionate marriage program was really very conservative, though they were willing to go along with it as an improvement over the status quo. Bertrand Russell asserted that, if he had his way, "no marriage ceremony would be valid unless accompanied by a medical certificate of the woman's pregnancy."[20] It was unfortunate for Lindsey that his essential conservatism was not better understood in his own country. He was soon to pay the price for having become a national symbol of radicalism. His days in Denver were numbered.

9 / "The Blue Menace"

IN 1928 AN OBSCURE UNITARIAN MINISTER IN MILTON, MASSA-chusetts, observed that the country had more to fear from the Blue Menace than it did from the so-called Red Menace. The Blue Menace, according to the Reverend Vivian T. Pomeroy, was the organized opposition by ultra-conservative forces against labor unions, civil liberties advocates, and any other group that did not conform to their own dogmatic notions in matters of politics, religion, and morals. Judge Lindsey, Pomeroy asserted, was among their prime targets.[1]

The spirit that animated the Blue Menace was unfailingly vindictive. It recognized its enemies and sought to destroy them, preferably by censorship, imprisonment, or deportation, as it had done during World War I and the Red Scare immediately following, or, when these methods were not legally available, by economic pressure, social ostracism, and sometimes even physical violence. Lindsey was a natural enemy of such self-anointed patriots, for they recognized that his liberalism was not confined to the realm of sexual conduct and that anyone who challenged the old orthodoxies in that vital sphere was probably a threat on other fronts as well. The Judge, who was never known for avoiding a good fight, fanned the flames of their hatred by his public denunciations of their foibles and inanities, and thoroughly enjoyed hitting back at the "boobs" and Neanderthals in language closely resembling that of his famous contemporary, H. L. Mencken. Among Lindsey's major targets were Prohibition, "one hundred percent Americanism," censorship, Fundamentalism, and, finally and consistently, the Ku Klux Klan.

Lindsey's opposition to Prohibition was the result of a genuine intellectual conversion. Indeed, after its repeal he was still an almost total abstainer, and in his early years his strictures on drinking and its relationship to "other vices" had a decidedly puritanical flavor. His first courtroom experiences with young offenders and some of their parents had convinced him that drinking was often associated with broken homes, truancy, and the whole pattern of juvenile delinquency. On several occasions the Judge accepted the political endorsement of the Prohibition party, and he was at first a strong supporter of the Eighteenth Amendment. Like many other progressives, however, Lindsey eventually became disillusioned with Prohibition. The rise of bootlegging and gangsterism convinced many Americans that the cure was worse than the disease. Another contributing factor to the disillusionment, which seemed to bother the Judge especially, was that the enforcement of Prohibition appeared to be working out inequitably along class lines. The wealthy were able to evade the law without much difficulty. The workingman had lost his saloon, but the rich man still had his wine cellar and, if worst came to worst, could always take a vacation to Europe or a short hop to Canada.

But the Judge's most fundamental reason for changing his mind about Prohibition went beyond matters of bootlegging and class discrimination in law enforcement. It reflected another aspect of the same viewpoint he had developed regarding sexual conduct. As he put it:

> Your attitude toward Prohibition is based on whether you believe human beings can be educated to decency and voluntary restraint in the indulgence of an appetite, or that they must be restrained by force and law. Your attitude on the time-honored sex taboos is based on precisely the same choice.

In retrospect the Judge thought the ideal of temperance had been a more realizable goal in pre-Prohibition days. Telling people they were forbidden to drink seemed to make many of them all the more determined to do so. As with sex, forbidden fruits were often the sweetest. Lindsey was now ready to label those who still supported Prohibition "busybodies who think that people can be legislated into heaven." He was convinced that they had set back the clock with their "direct action" and "bourgeois syndicalism," as he now described the Eighteenth Amendment. Looking back at his own support of Prohibition, he concluded:

> I still recognize the need for such control, but I understand now better than I did then, that morality and reasonable conduct cannot be made by the passing of statutes; and I know now, what many another citizen has come to realize, that the Eighteenth Amendment has proved a poor way to obtain a desirable end.[2]

There was much in Lindsey's experience that made him also a natural foe of those super-patriots of the 1920's who identified their prejudices and self-interest with "Americanism," and who were ever ready to use the labels "hyphenate," "alien," and "Bolshevik" interchangeably to describe any person or group who disagreed with them. The reactionary syndrome was not new, either to America or the Judge. In pre-war years Lindsey had personally found reasons for distrusting nativism in all its forms. He had always run well in the Jewish and Italian precincts of Denver, where he was loved for his pro-labor and humanitarian sympathies. He had heard his supporters called "foreigners" by some of the "respectable" citizens of Denver who swore that they would never be ruled "by cattle like that."[3] He was also familiar with the sanctimonious use of the phrase "law and order" as code words for saying, "We don't want workers to have unions." Exasperated by Colorado Progressives who refused to go along with him in supporting the coal miners in 1914, he wrote to William Allen White:

> Most of the . . . crowd have deserted us for "law and order," that in this state is simply Dr. Johnson's "Patriotism is the refuge of scoundrels" [*sic*]. When I see the infamous crooks wearing an American flag on the lapel of their coats—men who know no law and order, except for the other fellow—and observe the success

with which they are capitalizing the very flag itself in behalf of their tyranny and oppression, it makes me boil with indignation. I tell our fellows that we should not let them get away with that, but we should wear flags ourselves and have it out as to what that flag really represents.[4]

Lindsey's distrust of those who draped their causes in the flag grew stronger in the twenties when rampant xenophobia expressed itself in campaigns to restrict immigration, increase textbook censorship, and introduce loyalty oaths for teachers. The Judge deplored the censorship of "school histories that tell the truth about the American Revolution" and castigated what he called the " 'two hundred percent Americanism' attitude toward Roman Catholics—not to mention Jews, Negroes, and aliens" as a "yellow streak in our national life, a streak so yellow that a sane yellow dog would be ashamed to own it." As for the phrase "one hundred percent American," Lindsey declared, "I'd walk around the world to avoid having that label pinned on me."[5]

One of the Judge's major intellectual characteristics was his insistence on judging ideas and institutions by their relevance for the present and the future. Appeals to a real, or imagined, past were a stock in trade of chauvinists, Lindsey thought. A strong supporter of Woodrow Wilson's League of Nations, the Judge sarcastically observed:

I have often wondered that our national sense of humor should have been so dormant that it kept right on sleeping while Henry Cabot Lodge and his cohorts were presenting the fact that *Washington* had warned us against entangling alliances. And yet Henry Cabot Lodge was, in what seemed to me an evil way, intelligent. Perhaps that was why he used such an argument.[6]

Fundamentalism was another reactionary composite that drew Lindsey's fire. In the 1920's Fundamentalism was far more than a belief in the literal truth of the Bible. It was, as historian Richard Hofstadter has accurately demonstrated, "a religious style shaped by a desire to strike back against everything modern

—the higher criticism, evolutionism, the social gospel, rationalism of any kind." Obviously there could be no chance for Ben Lindsey to maintain cordial relations with this segment of the Blue Menace, and the Judge recognized the fact in his writings with a virtual declaration of open warfare. Referring to his pragmatic approach to sexual problems, he commented:

> I have been reading a good many letters of late, asking me how I reconcile some of the views I am expressing . . . with the Bible. I have one short and conclusive answer to that question. I don't reconcile [them] with the Bible. Moreover, I don't see why I should. Those of my views which are in accord with Holy Writ speak for themselves. Those which are not have to be classed with evolution, the roundness of the earth, and other matters which were not factors in the speculative thought of the ancient Jews. To say that modern sociology must deal with modern facts is not to flout or discount the Bible. It is to interpret that book in the light of changing conditions.[7]

Lindsey always emphasized that he was no scoffer at the spiritual element in man's nature and that he had no quarrel with "religion," or even with the churches. His antagonism was directed against those whom he called "Bible-olaters" who believed in an anthropomorphic God of very specific measurements and who, "if the record had said that Jonah swallowed the whale, would have believed that." Even these ideas would not have bothered him, Lindsey asserted, if the "true believers" had held them only as private convictions. Unfortunately it seemed to be a characteristic of the Fundamentalist syndrome to insist on foisting their beliefs on everybody else in the form of Prohibition, strict divorce laws, Comstockery, and statutes forbidding the teaching of evolution.[8]

Although Lindsey retained a certain admiration and even affection for the Catholic Church, he felt that its spokesmen were no better than the Fundamentalists when they subverted the principle of separation of church and state by imposing their views on divorce and birth control on the rest of society. Bracketing the Catholic and Protestant clergy who publicly fought the legalization of birth control as "clerical fanatics" and "Bible worshippers," the Judge excoriated them as the greatest producers of "immorality, wretchedness, crime, and black tragedy" in the country. Commenting on those who objected to his companionate marriage proposal on religious grounds, the Judge testily remarked:

> "Religious" people may find something holy—some hint of "holy" matrimony—in such a tangle, but I don't. [Lindsey had just described a particularly wretched loveless marriage.] I say the devil has never invented anything worse than this piece of "sacramental" poppycock that has been "sanctified" by the Christian church. I say that such absurdities are on an intellectual level with devil worship, and that we uphold and perpetuate the thing either because we can't think straight or are afraid to do so.
>
> It is mostly the so-called religious people of this country, don't forget, who rise up in arms when anybody proposes that we sweep their theological junk off the map and try to use a little intelligence in ordering our affairs. They appear to me to be in error when they call their system of superstition by the sacred name of Religion. Religion consists of putting oneself in harmony with reality; but they are not interested in that kind of harmony because they think it a sin. They hate "free thought" far more sincerely than they hate "free love."[9]

It is hardly surprising that such fighting words evoked an equally pugnacious response from the other side. Pickets and demonstrators protested the Judge's appearance when he spoke in Birmingham, Alabama, and the chief of police, accompanied by three plainclothesmen, escorted him back to his hotel in order to insure his safety. The National Defense Committee, a "patriotic" group, criticized the Lewis and Clark Chapter of the Daughters of the American Revolution for inviting Lindsey to speak in Eugene, Oregon. The Reverend Victor Capesius, president of the Evangelical Church of Austria, testified to the Judge's international fame when he charged that "Lindseyism" and Bolshevism were the "two destructive forces threatening to destroy . . . European civilization."[10] Perhaps the strongest sermon ever preached against the Judge was the fictional one by "Father Shannon" in *Studs Lonigan*. Although the sermon was a figment of James T. Farrell's imagination, its tone and content reflected Farrell's uncanny ear for the style of one type of clerical demagogue:

> And in Denver, there is a puny little man, whose mind would have to be seen through the lenses of a powerful microscope. A man who has sullied the sanctity and justice of the courts . . . one Judge Ben Lindsay [*sic*]. And what does he preach? (He sneered.) . . . Companionate Marriage! Companionate Marriage, another of those masked fads that rise from a cesspool of spiritual cravenness (sneering). Companionate Marriage! That is his sugar-coated seductive term. This little man, this human atom, this intellectual midget, what does he preach—at a price (with rising voice)? I'll tell you in straight language without any fake pretense of those abused words, liberality and tolerance. In simple words, this human rat, like the anarchistic, atheistic Bolshevists in unhappy Russia, says (his arms flung out in a gesture): "Away with the holy bonds of Matrimony!" Jesus Christ (his head bowing), our Lord, said "What God hath joined together, let no man put asunder!" . . . And Judge Ben Lindsay (with a sneer) says that this is all nonsense. It is not modern. It is old-fashioned. Away with it! . . . He tells the youth of America to go out, flirt, taste sin, ruin their souls, experiment, and that if it does not succeed, try again. He advises young men to take a girl, a pure, innocent, decent, perhaps even a Catholic, girl, and live with her in violation of one of God's Holy Commandments. Try her out! Ruin her! And if she doesn't powder her nose the right way, or burns the toast in the morning, or you stub your toe getting out on the wrong side of the bed, and think she is the cause, leave her. You are then incompatible. Leave her a ruined girl, unable to look her mother or her God in the eye, unable to find a decent young man who would want her! Incompatibility! Another of those masked, ambiguous, lying phrases used to clothe the intent of Satan who skulks in the low and depraved mentalities, like that of Judge Ben Lindsay![11]

Bitter as his struggles were with Prohibitionists, Fundamentalists, and Catholics, it would be hard to think of an organ-

ization whose ideology was as thoroughly incompatible with
that of the Judge as the Ku Klux Klan. The revived Klan of the
twenties, in keeping with the spirit of the times, had added a
lengthy list of "hates" to the original Klan's anti-Negro racism.
In each category, from the Klan's standpoint, Lindsey was
clearly identified with the wrong side. The Klan was pre-
eminently nationalistic, and Lindsey advocated international
cooperation. It was rabidly anti-Semitic, and the Judge proclaimed his pride in having Jewish supporters and allies. The
new Klan purported to be an uncompromising supporter of
"morality" (meaning, of course, sexual morality) against the
supposed wave of licentiousness that was sweeping the country.
The Judge was simultaneously preaching the joy and beauty
of the erotic side of life and attributing much of the tension and
hatred in the country to sexual repression. Finally, and ironically,
even the Klan's anti-Catholicism was a source of antagonism to
Lindsey, for was it not true that the Judge's mother's funeral
was held at the Roman Catholic cathedral in Denver in 1924, and
had he not himself sometimes committed wards of the court to
the care of a Catholic orphanage?[12] Even though the Judge
openly professed to be a member of a local Methodist church,
who in the paranoid realm of the "Invisible Empire" could be
certain that he was not a "secret Catholic" operating under
some Jesuitical dispensation to conceal his true identity? Bizarre
as these and other notions of the Klan were, they could not be
taken lightly. By the time Lindsey was ready to announce his
candidacy for re-election in 1924, the issue of Klan opposition
had become crucial, for in a period of scarcely three years the
Klan had become the most powerful political force in the state
of Colorado.[13]

The spectacular rise of the Klan to political power in Colorado was largely the result of the efforts of Dr. John Galen
Locke. Locke, who has been described as looking like Grover
Cleveland with a goatee, was a flamboyant physician who was
not sufficiently expert to be admitted to the Denver County

Medical Association. He managed to carry on a modest practice in Denver by organizing a small hospital of his own. In 1921, after a recruiting visit to Denver by William J. Simmons, Imperial Wizard of the Ku Klux Klan, Locke helped form the Denver Doers Club, which openly proclaimed its affiliation with the Klan in June of that year. Two of its most widely publicized early actions involved driving a caravan of automobiles down Curtis Street proclaiming its opposition to "the lawless element," and threatening to lynch a Negro custodian of an apartment house for "having intimate relations with a white woman." The latter effort was publicly fought by the district attorney, Philip Van Cise, who paid the price for his courage at the next election when he was succeeded by a Klan-backed opponent.

Negroes were not destined to be the chief victims of the Klan in Colorado, mainly because they were not the most convenient scapegoats. In 1920 Denver, which became the center of Klan activity in the state, had a population of approximately 250,000. The Negro population of the city was only about 7,000. Nor did their growing numbers constitute any kind of threat. In the decade ending in 1920 the total nonwhite population of the city had increased by only 649 persons. The Negroes were chiefly confined to a small ghetto just north and east of the capitol. Although there is some evidence that a handful of people living on the fringes of the ghetto were concerned about even the modest growth of the Negro population, the Klan leaders recognized early in the game that the biggest political paydirt on the hate front was to be found elsewhere.

It seems to have been found in approximately equal measure in the Catholic and Jewish communities. For predominantly Protestant, native American Denverites, and for Klan propagandists, the Catholics and the Jews were at once a more available and meaningful target. Although their numbers also were not large (approximately 35,000 Catholics and 11,000 Jews), among them were merchants who could be boycotted to the advantage of their Protestant competitors. Signs could be posted in shop windows—as they were—stating that the owners were "one hundred percent American" or even proclaiming their membership in the Klan. One Klansman apparently did his restaurant business no harm by putting up a sign which stated, "We Serve Fish Every Day—Except Friday." On the eve of the Jewish Sabbath, Klan hoodlums drove through the principal Jewish neighborhood of Denver and shouted obscenities.

In Denver, as in some other parts of the country, the "religious" argument helped the Klan appeal to some Protestant clergymen. One of the leading Klan officers in Denver was the Reverend William Oeschger of the Highland Christian Church, which he made a center of Klan activity. The First Avenue Presbyterian Church and the Grant Avenue Methodist Church (not Judge Lindsey's parish) were also active in Klan affairs. In an era when patriotism was often equated with uniformity and conformity, the Klan also made full use of traditional arguments that the Jews were unassimilable and that the Catholics owed allegiance to a foreign power.

Perhaps more important than all such "objective" appeals worked by the Klan was that composite of fear and hatred which compels some persons to make a particular race or group the embodiment of all that is evil. Social psychologists have explored in some depth the characteristics of this "authoritarian personality," as T. W. Adorno has labeled it. Apparently there was a wealth of such types in Denver in the 1920's. As Lindsey neatly capsulized the matter in describing the Klansmen (and women), "They had paid ten dollars each to hate somebody and they were determined to get their money's worth."

As early as January 1922 the Denver Klan had decided to make the defeat of Judge Lindsey one of their major goals in the 1924 election. A letter from the Kligrapp of Denver Klan Number One (as the secretary was quaintly called) to the Klan's national headquarters in Atlanta announced that they were determined to put "a clean man on the Juvenile Court."[14]

By early 1923 the Judge and the Klan were publicly denouncing each other. When the national Democratic convention met in New York City a year later to pick its national candidates, the party was torn asunder in a floor fight over a motion to condemn the Klan by name. From Denver the Judge enthusiastically endorsed the idea and issued a statement:

> As a Democrat, I heartily endorse the plank. The time has come when both parties must be frank with the people and courageously take a stand . . . for the open, free administration of government by all the people, or confess themselves on the side of hypocrisy and cowardice and privilege, for kliques, klans, and klasses, working under cover in the interest of a government that is invisible and not . . . as the Constitution and law of the land intended it should be.[15]

In Colorado, however, it was the Republican, rather than the Democratic, party that was to be the temporary agent of Klan domination. After gaining substantial influence in Denver after the 1923 municipal election, the Klan was now ready to make its bid to capture the Republican party and nominate candidates for governor, United States Senator, the state legislature, a vacancy on the state Supreme Court, and a number of county offices. Dr. Locke's assiduous work at the county level paid off at the Denver Republican Assembly in August 1924. Locke sat in the auditorium as if he were holding court. A few days later, when the Republican State Convention met, the Klan encountered some opposition from decent Republicans like Van Cise but not enough to prevent it from nominating its choices for all statewide offices. The ensuing campaign has been called by one historian "the bitterest and dirtiest in the history of the Centennial State." When it was over in November the Klan had won every major statewide office it sought as well as a majority of seats in the lower house of the state legislature. Its only important defeat was in the race for the judgeship of the Juvenile Court of Denver. Paradoxically, this defeat ultimately became its only long-range victory.

Although Lindsey was declared the winner, the returns reflected the intensity of the Klan campaign against him. Instead of his usual landslide margin running well into the thousands, the Judge defeated his Klan-supported opponent, Royal R. Graham, by only 137 votes out of a total of almost 90,000. In this slender margin the Klan leadership saw its chance to overturn the Lindsey victory. The strategy decided upon was to challenge the validity of the entire vote in District 6, Precinct J, where Lindsey had beaten Graham 548 to 15.

Lindsey's landslide in J-6 had come as no surprise to political observers in Denver. The Judge had lived there as a boy, maintained his neighborhood contacts, and had always done well in the district. In 1924 his opposition to the Ku Klux Klan was an important additional asset to his candidacy, since the district was located in the principal Jewish neighborhood of Denver. If J-6 could be disregarded, the Klan's candidate could take his seat as judge of the Juvenile Court of the City and County of Denver.

The case of *Graham v. Lindsey*[16] began in the court of Judge Julian Moore on March 31, 1925, and lasted two and a half weeks. Measured by newspaper headlines, the two most sensational episodes during the trial were Graham's admission that he was a member of the Klan and the appearance of the plaintiff's star witness, one William Unter. In his testimony Unter charged that he had been bribed by Charles Francis, an officer of Lindsey's court, to help swing the election of the Judge in J-6.

At the time he testified, Unter was already serving a six months' jail sentence for illegal conduct at the polls in J-6, a charge to which he had pleaded guilty two months earlier. When Lindsey's attorney had finished cross-examining Unter, however, his revelations seemed more damaging to those who had brought him forward than they did to Lindsey.

Two aspects of Unter's story which came out under the gruelling cross-examination by Lindsey's attorney, Philip Hornbein, made his testimony suspect. In the first place Unter conceded that when he first went to the chief of police on the advice of a "friend" and talked at length about his improper conduct on behalf of Democratic candidates, he never mentioned the alleged offer of a bribe by Francis. Hornbein's implication that the charge was an afterthought and pure fiction was not lost on the Denver press and probably not on Judge Moore, either. If Hornbein's implication were true, the thorough discrediting of Unter now required only that a motive be found. Unter then revealed that a man named Jack Martin had given him $100 and was supplying food and rent for his wife and children while he was in jail. Unter was not able to give any reason other than friendship why Martin, whom he had not even known five months earlier, was so generous. For those familiar with the Denver scene, the reason was not hard to explain. Jack Martin was widely regarded as the right-hand man of Dr. John Galen Locke.

Although Unter stuck to the line that Martin had only urged him to tell the whole truth in his testimony, it was hard to escape the conclusion that the witness, who gave the impression of being a weak and dependent young man, had probably been persuaded to testify against Lindsey by a combination of bribery and threats. The bribery was virtually self-evident, and the threats from law enforcement agents in a Klan-dominated administration could be easily imagined. Finally, the credibility of Unter's charge against Francis, and indirectly against Lindsey, was weakened by the fact that it rested exclusively on Unter's own statement that the bribe had been given to him at a private meeting with no other witnesses present.

Other witnesses testified, as Unter did, that there were many irregularities at the polls in J-6 (a condition hardly unique to that district), and Judge Moore eventually ordered a recount of the ballots for the entire city. After numerous challenges and "exceptions" in which sometimes Lindsey, sometimes Graham came out the winner, Judge Moore was finally ready to hand down a judgment on a motion by Graham's attorney to throw out J-6 altogether. The motion was a crucial one, since Judge

Moore's recount had reduced Lindsey's city-wide margin to thirty-five votes. Lindsey's greatest loss was in J-6, where the court found that a number of blank votes had been erroneously (but not necessarily fraudulently) counted in his favor. Nevertheless, even under the recount Lindsey had carried J-6 by a vote of 481 to 18. If J-6 stood, so did Lindsey's election.

Judge Moore ruled that the recount had purged the election of any possible fraud in J-6 and that there was "no sufficient evidence upon which the court could set aside this entire precinct vote." Even assuming that Unter had told the truth, Judge Moore held, there was no proof that he had actually marked a single ballot for Lindsey contrary to the wishes of a voter. It seemed to be all over. Judge Moore closed the proceedings by stating that no presentation by Lindsey was necessary since Graham had failed to show by a preponderance of the evidence that there was fraud in J-6. Judge Lindsey had won.

Immediately after Lindsey's victory, Royal Graham announced that he would appeal Judge Moore's decision to the state Supreme Court. For the remainder of 1925, however, events seemed to favor Judge Lindsey. In September Graham, the "clean man" whom the Klan had hoped to put in the Judge's place, turned on the gas jets in his kitchen and killed himself rather than face charges of fraud in connection with a public office he held in an adjoining county. Three months later Graham's lawyers moved to dismiss the case against Lindsey in the Colorado Supreme Court. Graham's widow was unwilling to consider the matter closed, however. In January 1926 her attorney petitioned the Supreme Court to substitute her name for that of her deceased husband in the case of *Graham v. Lindsey*. Cora Graham had two aims. First, she sought to have Lindsey's election invalidated, thus ousting him from the court. Second, as the administratrix of Graham's estate, she wished to receive the salary that Lindsey was paid for the period during which she claimed her husband should have been sitting as judge. From a technical standpoint the propriety of Mrs. Graham's petition was a sufficiently complicated legal question to divide the Supreme Court as closely as possible. Unfortunately for Lindsey, four of the seven justices voted to grant her motion. The ultimate issue would now be settled by the Supreme Court of Colorado.

On January 24, 1927, the Supreme Court unanimously held that the entire vote in J-6 was invalid.[17] For the next five months the Judge's lawyers made every possible legal move to undo the decision, including an appeal to the Supreme Court of the United States. The federal court exercised its right not to hear the case without ever touching on the merits of the controversy. Thus the decision of the Colorado Supreme Court stood, and on June 30, 1927, the best-known juvenile court judge in the world stepped down from the position he had occupied for almost a third of a century. The reasons behind the decision by the Colorado Supreme Court immediately became a subject of major controversy that extended far beyond the boundaries of Colorado and even beyond the borders of the United States.

On one level the opinion of the Colorado Supreme Court had considerable plausibility. Its major premise was that there had been so much irregularity at the polls in J-6 that it would be impossible ever to establish what the actual vote had been. Justice John W. Sheafor, using the transcript from Judge Moore's trial court, quoted at length from testimony that portrayed a condition of near chaos at the voting booth and in adjoining rooms. One witness testified that he saw voters go into the booth accompanied by as many as three or four persons who were neither election judges nor officials. Another testified that the ballots were left unsupervised at one time and on a subsequent occasion were left alone in the presence of persons with no official status. One witness seemed to sum up the whole scene when he observed, "There was so much trouble, my God, I couldn't begin to tell it." Under these circumstances, Justice Sheafor implied, even if there were no proof of "actual fraud," it would overtax the imagination to believe that fraud had not occurred.[18] In any event, he concluded on behalf of the court, a further recount of votes would be "abortive" since there was no possible way to separate legal from illegal votes. It would be purposeless, therefore, to remand the case to Judge Moore's court for further proceedings. The only proper remedy for the flagrant misconduct in J-6, which had violated at least four state election statutes, was to discard the entire vote.

Whatever the merits of the court's decision, the reaction to it in many quarters was that the Supreme Court had played the Klan's game by ousting Judge Lindsey on flimsy grounds. After all, there had been irregularities in other precincts in the Klan-dominated election of 1924. It seemed unfair that the Judge should lose his seat as a result of voiding the vote in the one district where everybody knew he was going to win by a land-slide. Judge Moore had seemed to appeal to common sense when he stated in his decision:

> Even assuming the entire truthfulness of the witness Unter ... there would be no sufficient evidence upon which the court could set aside this entire precinct vote. .... The evidence discloses that this precinct, J-6, was in a part of the town made up of the Jewish race [sic]; ninety per cent—perhaps more—of the votes in this precinct were Jewish votes. The evidence discloses that these were Lindsey votes....

Finally, William Unter, the only person who accused someone in Judge Lindsey's office of trying to buy votes for the Judge, had been a most unconvincing witness, especially in this totally unproven indirect charge against Lindsey. To many observers it seemed that the net result of the decision by the Supreme Court was that Judge Lindsey had lost his court through the malice of the Ku Klux Klan and a series of events for which he was in no way culpable.

At least one member of the Colorado Supreme Court even-tually concluded that the case should have been sent back to the lower court so that Lindsey could have an opportunity to refute the charges of fraud in J-6. When Lindsey's counsel petitioned the Supreme Court for a rehearing, Associate Justice John W. Denison dissented from the rest of the court's refusal to grant it. Justice Denison pointed out that Lindsey's attorneys had not introduced evidence that might have refuted the charge of fraud chiefly because Judge Moore's precipitous holding in their favor had seemed to make a defense unnecessary. Understandably, Lindsey's lawyers did not ask Judge Moore's permission to present their case in full when he had just announced that they had won. In Justice Denison's view, Lindsey was now being denied his day in court because his attorneys had relied on the rulings of Judge Moore. While Justice Sheafor's blunt but unproved assertion that Lindsey had no evidence to refute the charge of serious irregularities in the conduct of the election in J-6 might have been true, the refusal of the Supreme Court even to let him try strengthened the impression that the court was out to "get Lindsey."

Almost half a century after these events, surviving foes as well as friends of Judge Lindsey in Denver were convinced that at least some of the Justices of the Colorado Supreme Court were motivated by feelings of animosity. Most of them were Republicans of a conservative temperament, and Lindsey was undoubtedly the antithesis of their notion of what a judge should be. In addition to being a member of the opposite political party, the Judge had been a vocal critic of many aspects of the entire legal system. Many of the justices, no doubt, remembered his attacks on the courts in *The Beast* and his contempt of court in the Wright murder case. Perhaps most significantly, the Colorado Supreme Court heard the Judge's case at the very time he was receiving the greatest newspaper publicity in his lifetime as a result of his articles on companionate marriage, which had begun to appear in the *Red Book Magazine* in October 1926. To many conservative members of the legal profession it was vulgar and unseemly for a judge to write about his court experiences in a popular magazine and to travel around the country lecturing on (of all things!) the sexual revolution. Some citizens of Denver still believe that the emotions engendered by the Judge's articles were the crucial element in the court's willingness to oust him.

Certainly liberals outside Denver were convinced that Lindsey was being punished for his ideas and for having the audacity to advocate them in a public forum. From England Havelock Ellis attempted to console the Judge after his defeat: "I am afraid ... that the only thanks the moralist ever gets is to be crucified."[19] Dean Roscoe Pound of the Harvard Law School saw the Judge's ouster as part of the political repression that characterized one side of the 1920's. A few weeks before Judge Lindsey stepped down from the court, Pound wrote to him:

> We seem to be reverting to the seventeenth century period. These are indeed difficult times for those who take seriously the fundamental claims of the human spirit to form and express opinions with respect to human institutions. Apparently much that we supposed had been permanently won for human freedom in the seventeenth and eighteenth centuries must be won over again in the twentieth century.[20]

No final answer can be given as to the motives of the six justices who participated in the decision against Lindsey. At least one of them, Justice John T. Adams, had been elected in 1924 with the full support of the Ku Klux Klan and was widely believed to be a member of the organization. Under the circumstances it would have set an example for judicial propriety if Justice Adams had disqualified himself from sitting on the case, but judicial propriety was probably not a major characteristic of the man. Chief Justice Haslett P. Burke commented in his separate opinion that, given the legal precedents, he could see "no escape from the holding," possibly implying that he reached the conclusion regretfully. On the other hand Justice Greeley W. Whitford's concurring opinion in the decision to deny Lindsey a rehearing contained a phrase or two that could be interpreted as hostile toward Lindsey—a hostility that was unmistakably evident a few years later when disbarment proceedings were instituted against the Judge. Although the record does not reveal even an implication of motives in the other justices, including Adams, it is not unlikely that some of them welcomed an opportunity to rid the court of "this little upstart," as so many of the conservative bench and bar regarded the Judge. An illustration of the violent intensity of the feelings of one segment of the Colorado bar against Lindsey occurred as late as 1966 at a cocktail party which this writer attended in Denver. Informed that I was the biographer of Lindsey, an older attorney said, "Perhaps you can answer a question?" "Yes?" I replied. He then asked, "How could such a little guy have been such a big son of a bitch?"

A few months after Judge Lindsey relinquished his court the name of William Unter appeared again in the news. After Unter had testified against the Lindsey side at the original trial in 1925, he had been granted a parole by the governor of Colorado, Klansman Clarence J. Morley, thus strengthening the suspicion that a deal had been made between Unter and various officials who were also members of the Ku Klux Klan. Unter subsequently disappeared from the Denver scene and was not heard of again until a brief story in the *Denver Post* on March 2, 1927, reported that he and his family had settled in Los Angeles. Three weeks later Unter paid a visit to O. N. Hilton, a former Colorado judge then living in southern California, and expressed a desire to meet with Judge Lindsey. The purpose of the meeting, Unter told Hilton, would be to make a full retraction of the testimony he had given in Judge Moore's court.[21]

A conference between Lindsey and Unter was eventually arranged at the Ambassador Hotel in Los Angeles on August 1, 1927. After the meeting Lindsey prepared a statement which Unter signed on August 10. The statement, subsequently referred to as Unter's "confession" by Lindsey and the *Denver Post,* admitted that Unter had lied totally in testifying that he had been offered a bribe by an officer of Lindsey's court. It also asserted that no illegal votes had been cast for the Judge. The bulk of the statement recounted in lurid detail how Klansmen, including Dr. John Galen Locke, and public officials used bribes, promises, and even threats of physical violence to coerce Unter to help them by perjury in their plot to throw out J-6 and remove Lindsey. According to Unter, the Klan-backed district attorney had threatened him with "ten years in the penitentiary" if he ever told the whole story of their efforts "to get Lindsey." Nevertheless, Unter was willing to sign this unsworn statement in California in order to make partial amends for the wrong he had done to the Judge. He decided to do so, he declared, shortly after the Colorado Supreme Court reversed Judge Moore's decision, thus placing Lindsey's judgeship in jeopardy.[22]

It is not clear why so much time—almost five months— elapsed between Unter's first purported declaration to Hilton that he was willing to make a statement and the actual meeting with Lindsey in Los Angeles. Similarly, while it is easy to understand why Unter would not wish to return to Colorado jurisdiction, it is not clear why he had to have a personal meeting with Lindsey before issuing a statement, especially since Lindsey lost his court during the interval. Since Unter's eventual statement gave strong support to Lindsey's assertion that he had been framed, if it had been issued before June 30 it might conceivably have helped to bring moral pressure on the county commissioners to give the Judge an interim appointment, thus strengthening his position in the election of 1928 when he could have run as an incumbent.

Several reasons suggest themselves as possible explanations for the apparent slowness in following through on Unter's offer, at least as far as Lindsey is concerned. In the first place Unter's reputation might have made any story he told suspect. Furthermore, until June 5 at least, Judge Lindsey's petition for a writ of certiorari to the Supreme Court of the United States was pending and might be favorably acted upon. Even after that move failed, the Judge hoped that the county commissioners might give him an interim appointment, an option they chose not to exercise. Finally, and perhaps conclusively, Lindsey must have been aware that although a detailed statement from Unter would give him a great deal of moral and political support, it would almost surely be legally irrelevant as far as the Supreme Court of Colorado was concerned. After all, Chief Justice Burke, the one member of the court whose opinion intimated a possible twinge of regret over the decision in which he participated, had stated that even if Unter's testimony were completely disregarded (as he believed it should have been), the "undisputed condition of affairs" in J-6 left no alternative but to invalidate all the election returns.

Although Lindsey declared that the Unter "confession" completely vindicated him, no steps were taken to reopen the case. With the election of 1928 in the offing it seemed unwise to spend further time, energy, and money on new legal moves that would probably be subject to frustration in any event. It would be far more sensible for the Judge to concentrate on a new campaign. Before election time rolled around again, however, Lindsey found himself enmeshed in another crisis, in some respects even graver than the one through which he had just unsuccessfully passed.

10 / Defeat

THE DEFEAT THAT LED TO THE END OF BEN LINDSEY'S COLORADO career was not his ouster as judge of the Juvenile Court of Denver but his disbarment by the Supreme Court of Colorado in December 1929. Ironically, the disbarment proceedings were begun not as a result of any moves by Lindsey's many reactionary enemies but on account of a personal and public quarrel between the Judge and the courageously anti-Klan Republican Philip Van Cise in the summer of 1927.

The Lindsey–Van Cise feud had two related causes. Ten days after the Judge relinquished his court on June 30, 1927, Van Cise publicly accused him of making the effective operation of the court almost impossible by having persuaded a large number of its staff to resign in protest over his ouster. Van Cise wrote to the editor of the *Rocky Mountain News:*

> Yesterday, I had business in the juvenile court. I found it almost paralyzed. . . . Why? Because, under the direction of Judge Lindsey, an organized walk-out of practically all the employees of the court had left the court almost powerless to function until a new staff could be organized and put to work.[1]

Van Cise announced that he would request the Denver Bar Association to look into the matter with a view toward reprimanding Lindsey.

The Judge heard about Van Cise's action while he was in Los Angeles making arrangements to confer with William Unter. There followed a series of increasingly heated exchanges between the two men in the Denver press. Van Cise added a new charge that Lindsey had removed files, which Van Cise called "public records," from the Juvenile Court. The Judge replied that the files consisted of "voluminous notes and personal records" which in the hands of the wrong people might be used for blackmail and political persecution. Furthermore, Lindsey responded, the newly appointed chief probation officer of the Juvenile Court was a member of the Ku Klux Klan, and he, Lindsey, would do nothing to cooperate in any move that might lead to the placing of these papers under the jurisdiction of this man. Van Cise referred to Lindsey's actions as "czarism," and the Judge countered, "I'd see Van Cise in hell before I turned such papers . . . over to him and his snoopers." Subsequently the Denver Bar Association accepted Lindsey's theory that the papers were his personal property and announced that it would press no charges against him either on that count or in regard to the resignations of various officers of the Juvenile Court.

On September 18, 1927, Lindsey closed one phase of the controversy with a characteristically dramatic gesture. Two days earlier the Judge, with the help of Mrs. Lindsey and two former employees of the court, had torn the controversial papers into strips and repacked them in the living room of the Lindsey home on Ogden Street. Now, accompanied by friends and reporters in five automobiles, they would take them to a vacant lot at West 13th Avenue and Umatilla Street. Lindsey recalled four years later what happened next:

> At Washington Street the procession was held up—I had forgotten the gasoline and matches. Dashing back home and securing these, I resumed my place in the procession.
>
> Piled in the lot, the papers were sprinkled with gasoline. I struck a match and dropped it flaming into the mass and, as I watched the records of suffering shrivel, blacken and turn to ashes, I was happy in the knowledge that the secrets of thousands of humans whom I had helped were safe forever from the public gaze or blackmail use by agents of the Ku Klux Klan.

Lindsey's gesture caught the popular imagination. Many citizens of Denver, some of whom must have breathed a sigh of relief for personal as well as humane considerations, applauded the Judge's action as the *Denver Post* approvingly proclaimed, "Lindsey's Bonfire Wipes Out Shame Records."[2]

If ever there was a Pyrrhic victory, it was Lindsey's over Van Cise. A proud and somewhat flamboyant man, the former district attorney was so wounded in self-esteem that he determined to win the next round, albeit in a new fight. Where, he must have asked himself, might the Judge be vulnerable? As Van Cise scanned the events of recent years, his keen lawyer's mind settled upon one episode that might have possibilities—the Stokes case.[3]

W. E. D. Stokes, owner of extensive real estate holdings in New York City and of a major interest in the Chesapeake Western Railway, died in New York City in May 1926. At the time of his death he had been separated for many years from his wife, Helen Ellwood Stokes of Denver, and their two minor children, James and Muriel. Stokes had tried unsuccessfully to divorce his wife, and relations between them continued rancorous to the time of his death. When the terms of Stokes's will were disclosed, it was revealed that he had left his entire fortune to his son by a previous marriage, W. E. D. Stokes, Jr.

Mrs. Stokes decided to challenge the will in New York City. At first it appeared that the entire Stokes estate was worth less than $800,000, but Mrs. Stokes's able lawyer, the nationally renowned Samuel Untermyer, discovered that Stokes had transferred substantial assets to W. E. D. Stokes, Jr., shortly before his death. Untermyer's discovery was crucial, and the entire controversy was settled by private negotiation. Strictly speaking, the Stokes "case" never became a case at all, except that the final settlement was recorded and filed in a Manhattan probate court. Instead of receiving nothing, which the Stokes will proposed to leave them, or $200,000, which Mrs. Stokes was willing to accept during the first stage of the discussions, James and Muriel Stokes were eventually given one-third of the Stokes estate, an interest valued at almost $1.5 million.[4]

Judge Lindsey's involvement in the Stokes case was a matter of public information, duly reported in the Denver and New York City press. Back in 1920, after the Stokeses' separation, Judge Lindsey had made the children wards of the Juvenile Court at their mother's request, in order to prevent a possible attempt by Mr. Stokes to take them away from her. After Stokes's death, Mrs. Stokes, who had been a friend of the Judge since her childhood, wanted Lindsey to assume the guardianship of the children's estate, a step that would have been entirely legal but which the Judge declined. Instead he suggested to Mrs. Stokes that she file a petition, which he would help her prepare, requesting the Denver probate court of Judge George Luxford to appoint *her* the guardian of her children's estate. Technically, since James and Muriel were still "wards" of the Juvenile Court, Judge Lindsey "ordered" her to file the petition, but the technical language was in no way descriptive of the amicable relations existing between the Judge and Mrs. Stokes throughout the proceedings and afterward. On June 25, 1926, Judge Luxford appointed Mrs. Stokes guardian. Armed with the document, she departed for New York City to participate in the negotiations over the will.[5]

It was equally a matter of public record for readers of Denver and New York City newspapers that Judge Lindsey's role in the Stokes case went far beyond this minimal involvement. At the request of Helen Stokes, and with the enthusiastic approval of her attorneys, Samuel Untermyer in New York City and her brother, Victor Miller, an attorney in Denver, Judge Lindsey went to New York City in July 1926 to take part in the negotiations with the lawyers of Stokes, Jr. Although Lindsey had some early experience in probate law (not New York probate law, however), undoubtedly the Judge's major contribution to the Stokes children's cause was to lend his prestige as an internationally organized defender of children's rights. To many observers later it seemed that the Judge represented the public conscience which could not accept the view that a multimillionaire had a right to disinherit completely his minor children. Both sides in the controversy eventually acknowledged Lindsey's constructive role in the settlement that was reached on July 29. Certainly Samuel Untermyer's legal talents played the largest role in achieving the huge settlement; but the Judge's presence helped too.[6]

It occurred to Philip Van Cise, as it must have to any reasonable person, that Lindsey probably received some form of compensation for his services in New York City. In fact the Judge was compensated from two sources. In November 1926 Helen Stokes gave him $37,500 for investment toward a life pension of $200 a month. The next month Samuel Untermyer sent him a check for $10,000, as he had volunteered to do during the negotiations in New York City.[7] On the basis of the Judge's acceptance of these two "fees," as Van Cise described them, the former district attorney was now ready to petition the grievance committee of the Colorado Bar Association to bring disbarment proceedings against Ben Lindsey. In layman's terms, the charge against Lindsey was that he had practiced law while serving as a judge.

The hearing before the grievance committee encouraged Lindsey in the belief that nothing would come of the proposed disbarment proceedings. Victor Miller testified on behalf of his sister, Helen Stokes, that the idea of giving the Judge a gift was hers alone, and that there had been no prior understanding on this point. Perhaps even more impressive for Judge Lindsey's side was the testimony of Judge Luxford, who had issued the court order authorizing Mrs. Stokes to pay "certain local parties" for services rendered in connection with her children's estate. Although Lindsey's name had not appeared in that court order, Judge Luxford confirmed that Lindsey had fully and freely discussed the matter with him and that he, Luxford, was completely satisfied as to the propriety of what had been done. Since the colloquy on this matter was almost completely ignored by the Supreme Court of Colorado, it is worth repeating:

> MR. VINCENT: Did Judge Lindsey ask you whether, in your opinion, it was a thing he could receive with propriety—that is [*sic*] proper for him to receive?
>
> [JUDGE LUXFORD:] I rather suspect there was some conversation about that, and I told him I thought he was entitled to the fee.
>
> MR. LINDSEY: Judge, in our conversations a number of times, do you recall or not if I asked you if, in your judgment, it was perfectly ethical and proper if she wanted to make that to me, as a gift, it would be all right for me to accept it?
>
> THE WITNESS: Yes, that was brought up a number of times in the conversations which we had.
>
> MR. LINDSEY: And you told me you thought it would be perfectly all right, perfectly proper, [and] no one could make any objection to it, and people ought to be glad that she did it?
>
> THE WITNESS: That is exactly what was said.
>
> MR. VAN CISE: But you told Judge Lindsey you thought he was entitled to that as a fee?
>
> THE WITNESS: I don't know that I said it as a fee [*sic*]; but for the work that he had done in connection with the matter, I thought then and think now, that he was entitled to that sum of money.[8]

At the end of the hearing Lindsey was informed that he would be notified if further testimony were needed.

The members of the grievance committee eventually concluded that, whatever the extenuating circumstances, Lindsey had technically violated the law. The committee recommended to the Attorney-General of Colorado that it would be appropriate for the Supreme Court to give Lindsey a public reprimand. They did not recommend his disbarment. Nevertheless, in June 1928 the Attorney-General proceeded to file a petition with the Supreme Court recommending that it find that Ben B. Lindsey was "bereft of the qualifications to continue to hold the office of attorney at law and that 'he ought not to be suffered to pass for what he is not.' " The mills of the law grind slowly, and the Judge obtained several delays while his attorneys took various depositions and prepared their answer to the state's brief.

The most threatening—and ultimately fatal—turn of events for Lindsey's case occurred almost a year later when the Attorney-General moved for a judgment based on the pleadings.

A motion for judgment on the pleadings was uniquely menacing for several reasons. Such motions are governed by rigid rules which preclude the introduction of testimony and evidence that would be admissible in a regular trial or (as in this case) in a hearing before a referee. Only the specific allegations made in the plaintiff's complaint and the defendant's specific answers to these allegations may be considered. If the Supreme Court acted affirmatively on the motion there could be no appointment of a referee and no testimony by Victor Miller, Helen Stokes, or Samuel Untermyer, all of whom had indicated their willingness to testify on Lindsey's behalf. Finally, since disbarment was a matter within the original jurisdiction of the state Supreme Court, acceptance of the motion would mean an adverse decision without any full trial on the merits ever having been held and, for all practical purposes, without any chance of review by a higher court.[9]

On December 9, 1929, the fateful decision granting judgment on the pleadings was handed down by the Supreme Court.[10] Stripped of its verbiage, Chief Justice Greeley Whitford's opinion found that Lindsey had violated two Colorado statutes which provided:

> A judge of a court of record shall not act as attorney or counsel in any court or any cause. Civil Code, 1887.
> The Judge of the Juvenile Court . . . shall receive no other compensation for his services as such judge save the salary herein provided; nor shall he act as attorney or counselor at law. Law of 1923, Sec. 7, ch. 78, p. 211.

For the first time in thirty-five years Ben B. Lindsey was not a member of the bar of Colorado.

Chief Justice Whitford's opinion was written in such a way that it could be used (as indeed it later was) as an election campaign document against Lindsey. It frequently adopted a com monsense approach that would be persuasive to the unsophisticated layman. Whitford mercilessly attacked Lindsey's claim that his compensation was merely a "gift" or "donation." The *fees* were given, the Chief Justice asserted, because Lindsey's positions, both as judge and attorney, made him valuable to one of the parties in an essentially legal controversy. That Lindsey was chosen to participate in the negotiations in New York City because he was an old friend Whitford dismissed as an absurd and irrelevant argument. Mrs. Stokes and Untermyer did not seek his aid merely as a friend or general adviser. Mrs. Stokes could have gone to her clergyman or someone else for that purpose. Lindsey was chosen because he was an attorney with considerable knowledge of probate law and could be counted on to make a very practical contribution in a legal controversy. Nor was he merely a "mediator" or "arbitrator" as opposed to an attorney. Whitford waxed eloquent as he demolished this position. A major characteristic of an arbitrator or mediator was impartiality between the parties in a dispute. Clearly this description did not fit Lindsey, who was the friend and advocate of Mrs. Stokes's children and not of their half-brother.

Whitford's attack on the role played by Lindsey at the Denver end of the Stokes case was equally harsh. He emphasized the "fact" that Judge Lindsey "ordered" Mrs. Stokes to file a petition to become her children's guardian. That act, according to Whitford, demonstrated that Lindsey had used his judicial office to do something from which he knew he would personally profit. Whitford went on to point out that Lindsey helped Mrs. Stokes prepare (and actually drafted) several legal documents, including the very one that authorized his own compensation. One petition, dated October 11, 1926, stated that Mrs. Stokes was *"compelled* to employ the services of certain local parties," and Lindsey's own counsel admitted, Whitford declared, that the phrase "certain local parties" was intended to include Lindsey.

It is hard to escape the conclusion that Lindsey was justified when he later charged that Whitford had feelings of animosity and malice toward him. While it was true that honorable men, learned in the law, might believe that Lindsey's activities in the Stokes case violated Colorado law, the whole tone and impact of Whitford's opinion reflected a moral outrage against Lindsey that was not even remotely justified by the facts of the case. In sum the opinion was too much like a lawyer's brief at the beginning and too much like a district attorney's charge to the jury at the end. The net result was to bring Whitford's own credibility into question. Lindsey was portrayed by the chief justice as a venal, conniving, and devious man who had systematically prostituted his judicial office. Whitford extracted from formal legal petitions such words as "ordered" and "compelled" and quoted them in such a way that an inexpert reader would have been led to believe, contrary to fact, that the Judge had coerced Mrs. Stokes into obtaining his services, encouraged her to employ Untermyer in anticipation of getting a "kickback" from the New York lawyer, and bilked the estate of the Stokes children to the tune of $37,500.

That Whitford relished his condemnation of Lindsey and was anxious to go out of his way to impugn the Judge's character was an impression reinforced by his language at the conclusion of the opinion. "One of the prerequisites and indispensable qualifications . . . for the office of attorney," Whitford wrote,

is that he shall be of good moral character. . . . Unless one has the moral strength of character to stand immovable in fidelity to his duty, against the allurements of money, and to resist temptation to do those things that are prohibited by law to the judge, then he no longer possesses that indispensable moral character which the good of society and the administration of justice demand of an attorney and counselor at law. . . .

The respondent, by his acts, has set the law at defiance. He was false to his oath, taken as a judicial officer, and also false to his oath taken as an attorney and counselor at law, and has thereby proven himself unworthy of the trust reposed in him by this court, and withal, wanting in that indispensable moral character which the administration of justice demands of an attorney and counselor at law.

The judgment of this court is that the respondent be . . . removed from the office of attorney and counselor at law, and his license revoked, and his name stricken from the roll of attorneys and counselors at law, and with costs to be taxed against him.

Although there was no dissent from Chief Justice Whitford's opinion, one member of the court, Justice Charles C. Butler, did not participate because of illness. Four years later, when Lindsey petitioned the court for reinstatement and was refused, Justice Butler wrote a dissenting opinion that might, for its thoroughness, have served as a dissent which answered almost point for point the 1929 opinion of Chief Justice Whitford. Butler seemed to think so too, for he prefaced his remarks with the observation that his 1933 dissent "should be read in connection" with Whitford's earlier opinion.[11]

Butler's opinion, like Whitford's, appealed to common sense, but Butler's common sense brought him to an opposite conclusion. In the first place, Butler asserted, the major characteristic of a typical disbarment case was that somebody was injured by the guilty party's conduct. For example, an attorney had "sold out" his client or failed to disclose a significant conflict of interest. Here, by contrast, Lindsey had hurt no one and had helped bring a "substantial benefit" to everybody concerned. Even the attorney for Stokes, Jr., had taken the unusual step of writing to Lindsey at the end of the negotiations in New York:

> While you were naturally keen to protect the interests of the children to the fullest extent, your attitude was such as to enable us to handle the situation on broad lines of substance and fairness.

Furthermore, Butler pointed out, the deposition by Samuel Untermyer, which could not be considered in the original case because of the technical rules governing a motion for judgment on the pleadings, completely supported Lindsey's claim that the idea of compensation originated independently and unilaterally with Mrs. Stokes and Untermyer. Similarly, at the grievance committee hearings Victor Miller had testified to the same effect and had also described the long friendship that existed between his sister and Lindsey. Thus, said Butler, there was no semblance of the "at arm's length" atmosphere that characterized negotiations over legal fees, and the terms "gift" or "donation" were not examples of sophistry or deception but were really more descriptive of what actually transpired than "fee."

Justice Butler maintained that Lindsey's conduct in Denver was also above reproach. The only order ever issued by Lindsey's own court that had had any legal effect on the case was the original 1920 order making Mrs. Stokes the legal guardian *of the persons* of her children. That order had nothing to do with their property rights. Mrs. Stokes's appointment as guardian of her children's estate was made by Judge Luxford, who was in no way bound by Lindsey's wishes or recommendations as judge of the Juvenile Court. Finally Justice Butler quoted at length from the testimony of Judge Luxford before the grievance committee to demonstrate that Lindsey had fully and frankly discussed his part in the Stokes proceedings. He described in detail the circumstances surrounding the making out of Mrs. Stokes's check for $37,500 to Lindsey's wife, which had aroused some suspicion. The Judge was simply going out of town and wished Mrs. Lindsey to sign the check and send it to her father immediately for investment purposes. "Surely," Justice Butler concluded,

> from such a transaction no sinister motive can reasonably be inferred; no purpose to conceal the facts through consciousness of having done wrong.
>
> It seems not to have occurred to any person connected with the transaction, not even to the judge of the county court (a high-minded, able, and experienced jurist) that there was anything improper in what [Lindsey] did.

The points made by Justice Butler in 1933 were recognized by others in 1929, though they were never so eloquently or thoroughly stated. In the disbarment case, as in the ouster case the belief persisted, and not only in liberal circles, that Lindsey was being punished for what he was rather than what he did, that somehow the court would have found a way to reach a different result if the "respondent" had been someone other than Ben Lindsey. After all, as Justice Butler was to remind his colleagues, disbarment or full condonation were not the only options available to the court. It could have accepted the view of the grievance committee that Lindsey merely be "rebuked." Even after the court disbarred an attorney there was precedent for immediate, even simultaneous, reinstatement. There were even times when the court had refused to disbar attorneys who had violated the criminal law, and Lindsey's actions were at most a civil infraction.

Immediately after the disbarment decision Lindsey received hundreds of letters of sympathy. Clarence Darrow combined his well-known fatalism with a note of compassion:

> It is the way of the world—always has been and always will be. There are many young boys and girls in Denver whose lives you have made easier, and many others whom you have caused to think, and this must be your consolation.[12]

Leaders of American liberalism saw the disbarment as one more proof of reactionary power and vindictiveness. John Dewey wrote:

> Aside from any personality, the serious phase of the whole matter is the additional proof that it gives of the organized control that certain interests have at the present time. I confess I get rather pessimistic at times when it seems as if we were headed for a smash unless these interests modify their desires and methods.[13]

In the same vein Roger Baldwin commented to Lindsey:

> I am more shocked than surprised that the Supreme Court could play such a dirty political game—openly. And such bosh about ethics! The whole crew of them haven't as much as you have shown in any *one* day of your long service and championship of right, at a sacrifice your enemies can never understand. *We* do.

Your friends honor you for this—and know to what lengths the forces you have aroused will go.[14]

To some extent each writer put the episode in the context of his own special concerns. Bertrand Russell saw the disbarment as a response to Lindsey's views on sexual freedom and wrote sympathetically from London:

> I am much disgusted by the injustice and persecution to which you have been subjected. I suppose it was only to be expected, but I continue to be surprised by the fact that America persecutes Americans for the opinions which it hires foreigners at great expense to express.[15]

For Lindsey's old friend, Lincoln Steffens, the disbarment simply confirmed what both men had known two decades earlier:

> That act bears out all that you have said of the court itself and of conditions in Colorado. If you were sincere in your exposures, you cannot be astonished and hurt by the way things are running true to form and by the illustrations they give ... of the thesis you have spent your life proving. Suppose that instead of being disbarred, you had been elected a Supreme Court Justice. I would have had to suspect that you had gone crooked or that all you had ever said was the bunk. As it is, you are disbarred and all is well; all is as you said it was; and as I said it was. The Beast has got you.[16]

Shortly after the Attorney-General had filed the disbarment suit against him, Lindsey decided he would not be a candidate for re-election in 1928. There were simply too many arguments against it. The companionate marriage controversy had now earned him the hostility of the local Catholic clergy, most of whom had probably supported him in 1924 when he was fighting the Klan and had not yet made so many highly publicized statements on birth control. To be sure, the Ku Klux Klan had largely discredited itself after two years in office and had begun to retreat from the Colorado scene after major election setbacks in 1926. Nevertheless, the Klan mentality had not entirely dis appeared, and the Judge's image as a radical would still be no asset in the political climate of Colorado in 1928. After all, even if the Supreme Court had allowed the returns from precinct J-6 to be counted in the earlier election, Lindsey's victory would have been razor-thin—and by 1928 he was a far more controversial figure. Finally, the disbarment case, which would not be settled by election day, hung like a cloud over his future and would guarantee a bitter, mud-slinging campaign that would inevitably put him on the defensive. Under the circumstances Lindsey's decision not to run was almost surely the right one.

Even before disbarment became a threat Lindsey had tentative thoughts about moving to Los Angeles. Both the Judge and his wife were attracted by the glamour of the movie colony which made isolated Denver seem pale and unexciting, especially to Mrs. Lindsey. For several years the Judge had maintained a peripheral relationship to the movie industry. On one occasion, during a court recess in 1920, he had briefly traveled to Hollywood and played a bit part as a juvenile court judge in a film called *The Soul of Youth*. At other times during the twenties he served sporadically as a public relations figure for the industry, writing articles or granting interviews in which he opposed various proposals in Congress for censorship of motion pictures. After his ouster from the Denver court he briefly served in an advisory capacity to Cecil B. DeMille's studio, helping with a script that dealt with reform schools. Perhaps, the Judge speculated, his unique background in law and human relations might some day find an exciting and profitable outlet in the film industry.[17]

The Hollywood connection was destined always to remain peripheral, but the idea of a move to Los Angeles was appealing enough, after his removal from the Juvenile Court, to cause Lindsey to seek membership in the California bar as early as September 1927. For an attorney already admitted to practice in another state, the California procedure was then relatively simple, and there was no harm in having another iron in the fire. Lindsey had no definite plans for moving to California at this time, nor was such a move required by California law. While Lindsey's application was still pending, Van Cise filed the charges against him which eventually led to the Colorado disbarment. Lindsey gave full notice to the California Bar Association of these proceedings, which had not yet been acted upon by the Attorney-General of Colorado. On May 4, 1928, a month before the disbarment proceedings formally began in Colorado, Ben Lindsey was admitted to the California bar. The timing of his admission, though unplanned, was ultimately to be crucial for his career—and for once, at least, in his favor.[18]

The years 1928 through 1930 were by no means all bad for Lindsey in spite of the disbarment episode and the decision not to run for re-election. The Judge was still much in demand as a lecturer, and his agency managed to arrange debates on companionate marriage in every part of the country. Often the audience was asked to decide who won the debate, and Lindsey usually came out on top, especially when he spoke to college students. The Judge kept himself in the national limelight when he made a number of personal appearances at opening-night showings of the film *The Companionate Marriage* in Cleveland, Toledo, and Denver. Abroad, book publishers were seeking translation and distribution rights for the Judge's book, which enjoyed a wide vogue in England, Japan, the Soviet Union, and the Scandinavian countries. Thomas Mann gave the Dutch edition a warm endorsement, and the German edition, *Die Kameradschaftsehe,* became a best-seller in the Weimar Republic. In February 1929 American journalist Edgar Ansell Mowrer wrote that Lindsey's book "was found a few months ago on nearly every parlor table in Berlin." In Prussia the Society for the Protection of Mothers and Sex Reform overwhelmingly endorsed companionate marriage. Some foreign critics thought Lindsey's book demonstrated that promiscuity was rife in the United States, a reading not so different from that of certain American critics. The chief lesson of the book, according to a lady journalist in India, was that the American system of coeducation would be unsuitable for Indian youths. Meanwhile, interest in the Judge's proposals continued unabated in the United States, even into the early 1930's. Many radio broadcasts dealt with Lindsey's theme, and sometimes featured the Judge. Other popular treatments of the sexual revolution, such as V. F. Calverton's *The Bankruptcy of Marriage* (1928) and Floyd Dell's *Love in the Machine Age* (1931), drew heavily on Lindsey and acknowledged their debt to him. The Judge was still news, and the media were not ignoring him.[19]

In one sense the beginning of the end of the companionate marriage issue occurred in the Cathedral of St. John the Divine in New York City on December 7, 1930. On that Sunday morning Bishop William T. Manning preached a sermon against companionate marriage and specifically against Ben B. Lindsey. The Judge, who had managed to enter the church unnoticed, openly challenged the Bishop's presentation of facts and was forcibly removed from the cathedral. The incident was hardly spontaneous, for the Lindsey-Manning controversy had a long history.[20]

As early as 1927 Lindsey, learning of Bishop Manning's criticisms of his proposals "for a new kind of marriage," had challenged the Bishop to a public debate on the subject. At that time Manning replied:

> In reply to your telegram I beg to say that for Christians the moral standards given to the world by Christ are not open to debate in spite of your assertions to the contrary. The temporary so-called companionate marriage advocated by yourself and others is not marriage but only another name for free love. Your teachings would not lead forward but backward to those conditions which destroyed the old pagan world. In your writings you reject and hold up to contempt the Christian ideal of morality and purity. Such teaching is a sin against God, an insult to the womanhood and manhood of our land, and should be condemned by all good citizens.[21]

The Bishop's reply closed the subject until 1930 when a liberal group of Episcopal ministers invited Lindsey to give a luncheon address on the topic of marriage and divorce to the New York Churchmen's Association.

Bishop Manning was appalled at the idea of extending an official invitation to this "most un-Christian man," and personally tried to have the invitation withdrawn. The Bishop always insisted afterward that he had merely suggested the withdrawal, but the Reverend Eliot White, chairman of the committee that formally invited Lindsey, maintained with equal fervor that the Bishop had ordered him to cancel it. By the first week of December 1930 the issue had become a public controversy. The Bishop added to the excitement at the end of the week when he announced that his Sunday sermon would deal with "certain matters of concern" in the diocese.

Lindsey, who was in the East for a number of lecture engagements, was staying at his usual Manhattan retreat, the Algonquin Hotel. On the Saturday evening before the Bishop's sermon the Judge talked with several good friends about Manning's apparent belief in suppressing freedom of speech. Among those present were Dr. Harry Benjamin, internationally recognized endocrinologist, and Arthur Garfield Hays, outstanding attorney in civil liberties cases who had served with Clarence Darrow four years earlier as defense counsel in the famous Scopes "monkey trial" in Tennessee. As the evening wore on Lindsey's resentment at Manning grew. Dr. Benjamin later recalled Lindsey's words at the Algonquin: "I am going there tomorrow and if the Bishop criticizes only my book, I won't say a word; but if he attacks me personally, I shall answer right back."[22]

As it turned out, Manning did attack the Judge personally. After describing *The Companionate Marriage* as "one of the most filthy, insidious, and cleverly written pieces of propaganda ever published in behalf of lewdness, promiscuity, adultery, and unrestrained sexual gratification," the Bishop launched into a stinging attack on Lindsey himself. He reminded his listeners of Lindsey's disbarment and quoted verbatim from Chief Justice Whitford's opinion the most damaging passage regarding the Judge's moral character. If Lindsey had any doubts about challenging the Bishop in his own church, these remarks resolved them. At the end of Manning's sermon the Judge rose, stood on a table, and shouted: "I have been misrepresented. If this is a house of justice, I demand five minutes of your time. Bishop Manning, you have lied about me. . . ."

Eyewitness accounts of what happened next embraced the usual discrepancies, but there was general agreement on some points. Before Lindsey could finish his remarks a combination of ushers and city detectives forcibly removed him through a side door to Amsterdam Avenue, where he was whisked away in a detective's car to the local police station. Several members of the congregation were enraged by Lindsey's action; there had been shouts of "Put him out!" and "Throw him out!" According to the *New York Times,* at least one member of the congregation shouted, "You ought to be lynched!" A few moments after Lindsey's exit the congregation broke into an unaccustomed outburst of applause when the Bishop announced, "We will sing 'Fight the Good Fight.' "

The episode created quite a stir for a few weeks. Lindsey, after agreeing to appear in a Manhattan magistrate's court in ten days, was released and promptly announced that he was considering a lawsuit for slander against the Bishop. A few liberal clerics announced their support of the Judge. Most clergymen who were quoted in the press sided with the Bishop. About five hundred students at Dartmouth signed a statement supporting Lindsey. The *Nation* caustically referred to the Bishop's "bad temper, bad taste, and bad judgment," but feared that Lindsey's cause was hurt by his "ill-timed response." The *New Republic* was wholly sympathetic to the Judge and sardonically expressed its satisfaction that Manning, "who seldom knows what is going on in the modern world," had for once in his life preached on "a live public topic." In an even lighter vein one newspaper reported that some Episcopal clergymen in New York were circulating the following limerick:

> A Bishop who's quite fond of banning,
> Whatever he haps to be scanning,
> Made someone so wroth, that he shouted with froth,
> "You can't serve both God and Manning!"[23]

The end of the Lindsey-Manning episode was somewhat anti-climactic. On December 17 Lindsey, accompanied by Arthur Garfield Hays, appeared before Magistrate August Dreyer at the courthouse on Mulberry Street in lower Manhattan. The magistrate conveniently discovered a technical flaw in the complaint against Lindsey. The Judge should have been accused of "making unnecessary noise in a church." Dreyer asked if there were anyone in the crowded courtroom who had been in the cathedral on December 7 and was willing to sign an amended complaint. There were no takers. Bishop Manning had previously announced that he would not sign a complaint. The magistrate made a brief speech criticizing Lindsey for his conduct and expressing the hope that no one would falsely conclude that church services could be interrupted with impunity in the future. Lindsey then left the courtroom and was surrounded by well-wishers. He announced that he had no plans to sue the Bishop for slander.[24]

As 1931 opened, the gloom that lay heavy over the nation was beginning to affect Ben Lindsey, and for some of the same reasons. Like many other Americans the Judge had made some bad investments and had only limited savings to fall back on. Royalties from *The Companionate Marriage* were dwindling. No regular employment had yet appeared on the horizon. Although Lindsey was now sixty-two, he was vigorous and active and had not anticipated an early retirement. Besides himself, there was his wife to support as well as an eight-year-old daughter. A steady income would be welcome. Once again California attracted the Judge. True, there were no specific prospects in the Golden State either, but at least he was still recognized there as a member of his profession. In mid-year he moved to Los Angeles where he opened a small law office. Mrs. Lindsey remained in Denver for a brief time to keep their house occupied until the future became more certain. Both the Judge and his wife feared that private practice in Los Angeles was a dead end. Lindsey's old friends Roger Baldwin, Clarence Darrow, and Upton Sinclair sent words of encouragement. Darrow advised the Judge to stay with private practice "and let the world go to hell in its own way." Baldwin and Sinclair, somewhat more realistically, recognized that Lindsey had not been a practicing lawyer for almost a third of a century and that his long-range answer, if it ever came, would still be a public career.[25]

The one event of 1931 on which the Judge placed his hopes was the publication of his autobiography, which he called *The Dangerous Life*. Two years earlier Lindsey had met Reuben Borough, a sympathetic and liberal journalist associated with the *Los Angeles Record*. Borough wrote a favorable series of articles on the Judge for the *Record*, and the two men eventually formed the idea of enlarging them into an autobiography. In the spring of 1930 Borough drove from Los Angeles to Denver and spent several weeks taking copious notes on Lindsey's oral reminiscences. Frequently they worked in Cheesman Park. Borough later liked to recall how a gusty wind once blew his notes in many directions and how he and Lindsey frantically scampered about the park recovering them. During their talks the Judge would pace back and forth waving his arms and denouncing his enemies. Sometimes he became quiet and morose, other times he would ramble, trying his collaborator's patience. But Borough never lost his strong affection for "the little Judge" and was relieved to observe, as the weeks went by, that Lindsey's deep involvement in the book "seemed to pick him up."[26]

The book was not the answer. Its sales were disappointingly small. The publisher reported to Lindsey after three years that he had suffered a final deficit of more than $400 on the enterprise. The public no longer seemed interested in juvenile courts, companionate marriage, and the nefarious activities of the Ku Klux Klan back in the twenties. Nor had *The Dangerous Life* provided the shot in the arm that Lindsey hoped it would give to his speaking itinerary. Actually the book, which generally received good reviews, was probably not to blame on this score. In the 1930's radio stations and popular serials were mushrooming, and the "talkies" were entering their golden era. The chautauqua format represented a vanishing America. By the end of 1932 a note of gloom had become pervasive in Lindsey's letters to his friends. Modern technology, he wrote to one of them, had become "the new Frankenstein."[27]

For some Americans, at least, a ray of hope appeared a few months after Lindsey wrote those words. On March 4, 1933, Franklin D. Roosevelt became President of the United States. For Ben Lindsey the meaning of the New Deal would become very personal and direct. It paved the way for his return to public life.

11 / Vindication, and New Crusades

T HE NEW DEAL BROUGHT TO WASHINGTON A NUMBER OF Lindsey's old friends and associates. Among them were former correspondents from Progressive days such as Gifford Pinchot and Frederic C. Howe. Another was Donald Richberg, who had written approvingly of *The Beast* more than two decades earlier and who now held the exalted position of general counsel of the newly formed National Recovery Administration. In a special category was George Creel, a close friend of more than twenty years' standing who had loyally stood by the Judge in his trials and tribulations since 1927. By 1933 Creel was a key figure in the California Democratic party, having attached himself to that old Wilsonian William Gibbs McAdoo, son-in-law of the late President Wilson and now United States Senator from California. Creel was soon commuting regularly between California and Washington and was being groomed by the McAdoo "machine" (alas for Creel, it was all too slight an organization) to become governor of California in 1934. In the spring of 1933 Creel became West Coast Administrator of the NRA, hoping the position would be a useful stepping-stone to the governorship. The presence of so many friends and former associates in the New Deal encouraged Lindsey to seek a federal post for himself.

Lindsey also had a cordial though peripheral relationship with Franklin D. Roosevelt. In 1913 the Judge had congratulated the young New Yorker upon his appointment by President Wilson as Assistant Secretary of the Navy and had received a warm reply. Lindsey actively supported the unsuccessful Cox-Roosevelt ticket against Harding and Coolidge in 1920. In 1932 he was an early supporter of Roosevelt's nomination when it was still much in doubt on account of Democratic factionalism. Under the circumstances the Judge was not diffident in 1933 about pressing his case personally with the President.[1]

The results were at first rather disappointing. Lindsey expressed his interest in a juvenile court vacancy in the District of Columbia, but the appointment ultimately went to a candidate with stronger claims to patronage. For a while there were rumors that the Judge might become Territorial Governor of Hawaii, but his lack of residence in the Islands was a serious barrier to this somewhat dubious move. In October 1933 Lindsey urged the President to appoint him as deputy administrator of the Motion Picture Code under the NRA. Roosevelt sent a cordial personal reply and promised to take up the matter with national administrator Hugh S. Johnson. Meanwhile, George Creel wrote supporting letters to the President and to Donald Richberg, suggesting that Lindsey would have "the very fullest measure" of support in California except for "a certain reactionary element among the motion picture producers." The appointment finally went to a candidate who had more established ties with the movie industry.[2]

As Lindsey continued his efforts to obtain a federal appointment, he also was looking elsewhere. Since he had not permanently ruled out the possibility of returning to Denver, he decided to appeal to the Supreme Court of Colorado in the spring of 1933 for reinstatement as a member of the Colorado bar. Among those supporting Lindsey's petition were Senator Edward P. Costigan and two former United States Senators from Colorado, two former presidents of the Colorado Bar Association, the newly elected Attorney-General of Colorado, and two former presidents of the Denver Bar Association. Nevertheless, Lindsey lost another round in his six years' confrontation with the Supreme Court. On this occasion, however, there were some aspects of moral victory in the defeat.[3]

The Supreme Court based its refusal of reinstatement solely on the ground that Lindsey was unwilling to apologize for certain caustic remarks he had made in *The Dangerous Life* about some members of the court, particularly Chief Justice Whitford, who had been defeated for re-election in 1930 and was no longer on the court. Four of the justices who participated in the original disbarment decision were still present. Whitford's successor as chief justice was John T. Adams, one of the four holdovers. To him fell the task of assigning the writing of the court's opinion. He gave it to Francis E. Bouck, a newly elected member of the bench. Thus Bouck spoke for himself and four colleagues who had sat on the court continuously since Lindsey's disbarment. Bouck's opinion was relatively brief. After a few Portia-like remarks about the appropriateness of mercy, he asserted that Lindsey had proved himself unworthy of it by refusing to apologize for having accused the court of participating in a "political disbarment." "The mercy invoked," Justice Bouck declared,

> . . . is for those who freely confess and sincerely repudiate the wrong they have done. By his failure to meet that reasonable test, the petitioner has disentitled himself to readmission. . . .

On this occasion the opinion of the Supreme Court was not unanimous. Justice Butler's lengthy dissenting opinion, dealing with the substantive issues in the original disbarment case and questioning its fairness, has already been mentioned. An added dissent was written by a new member of the court, Justice Benjamin Hilliard. Hilliard expressed his agreement with Butler and went further. He took the court to task for its main premise in the present case, and accused his colleagues of pettiness. It was only human, after all, Hilliard thought, for a person who had suffered as much as Lindsey to strike back verbally at those who had tried to destroy him professionally. "We have graver duties than defending ourselves," Hilliard admonished his fellow justices. Denver's *Rocky Mountain News* concurred with the dissenting justice in a lead editorial entitled, "Not Justice, But Wounded Vanity."[4]

Faced with another failure in Colorado and with uncertainty on the Washington front, Lindsey worked simultaneously on another plan of action as he grew increasingly doubtful that paying clients would ever appear in Los Angeles. For many years the Judge had dreamed of replacing the criminal courts and even the prisons with a new system, patterned to some extent on juvenile court procedures, which he called a House of Human Welfare. The idea was to replace "the punishment machine of the State," as Lindsey described the institutions that enforced the criminal law, with an organization staffed by physicians, psychiatrists, sociologists, and social workers. The concept was a logical corollary of the juvenile court movement, Lindsey explained, because many adult criminals were merely "children grown large." As he had done in the past, the Judge denied that he was being sentimental about criminals. He conceded that a hard core of the criminal population would have to be confined indefinitely, "like any other lunatics." The fault with the existing system, he asserted, was that it confined many who could be "healed."[5]

In 1933 Lindsey tried to establish a private foundation called the Institute of Human Relations to carry these ideas forward in somewhat modified form. Although the institute would concern itself with the problem of adult crime, its emphasis would be on domestic relations problems, particularly as they affected the welfare of children. Since the institute would deal with a broad range of human problems, including juvenile delinquency, divorce, marriage counseling, and "sex education," one of Lindsey's friends suggested, not entirely tongue-in-cheek, that "institute" might be a more judicious term than "house" to describe the organization over which the Judge proposed to preside.

Although Lindsey spent considerable time and energy in

his search for private subscriptions to the proposed institute, the movement never really got off the ground. Aside from the fact that 1933 was not a very propitious year for fund-raising, the proposal suffered from an inherent defect. The brochures and form letters that were sent to potential donors were excellent in their criticisms of some aspects of the legal system, but extremely vague and general when they attempted to describe the future operations of the institute. It was never clear to what extent the organization would serve as a clearing house for existing public and private agencies or act independently. In one respect, however, the literature was realistic. It recognized that the goals it sought would eventually have to be implemented by legislation. How this was to be achieved was left unanswered. At this point Lindsey began to wonder whether such an institute was the best way to establish a "House of Human Welfare." The lack of private subscriptions suggested that it was not.[6]

Yet Lindsey was convinced that there must be *some* way. After all, he was fond of pointing out, some of the goals of such an institution as he proposed had once been achieved in Denver. For years he had been the chief lobbyist in Colorado for extending the juvenile court system. It was he who had drafted the laws that gave the Juvenile Court a partial jurisdiction over adults. In the domestic relations work of the court he had tried to apply the same principles he was now advocating in California. Although some of his bills had been modified or rejected in the Colorado legislature, and one had been emasculated by the state Supreme Court, he had nevertheless enjoyed an impressive degree of success. In those days, of course, he possessed an asset he no longer had: the prestige of being a presiding judge. Perhaps he needed that status as a first step for success in California.

For liberal Democrats in California, 1934 opened as a promising year. Two years earlier the traditionally Republican state had joined the national Democratic landslide, voting for Roosevelt as President and McAdoo as Senator, and sending a majority of Democrats to Congress. In 1934 there seemed little doubt that many Democrats would benefit from the ineptness of the Republican administration in Sacramento and even more from the charisma that emanated from 1600 Pennsylvania Avenue. Technically, judges ran on a nonpartisan basis in California elections, but it would be easy to remind the electorate of Lindsey's Democratic connections. The office for which he would become a candidate, if he decided to run, was one of the Superior Court judgeships of Los Angeles County. William N. Neblett, a law partner of Senator McAdoo, urged Lindsey to announce his candidacy, arguing that 1934 was an opportune time for Democrats to return to office. According to Neblett, Lindsey made his final decision over a luncheon the two of them had at the Biltmore Hotel early in the spring.[7]

Meanwhile the efforts of Lindsey's friends in Washington had finally paid off, though modestly. In February 1934 the Judge was appointed Labor Compliance Officer for the NRA in southern California. He served for only three and a half months. In May he simultaneously announced his candidacy for the Superior Court judgeship and his resignation from the NRA. The decision made sense. Lindsey had neither the temperament nor the background to handle the intricacies of labor law, and, as it turned out, the job had no future. Almost a year to the day after Lindsey's resignation, the Supreme Court of the United States declared the NRA unconstitutional.[8]

Now it was necessary to organize a campaign. The Judge was fortunate in winning the support of Albert Mellinkoff, a successful Los Angeles businessman prominent in civic affairs and a well-known friend of liberal causes. Lindsey's relationship with the Mellinkoff family had begun a year earlier when the Judge was introduced to Mrs. Mellinkoff by her son's high school English teacher. Mrs. Mellinkoff, whose interest in civic affairs was as intense as her husband's, soon became a close friend and confidante of the Lindseys and was enthusiastic about the Judge's decision to run. She knew that Lindsey hoped to preside over the juvenile court department of the Superior Court, and she liked the idea of having the best-known juvenile court judge in the country serving in that capacity in Los Angeles. She also felt that Lindsey's election would serve, in some measure, to restore and vindicate him after the shabby treatment she felt he had received in Denver. Mrs. Mellinkoff had no difficulty in transferring her enthusiasm to her husband. By 1934 Albert Mellinkoff generally confined his business activities to investments and had the time and the means to devote much of his energy to politics. In May he became Lindsey's uncompensated campaign manager. An official campaign headquarters was opened in downtown Los Angeles. The Mellinkoff home in Beverly Hills became the unofficial headquarters where Lindsey and his friends mapped out the grand strategy of the campaign.[9]

The first goal in the Lindsey campaign was to win in the forthcoming primaries. Twelve candidates in addition to Lindsey were competing for the nomination. Eight of them were municipal judges. None, of course, was as widely known as Lindsey, who at sixty-four was still vigorous. Although a whispering campaign about the Judge's "radical" ideas began as early as June, it was not enough to counteract the effective work of the Mellinkoff organization. The Beverly Hills Democratic Club unanimously endorsed Lindsey. Albert Mellinkoff sent out form letters stressing the Judge's early support of such legislation as aid to dependent children and old-age pensions. In one form letter, in the left-hand column traditionally reserved for the names of individual sponsors, Mellinkoff proclaimed Lindsey's "sponsors" to be "THOUSANDS of children whom his juvenile court system has saved from a life of crime, THOUSANDS of Americans who honor him for his courageous battles against injustice, THOUSANDS of women who have the right of suffrage," and so on for "thousands" of working people, babies, and mothers who enjoyed the benefits of laws for which Lindsey had fought in Colorado and elsewhere. The Mellinkoffs successfully solicited contributions and support from friends in the movie industry. Charlie Chaplin gave a large contribution and commented to Albert Mellinkoff, "Call me again if you need to." Finally, the Judge himself was a most effective campaigner. In a radio broadcast on the eve of the primary election in August he reminded his listeners of a warm commendation he had once received from Franklin D. Roosevelt. Lindsey's script read:

> I may be defeated in tomorrow's primary, but I carry to my grave the accolade that a great president of a great nation declared that he would be ashamed if he did not raise his voice in defense of me—(soften voice)—and I say this in the humility of my soul and only because I have a great desire to serve, perhaps he has been too kind, and I accept his praise and his endorsement [sic], not as a tribute to myself but to the causes to which I have dedicated my life.[10]

When the returns were counted Lindsey easily led the list of candidates with 203,207 votes. The runner-up, Municipal Judge Ida May Adams, received 58,210. The remaining eleven candidates had a combined total of 246,331. A final contest between Adams and Lindsey was next.

In many ways the Lindsey-Adams campaign resembled the ugly contest that was being simultaneously waged for the governorship. In the same primary election that Lindsey won, his old friend Upton Sinclair amazed political professionals by capturing the nomination for governor on the Democratic ticket. The former Socialist had formed an organization called EPIC, the letters standing for his campaign slogan, "End Poverty In California." Its activities were so successful that the "erstwhile Socialist," as the hostile press invariably called Sinclair, won more votes in the Democratic primary than all of his opponents combined, including runner-up George Creel. Sinclair's Republican opponent, Governor Frank F. Merriam, as well as some disgruntled Democrats, were now ready to cull Sinclair's record over a period of thirty years in order to prove that his election would inflict every imaginable horror on California from the "nationalization of women and children" to the loss of the motion picture industry (in that ascending order, presumably). Realizing that Lindsey might be hurt if he became closely identified with the EPIC campaign, Sinclair endorsed the Judge as a liberal Democrat but did not insist on Lindsey's endorsement in return. "The election means more to Ben than it does to me," Sinclair confided to Albert Mellinkoff. In some respects, of course, Lindsey suffered from the same disabilities as Sinclair. He too had a "record," though the larger stakes in the gubernatorial campaign diverted attention somewhat from the Lindsey-Adams contest. Nevertheless, a miniature replica of the smear campaign against Sinclair was soon under way against the Judge.[11]

By October 1934 thousands of circulars were being distributed with the heading, "Judge Ben B. Lindsey, Juvenile Court Authority and Advocate of Companionate Marriage." Billy Sunday's phrase, "barnyard marriage," was rediscovered and quoted approvingly. A local minister interpreted Lindsey's comments in *The Companionate Marriage* regarding the relationship between changing technology and social mores as proving that the Judge advocated adultery and aviation with equal fervor. Many of the circulars dealt with the Stokes case and carried lengthy quotations from former Chief Justice Whitford's opinion. Whitford may even have encouraged the move, since he provided Lindsey's opponent with an updated endorsement of his 1929 views on Lindsey's character. Perhaps the lowest point in the campaign was reached when a fictitious organization called "The Los Angeles County Judiciary Committee" made a crude appeal to racial and sexual fears by circulating discredited charges going back to 1909 that Lindsey had been lenient toward rapists when he was a judge in Denver. In several instances the beneficiaries of his putative leniency were described as "Negroes" or "Colored." In capital letters the language of a 1912 campaign document was repeated verbatim:

THE RAVISHING OF YOUNG GIRLS HAS
INDEED BECOME A JOKE IN DENVER.

The pamphlet concluded with an emotional appeal to save "the little girls of Los Angeles County" from the consequences of an election victory by "the former Judge of the Denver Juvenile Court."[12]

Yet the Adams campaign was no match for Lindsey's. The great strength of the Mellinkoff organization was its dedication. Volunteers from many walks of life appeared and offered their services. A number of shoeless volunteers (shoeless from economic rather than ideological considerations) in their late teens and early twenties, who remembered or had heard of the Judge's reputation, distributed pro-Lindsey pamphlets. Two men in early middle age whom the Judge had placed on probation many years ago designed posters and performed other services in the campaign. Two brothers, Jacob and Harry Milstein, who had achieved success in the movie industry put together a documentary film about Lindsey. Although they had never been delinquents, the Milsteins had been active in boys' clubs during their Denver youth and remembered the Judge fondly. Through Mellinkoff's efforts the film was shown at no cost in various Los Angeles movie houses. In the entire Lindsey campaign only one person—a stenographer—worked for pay.

This dedication was equaled only by the organization's mastery of strategy. Again, as in the primary, the accent was on the positive, with emphasis on the Judge's specific contributions to economic and social reforms. It was sensibly decided to play down the companionate marriage issue as much as possible. If hecklers persisted in mentioning the subject, the first "stopper" was, "Have you read the book?" In case the answer was "yes," the next comment was, "You've misinterpreted it." Recent favorable press comments about Lindsey from Colorado, particularly from the *Rocky Mountain News,* were good antidotes to the charge that the Judge had no friends "in his own state." Perhaps the most difficult issue to handle was Lindsey's disbar-

ment. Because the legal aspects of the case were complex, explanations could easily become confusing and sound defensive.
A week before the election Albert Mellinkoff came up with the
best possible solution. Accompanied by Lindsey, he visited Mrs.
Stokes, whose presence in Los Angeles was completely fortui-
tous, and obtained an endorsement for the Judge. Helen Stokes
expressed her "everlasting gratitude" to Lindsey and deplored
the fact that he had been disbarred for an act of kindness on
behalf of her children. The endorsement concluded:

> I appeal to you in behalf of the motherhood and childhood of
> America, in behalf of justice and humanity, to rebuke this unjusti-
> fied onslaught upon Judge Lindsey by electing him to Office 19,
> Superior Court, on November 6th by an overwhelming majority.

Mrs. Stokes got her wish. On November 6, 1934, Ben Lindsey
received the largest vote for a county judicial office ever won by
a candidate in the history of California. After seven years the
words "Judge Lindsey" were no longer merely honorific.[13]

Even before he assumed his new position as judge of the
Superior Court, Lindsey became involved in a controversy with
one of his future colleagues. To a large extent the conflict soured
all of his future relations with a majority of the judges on the
Superior Court bench. The issue involved was the right to preside over the Juvenile Department of the Superior Court, as the
Los Angeles Juvenile Court was called. The incumbent was
Judge Samuel Blake. Under Superior Court procedure the entire
panel of fifty judges made the annual assignments of their membership to the various departments. Before Lindsey had announced his candidacy, Judge Blake had apparently given him
a verbal assurance that it was his intention, if Lindsey entered
the 1934 campaign and won, to give up the Juvenile Court and
request another department in the Superior Court system. Both
men had something to gain under such an arrangement. Blake,
who had the advantage of being the incumbent in the Juvenile
Court department, was virtually assured of re-election against

any candidate other than Lindsey. For Lindsey there was a different advantage. There was a vacancy in Department 19 (a general department of the Superior Court) which would give him the advantage of not having to run against a presiding Superior Court judge. During the campaign Lindsey referred to Judge Blake's earlier promise and requested him, just before the election, to repeat it publicly. Blake neither confirmed nor denied that there had been a commitment, but announced that he would acquiesce in whatever decisions regarding assignments were made by the other judges. Lindsey bitterly resented Blake's action and urged his colleagues to appoint him to the Juvenile Court. In January 1935 the judges voted to continue Samuel Blake in his present office.[14]

The controversy continued for several years but always with the same result. Lindsey continued to circularize his colleagues, recalled that he had publicly campaigned on the assumption that he would be selected for the Juvenile Court, and reminded them that he was the best-known juvenile court judge in the country. Even after Blake ceased to preside over the Juvenile Court of Los Angeles, a majority of the judges still would not vote for Lindsey, asserting that he was too inclined to be a publicity seeker. The repeated rebuff from all but a few of his colleagues continued to embitter Lindsey's years on the Los Angeles bench even after he was re-elected by an even larger majority of the voters in 1940 to another full term on the Superior Court.[15]

Shortly after he began his new career in California the Judge was finally restored to the Colorado bar. Following Lindsey's election a few old Denver friends suggested to Charles Butler, author of one of the two dissenting opinions in the 1933 reinstatement defeat and now chief justice of the Colorado Supreme Court, that Lindsey's reinstatement would be an appropriate Christmas present at the end of his first year on the Los Angeles bench. Instead of waiting until Christmas the Supreme Court acted on Lindsey's sixty-sixth birthday, November 25, 1935.

There is a characteristic Lindsey legend that the court acted at that time not because it was Lindsey's birthday but because rumors were already circulating about the planned reinstatement and it was feared that the Judge would make some comments about the Supreme Court before Christmas that would make his reinstatement impossible. By November 1935 only two members of the court remained who had participated in all the votes against Lindsey since the original ouster decision in 1927. One was Justice John Campbell, who had been on the court since the 1890's. The other was Justice Burke. In the final vote to reinstate Lindsey in 1935, there were no abstainers. Only Justice Campbell recorded his dissent. He did not write an opinion.[16]

In his first four and a half years on the Superior Court of Los Angeles, Lindsey performed the usual services of a neophyte judge on a county court of general jurisdiction. He served in both the civil and criminal departments of the court and also presided over the Psychopathic Department, which had the duty of committing the mentally ill to state institutions. At one point the Judge was doing the "psychopathic work" in the morning and hearing domestic relations cases in the afternoon. In the latter work he professed to be horrified at the callous and perfunctory attitude of some members of the legal profession toward divorce, particularly when small children were involved. As he put it to a friend, "I serve in the insane court in the morning and the insaner court in the afternoon."[17]

The old reformist spirit in the Judge never died—nor even slept. Among the widely varied issues that aroused his zeal in his adopted state were the lack of effective sanctions against usurious rates of interest, the harsh foreclosure rules on car buyers, the absence of a required pre-marital test for syphilis, the inadequate financing of rehabilitative measures for alcoholics and sexual "degenerates," and the lack of protection for the earnings of child actors from parental bad judgment and costly lawsuits, a topic that was currently in the news because of lengthy legal controversies involving a former child star, Jackie Coogan, and a contemporary one, Freddie Bartholomew. Soon the Judge was making statements to the press, writing letters to the district attorney, and beginning to enlist support among California lawmakers for a number of bills to remedy some of the defects. Finally, on various occasions he took the train north to Sacramento and appeared before committees of the legislature to testify on the need for different parts of his program. At one time he asserted that if the legislature did not see the light soon on the matter of child actors, it might be necessary for "the kids" to come to Sacramento and lobby in person. It was the turn-of-the-century Denver scene all over again.[18]

Various Lindsey bills were introduced at the four regular biennial sessions of the California legislature between 1937 and 1943. Most of them were introduced by the Judge's former colleague Robert W. Kenny, who had recently left the Superior Court bench to become state senator from Los Angeles and who was later to become Attorney-General when Earl Warren vacated that post for the governorship in 1943. After 1938 the Judge was able to count on at least the passive support of Culbert L. Olson, the first Democrat in the twentieth century to serve a term as governor of California. On the whole, however, Lindsey's proposed legislative program did not fare very well in Sacramento. Its one outstanding success, the creation of the Children's Court of Conciliation, came in 1939. Since the law establishing the court was personally drafted by the Judge with the aid of the State Legislative Counsel, was introduced at his request by Senator Kenny, and was adopted substantially as written, it was a uniquely personal triumph.[19]

Lindsey called his legislative program "The Children's Bills," since their common purpose was to give new kinds of legal protection to children. The protection provided in the Children's Court of Conciliation was the effort to save troubled marriages when children were involved. On the face of it, it seemed ironic that the man who was so often associated in the public mind with the notion of easy divorce should have written what was essentially an anti-divorce law. Yet careful readers of *The Companionate Marriage* should not have been surprised. In that "radical" book the Judge had criticized existing divorce legislation for not sufficiently taking into account the welfare of the children. As far as *family* marriage was concerned, Lindsey maintained, a couple should be morally *and legally* required to demonstrate that they had considered their children's interests before a divorce was granted. The Judge developed this theme in several articles after 1927 and again in *The Dangerous Life.* His proposal for an Institute of Human Relations had made a reduction in the divorce rate through marriage counseling (as well as pre-marital education) a major goal of a more rational social order. The Children's Court of Conciliation was a modest first step in this direction.[20]

The new law, signed by Governor Culbert Olson on July 13, 1939, permitted the creation of a Conciliation Court as a new department of the Superior Court. Basically the Conciliation Court would act in either of two contingencies. On the request of either husband or wife, or both of them, it would try to prevent a threatened dissolution of a marriage. In cases in which a divorce action had already been filed, the court would try to bring about a reconciliation of the couple. In both situations, if at least one minor child were involved, the use of the court was mandatory. Its primary object was to prevent the dissolution of a family. If the aim proved impossible, a secondary goal was to assist the couple in making an amicable settlement. In Lindsey's opinion the underlying philosophy of the law was as important as the procedures it established. The principle behind the statute was the recognition that children had a right to a home and that "the People," as the State of California was described on legal forms, had a discrete interest in the case because it concerned the preservation of the family. In an effort to stress this underlying philosophy Lindsey introduced into the law the same language that he had used in Colorado juvenile court legislation. When the parents of Johnny and Susie Smith in Los Angeles contemplated a divorce, a legal document would no longer carry the traditional adversary form of *Smith v. Smith* but would read:

In the Superior Court of the State of California
in and for the County of   Los Angeles

The People
For the best interest and protection of
    Johnny Smith,   Susie Smith
Upon the petition of
Mary Smith   (petitioner)
    and concerning
John Smith   , and
Mary Smith   , Respondents.

Although the *jurisdiction* of the Court was mandatory, neither Lindsey nor the legislature was willing to force a reconciliation on unwilling parties. In this respect the law was not unique. Neither Michigan nor Wisconsin, the two states that already had limited experience with conciliation courts, had introduced the principle of compulsion into the process, nor has any state which has adopted such procedures since 1939. Under the Lindsey plan the Conciliation Court was given jurisdiction for a period of thirty days. During this time a salaried director of conciliation would work closely and informally with the couple, their attorneys, and the judge in an effort to save the marriage. The court was also authorized to use the help of "physicians, psychiatrists, endocrinologists, or other specialists," as well as clergymen of the couple's faith or faiths. In cases where such aid was invoked, however, the consent of both parties was required. These provisions of the law were weakened somewhat by an express limitation that there could be no financial compensation for such outside assistance unless specifically authorized by the county Board of Supervisors. Finally, the law emphasized the voluntary aspect of the conciliation process by disavowing any intent to change the law of divorce. If the efforts of the Conciliation Court were not successful during the thirty-day cooling-off period, either party was free to move for a divorce, annulment, or separate maintenance agreement under the same general laws governing such matters before the enactment of the 1939 law.[21]

The Children's Court of Conciliation Act was hardly a panacea, but it has survived and after thirty years has even been praised by some who were once hostile to the idea. Over the years the professional staff has added trained counselors; thirteen California counties have followed the lead of Los Angeles in creating conciliation courts; and some features of the California law have been adopted by seven other states. In 1955 the statute was amended to make the court's jurisdiction optional in cases where divorce suits had already been filed, but this move did not thwart the continued growth of the court, which appears to enjoy a high degree of success in the cases submitted to it.[22]

Aside from the Children's Court of Conciliation, Lindsey's legislative successes in California were strictly peripheral. In 1939 the legislature did pass a law providing that at least half of the earnings of child actors must be placed in trust funds under court-approved contracts. The statute is sometimes called the Bartholomew Law in recognition of the part that earlier litigation involving Freddie Bartholomew played in its inception. At the same session the legislature passed the first California law requiring a serological test for syphilis as a condition for obtaining a marriage license. Such laws, the Judge liked to remind people, were also "children's legislation," since they gave "unborn children" the right not to come into the world blind or maimed. The bills that were finally adopted on these subjects were not the ones Lindsey had caused to be introduced in the legislature, though they bore a substantial resemblance to the Judge's proposals. Lindsey was nonetheless able to feel some satisfaction in knowing that he had helped create a climate of opinion that made the legislature responsive to the demand for such laws. He had lobbied for them for two years and had appeared before a legislative committee in Sacramento in 1939 on behalf of the "Bartholomew" legislation.[23]

These victories in 1939 were more than offset, in Lindsey's opinion, by the failure of the legislature to enact what he considered "the most important" single item of the Children's Bills. This was a proposed amendment to the California Juvenile Court Law which would have given juvenile court judges the right to use a civil proceeding in equity to deal with persons accused of contributing to the delinquency of a minor. It was needed, the Judge argued, for the same reasons that had caused him to introduce it in Colorado in 1909,* and it would be useful in curbing juvenile delinquency in Los Angeles. The defeat of the bill was doubly disappointing to Lindsey because he had hoped that its adoption would be a reminder to his judicial colleagues of his constructive leadership in juvenile legislation and his continuing interest in presiding over the work of the Juvenile Court of Los Angeles.[24]

The pace of the Judge's life did not slow as he approached his seventieth birthday. In the fall of 1939 he was chosen by his colleagues as first presiding judge of the Children's Court of Conciliation. He threw himself into the work with enthusiasm, was ready after six months to write an article for *Liberty Magazine* on his "Court of Mended Hearts," and was gratified to receive accolades from Justice Frank Murphy of the United States Supreme Court and Secretary of Labor Frances Perkins. In September 1940 Lindsey was assured that an audience of millions would read about his court when *Reader's Digest* reprinted an article about it under the eye-catching title, "The You-Don't-Want-A-Divorce Court." Meanwhile the Judge was preparing to do battle with the legislature again in 1941. Before the year was out, however, his energies were temporarily diverted by a request from Governor Olson to investigate a situa-

* See Chapter 2.

:ion at the Whittier State School that had attracted statewide attention.[25]

In August 1939 Benjamin Moreno, a thirteen-year-old Chicano, escaped from the Whittier correctional institution and roamed about the citrus area of southern California for two days before being captured. Upon his return to Whittier he was placed in the Lost Privilege Cottage, an apparent euphemism for the juvenile equivalent of solitary confinement. The next morning young Moreno was found hanging from a bar in his room. Two separate investigations were conducted in 1939. Although one investigating committee was critical of certain procedures at Whittier, both investigations exonerated the authorities from any responsibility for Moreno's apparent suicide. The issue might have been closed permanently but for an additional tragedy that occurred on July 23, 1940, less than a year after the Moreno episode. The circumstances were remarkably similar. Again a young inmate, one Edward Leiva, escaped and was found a few days later (on this occasion, at the entertainment area in nearby Long Beach), was returned to Whittier and placed in the Lost Privilege Cottage, and committed suicide a few hours later. Again an investigating committee headed by Dr. Aaron Rosanoff, State Director of Institutions, found the Whittier authorities innocent of misconduct. The press, led by the *Los Angeles Examiner,* was not satisfied, however, and demanded a new investigation of conditions at Whittier.[26]

Governor Olson responded by asking Judge Lindsey to recommend two persons to serve under his chairmanship on an investigating committee. Lindsey's choices, immediately approved by the governor, were Mrs. Albert Mellinkoff and Dr. Ernest Caldecott, a well-known liberal Unitarian minister in Los Angeles. After an intensive study the committee, in a report prepared by Mrs. Mellinkoff and personally handed by her to Governor Olson on December 6, 1940, concluded that the earlier investigations of both the Moreno and Leiva cases ranged from incomplete to grossly inadequate. In its findings the committee criticized the administration at Whittier for brutal use of corporal punishment, administrative apathy, and a counseling system that was deficient in general and worthless in particular for Spanish-speaking boys. The committee concluded its report with a recommendation that the governor appoint a new advisory group composed of the nationally prominent Father Edward Flanagan of Boys' Town, a representative of the United States Department of Justice, and a third member representing the Osborne Society, a respected private foundation concerned with penology research. The new committee would be asked to make long-term recommendations for the improvement of Whittier, including changes in personnel.[27]

The committee report brought to an end Judge Lindsey's formal involvement in the Whittier episode. The governor's secretary praised the report for its "brevity and good sense," and Governor Olson soon appointed a new committee along the lines recommended. Father Flanagan and William B. Cox, a representative of the Osborne Society, were available, but Olson failed to obtain a representative from the Department of Justice and appointed Mrs. Mellinkoff to the new committee as the third member. After several months the committee helped inaugurate a series of changes at Whittier, including the appointment of a new superintendent. A by-product of the entire episode was the creation by the legislature in 1941 of a California Youth Authority, an agency intended to achieve a more scientific and humane treatment of youthful offenders throughout the state.[28]

Lindsey's plans for spending the early part of 1941 in renewed lobbying for amendments to the Juvenile Court Law were upset by two serious threats to the future of the Children's Court of Conciliation. The first grew out of a public quarrel that arose between the Judge and the director of conciliation attached to the court, Mrs. Rosalind Bates. In essence Lindsey accused Mrs. Bates of improperly referring couples who came to the Conciliation Court to lawyer friends, indiscreetly discussing with them her personal and professional contacts with other judges, and making disloyal statements about himself and the operation of the court. When Lindsey announced his intention to fire her, Mrs. Bates responded by publicly accusing the Judge of permitting serious irregularities in court procedure and of concealing records that would prove it.

The Lindsey-Bates controversy reached its climax in late January when a majority of forty-three attending judges of the Los Angeles Superior Court voted to remove Mrs. Bates from office. Some of Lindsey's closest friends among his colleagues, led by Judge William J. Palmer, introduced a resolution that would have required her to put her accusations against Judge Lindsey in the form of an affidavit, and recommended that she be prosecuted for perjury if they proved false. The Palmer motion was defeated and, in its stead, a resolution providing for an investigation of the Conciliation Court was passed.

The Judge was annoyed over the creation of an investigating committee, since it seemed to imply that there might be some substance to Mrs. Bates's charges. While conceding that there might be some minor irregularities in the operation of the Conciliation Court, the Judge insisted they were no more serious than those found in other departments of the Superior Court which nobody was proposing to investigate. When the six-member committee, composed of three Superior Court judges and three representatives of the Los Angeles Bar Association, reported to the entire panel of the Superior Court two months later, Lindsey's position was substantially vindicated. The committee based its findings on one hundred cases selected at random. It found certain irregularities in procedures but concluded that the interests of litigants had never been damaged as a result and found that all court rulings were valid. The committee could find no "concealment" of records. The Superior Court judges voted to continue Lindsey as judge of the Conciliation Court.[29]

At the same time he was defending himself before the investigating committee, the Judge was fighting for the very existence of the court itself. At the beginning of the 1941 session of the California legislature, senators from two rural counties had introduced a bill to abolish the Conciliation Court. The reason behind the move, according to the Yuba-Sutter Bar Association which caused the repeal measure to be introduced, was the fear that such courts would introduce vexatious procedures and delays and thereby increase the costs of divorce litigation without a commensurate increase in attorneys' fees. When the California Senate passed the DeLap-Rich repeal bill in March 1941, by a vote of 22 to 14, the "Lindsey organization" went into action. Mrs. Mellinkoff addressed PTA groups in southern California, the Judge issued reports on the accomplishments of the court to date, and the support of clergymen of all faiths was enlisted in sending letters and telegrams to Sacramento. In Los Angeles Archbishop Cantwell (Catholic), Bishop Baker (Methodist), and Rabbi Magnin all supported the continuation of the court. On April 10, 1941, Judge Lindsey appeared before the Committee on Judiciary Codes of the State Assembly to testify against the bill. The campaign was successful. On June 14 the assembly defeated the DeLap-Rich bill by a margin just one vote short of two to one. The Children's Court of Conciliation was saved.[30]

The Judge's final years in California were a mixture of victory and unfulfillment. On the positive side of the ledger he had made a comeback in his sixties from defeats that would have destroyed many younger men. He had almost single-handedly created a new institution in his adopted state and was actively engaged in presiding over it. On the debit side was the continuing rebuff of his efforts to preside over the Juvenile Court. As late as 1941 scores of persons in Los Angeles who remembered his reputation as a juvenile court authority wrote to him, asking his advice about dealing with their children. Sometimes they pleaded with him to help in having their children removed from reform schools. The Judge tried to acknowledge all such requests but usually confined himself to expressing his sympathy and regrets. Sometimes he added that the Conciliation Court was taking up all of his time, and occasionally he corrected a writer's false impression that he actually was the judge of the Juvenile Court.[31]

In January 1943, as the California legislature began a new session and the Superior Court of the County of Los Angeles made its annual refusal to appoint him to the Juvenile Court, the Judge resumed his biennial campaign on behalf of the "Children's Bills." At the top of his agenda were two proposals to extend the chancery jurisdiction of the Juvenile Court over all adults who contributed to the delinquency of minors. At last, however, the toll of battle was beginning to show on Lindsey. Although he continued to serve on the Conciliation Court, his blood pressure was uncomfortably high and he had begun to show signs of excessive fatigue. On Wednesday, March 24, 1943, after a day in court, he wrote to Senator Jack B. Tenney of Los Angeles:

> My hard work and health are such that my doctor and my wife do not wish me to go to Sacramento to indulge in the kind of activities in which I cannot refrain from putting all my strength. It may be possible, however, that I could prevail upon them to let me go if you think there is a fairly good chance of getting the legislation through.[32]

As the Judge returned to his home in Bel Air that evening, he expected to be back in the Conciliation Court in downtown Los Angeles on Thursday morning. After a restless night following what was subsequently diagnosed as a heart seizure, he spent the day, instead, in the Good Samaritan Hospital, in the same building where Senator Robert Kennedy was to die twenty-five years later. A second heart attack less than twenty-four hours after the Judge's arrival at the hospital, at 7:30 in the morning of Friday, March 26, 1943, was fatal.[33]

12 / Maverick Judge

"H E WAS NEVER GIVEN CREDIT FOR WHAT HE DID." PHILIP
B. Gilliam, judge of the Juvenile Court of Denver,
said this of Ben Lindsey. For more than thirty years
Gilliam has held the office that Lindsey almost single-handedly
created. Two of Lindsey's surviving colleagues on the Superior
Court of Los Angeles, who never met Judge Gilliam, made
almost identical remarks in appraising Lindsey's career. If the
Judge had wanted a tombstone for himself, the words would
have been an appropriate epitaph. Although they do not tell the
whole story, they are the essential truth.

A certain tendency to make light of Lindsey was evident
throughout his career. Some of it, at least, was attributable to
his enemies in Colorado. Most of these enemies were not the
kind of people who write books, but their efforts to portray the
Judge alternately as a mere publicity-seeker and even as a thoroughly evil man were unrelenting and doubtless had some effect on his reputation. The scurrility of the rumors was widely
imaginative. On the gentler side they included charges that he
faked illness in order to stay home from court and write political
speeches. Another favorite was that his aged mother's eyes were
bandaged because he had beaten her while he was in a drunken
rage. Because Lindsey was a bachelor until he was forty-four, his
opponents intimated that his interest in children was unnatural,
a rumor that finally culminated in a vile and crudely constructed
false charge that he had sexually molested two young boys in his
court chambers. The rumor received the *coup de grâce* when
Theodore Roosevelt confirmed that the Judge was his house
guest on Long Island when the alleged incident occurred in

Denver. The abuse of such rumors was matched only by the venom and persistence of Lindsey's enemies. After his disbarment in Colorado they tried unsuccessfully to have him disbarred in California as well, on the ground that his role in the Stokes case justified taking away his chances of making a livelihood in his adopted state. When he was elected to the Superior Court of Los Angeles in 1934, an effort was made to have his election invalidated on the ground that he did not have sufficient legal residence in California. Those who sometimes accused the Judge of near paranoia perhaps needed to be reminded that he had a real collection of enemies. An implication by Bernard De Voto in 1927 that Lindsey deserved to be loved for the enemies he had made had considerable merit.[1]

Ben Lindsey had one special enemy—perhaps his worst—whose characteristics must be described if the story of the Judge is to be complete. His style and actions sometimes made the greatest contribution to the Judge's image as shallow and irresponsible. At his worst this enemy was successful in making people forget Lindsey's significant accomplishments in the field of social legislation, his stirring and eloquent appeals to the best humanitarian sentiments of the American people, and his insights into the nature of some of the changes that were necessary in order to build a healthier society. The enemy's name, of course, was Ben Lindsey.

At his best Lindsey could be warm, humorous, empathetic, and even objective about himself. But these virtues were sometimes offset by weaknesses that seriously compromised the favorable image. Perhaps the Judge's greatest vice was his need to boast. Despite the fascinating anecdotes he recounted in his books, even the sympathetic reader becomes a little weary, and eventually a little skeptical, about a person who invariably portrays himself as the embodiment of wisdom and virtue. Lindsey's autobiography, *The Dangerous Life,* prepared during the most trying time of his life since adolescence, revealed this trait in its most glaring form. Instead of being satisfied with describing his very substantial achievements in Colorado and elsewhere, the Judge continually conveyed the impression that he had done it all by himself. Nowhere in the book did he discuss, for example, his extensive correspondence with other judges and lawyers whose suggestions he solicited while drafting laws, just as other judges and lawyers borrowed from him. True, he mentioned in passing that his accomplishments "would have been impossible without the help of thousands of loyal, understanding friends," but one still came away feeling, to paraphrase Mr. Dooley's remark about Theodore Roosevelt and the Spanish-American War, that Lindsey's autobiography might well have been entitled *Alone in Denver*.

An example of Lindsey's bad judgment that caused many people to think of him as an egoist was his reference in *The Dangerous Life* to a list of 151 "systems and laws inaugurated by Judge Lindsey." The list came from an old campaign document used in 1912 and 1916 and later reprinted under the title *Twenty-Five Years of the Juvenile and Family Court of Denver*. A careful reader would notice that the large figure was reached by occasionally duplicating certain items—listing a general law first, then giving its specific provisions separately. A really expert reader, including some of the leadership of national social welfare agencies, would also know, in a few instances, that it was misleading to call some of the items successes. Take, for example, Items 133–135 as they were listed in the pamphlet:

133. The International Juvenile Court Association formed at Hull House, Chicago, in 1905, grew out of the suggestion of Judge Lindsey.

134. It brought to the attention of the Sage Foundation the necessity for the work it proposed to do and asked its financial aid to carry out a big national program for the better protection of children.

135. After several conferences with its secretary, Mr. John M. Glenn, the Sage Foundation took up much of the work proposed, furnished the money and got it done.

In fact the International Juvenile Court Association was one of Lindsey's less successful ventures. Lindsey did play the dominant role in it, but the Sage Foundation turned down repeated efforts to persuade it to fund the association and went ahead on its own. A completely accurate statement would have added, at the end of Item 135, the words: *but not through the International Juvenile Court Association, as Judge Lindsey wished*.[2]

These illustrations should not lead one to conclude that Lindsey's claims were mostly false. The saddest part of the story is that Lindsey could have accurately claimed a major role, and often *the* major role, in bringing about the reforms in Denver and in Colorado that were listed in the 151 items. *The truth was good enough*. The Judge's weakness lay in his insistence on overstating his case. His friends excused such episodes as rather amusing examples of his supersalesmanship, or as standard political campaign tactics used by candidates for even the highest political office. His enemies, needless to say, claimed that they proved him an egomaniac.

Another feature of Lindsey's personality that sometimes caused his contributions to be either overlooked or consciously ignored was a certain tendency in the Judge to be a loner. The trait was paradoxical in a person who on many occasions demonstrated qualities of near genius in public relations and in the political mobilization of electorates and legislative bodies. Perhaps a key to the paradox is that Lindsey showed these qualities to the fullest when he was fighting for his own favorite measures. The Judge was no organization man. For example, when the National Child Labor Committee, of which he was a member in 1911–1912, was considering a strong motion against the employment of children on the stage, Lindsey took a middle ground between laissez-faire and prohibition in favor of regulation with adequate safeguards to insure parental supervision, limits on the number of performances, and sufficient schooling. While the discussion was still going on the Judge took his case "to the people" by means of the public press, basing his argument on his own experiences under a law that he had drafted and that was in force in Colorado. Several members of the committee were furious, charging that the Judge acted with impropriety in publicly advocating a position on a matter that was still under discussion in a committee of which he was a member. Julia Lathrop and Florence Kelley were among the powerful forces in the child welfare movement whom Lindsey thus alienated. In later years the Judge was convinced that Miss Lathrop, who became first chief of the federal Children's Bureau, was responsible for keeping him off important national committees dealing with child welfare. Lindsey's habit of referring to many social workers as "scientific robots" probably struck a responsive chord among some of the alleged beneficiaries of their ministrations—but won him few allies in professional social service organizations.[3]

One of Lindsey's greatest strengths was his showmanship. It played an important part in winning the political support that re-elected him regularly in Denver and Los Angeles, and it helped the Judge to spread the juvenile court idea throughout the country and even beyond its boundaries. It also played a significant role in achieving legislative victories for other reform measures not directly related to child welfare. Without it Lindsey's influence might well have been confined to Colorado. But another facet to Lindsey's showmanship was a liability. At its worst it detracted from the Judge's credibility as a serious reformer. At times Lindsey seemed almost to follow the reputed Hollywood maxim that the only bad publicity is no publicity. His willingness to pose for commercial photographs of himself listening to the confessions of young women as a part of the advertising campaigns for his books and articles was a case in point. There was nothing intrinsically wrong in the act, but the Judge seemed unwilling to realize what such publicity would cost him among large conventional segments of the public. Similarly, his endorsement of a book called *The Future of Nakedness,* his willingness to accompany the film *Companion-*

ate Marriage on a publicity tour, and his acceptance of an offer to write an article for *True Confessions* played directly into the hands of enemies who enjoyed portraying him as a ridiculous figure. Finally, the episode in the Cathedral of St. John the Divine achieved nothing but a transient notoriety for the Judge and did little to enhance his reputation. Given Bishop Manning's provocative and ill-tempered remarks, a dignified silence (or perhaps a letter to the *New York Times*) would have scored more points for the Judge than challenging the Bishop during a religious service.[4]

Lindsey often shot from the hip intellectually. A great American lawyer, Adolf Berle, once characterized Lindsey's mental processes as emotional and intense rather than incisive or accurate. His speeches and writings often contained shrewd insights into social causation and human motives, but they were also often diffuse and lacking in any central theme or theoretical framework. *The Companionate Marriage* suffered from some of these defects. The original articles that went into the book were convincing in their portrayal of certain aspects of the human condition. But, as one member of the editorial board of an eastern magazine complained with considerable perception, the Judge did not clearly relate the cases to his many years in domestic relations work or even show very convincingly that his companionate marriage program would solve most of the problems described in the articles. Related to this analytical deficiency in Lindsey was an occasional tendency to accommodate himself intellectually to changed circumstances with too great speed, especially in those areas where he had no special competence and where silence would have been a wiser course. His sudden turnabout in regard to American policy during the First World War is illustrative. Until American intervention the Judge, like many other Americans, was highly critical of the favoritism allegedly shown to the Allied side by the Wilson administration, and publicly declared that it should be a matter of indifference in the United States whether one group of European belligerents or the other won the war. Once America was at war, however, he was eager to offer his services to the Committee on Public Information and to start writing about the threat of "Pan-Germanism." If the change resulted from any intellectual process, the evidence has never been discovered. As historian Louis Filler has suggested, the most that can be said for such converts is that they had plenty of company.[5]

A final weakness in the Judge was his combativeness. The word "feisty" frequently came to mind when people tried to describe "the little scrapper," as one observer called him. Like his showmanship, Lindsey's combativeness was often a necessary virtue. A man without prestigious social background, with only a modest formal education, attacked by entrenched economic and political powers who stooped to almost any depth to destroy him, the Judge needed a combative spirit to do what he had to do. Child labor laws, employers' liability laws, and electoral reform legislation do not become realities because those who oppose them are converted by kindness and moral appeal. Without his feisty temperament the Judge would never have become one of the greatest single contributors to such Progressive transformation as there was in Colorado during the first decade and a half of the twentieth century. When he was striking back at the Women's Protective League, the Speer machine at its worst, and later at the Ku Klux Klan, his broadside attacks were fully justified. On other occasions, however, they revealed poor judgment at best, peevishness at worst.

Two examples from the early and late Colorado phases of the Judge's career are in point. After he bolted the Democratic party to run for governor as an independent candidate in 1906, Lindsey denounced his Democratic opponent, Alva Adams, as a virtual "tool" of the corporations. Annoyed at Senator Thomas W. Patterson, publisher of the *Rocky Mountain News,* for supporting Adams, Lindsey patronizingly wrote that he believed Patterson was "honestly deceived." In other words, he was a fool. The fact of the matter was that Lindsey had shown poor judgment in running for the governorship, and his attacks on Adams as a tool and Patterson as an unwitting tool of "the Beast" were supported only by hearsay and innuendo. Such charges may have been fair play under the rules of the game in a hotly contested election, but Lindsey's gratuitous repetition of them three years afterward in *The Beast* showed a waspish quality that did him no credit and caused an unnecessarily protracted coolness between himself and Senator Patterson, who often supported both liberal causes and Ben Lindsey.[6]

A second example, from the later period of the Judge's Colorado career, illustrates an unfortunate tendency on his part to operate on the principle that "he who is not with me is against me." The episode involved his immediate successor, Judge Robert W. Steele, who was appointed by the county Board of Commissioners as Lindsey's interim replacement on the Denver Juvenile Court pending a new election. The event had an interesting historic parallel. Twenty-seven years earlier Steele's father had gone to the Colorado Supreme Court, vacating a county judgeship to which Ben Lindsey had been given an interim appointment. The young Robert Steele had been a friend of Lindsey since childhood and had once been deeply touched as a rather shy freshman at Princeton when Lindsey, visiting the campus as a nationally famous guest lecturer, singled him out in an audience. They remained friends until 1927. When Lindsey heard of Steele's acceptance of the appointment to the Juvenile Court, he was deeply hurt. According to Judge Steele, Lindsey told him that he was convinced that the Board of Commissioners would have continued him in office if Steele had declined the appointment. Steele told Lindsey that he was equally convinced that the Board would simply have looked for another candidate. It was the end of their friendship.

The Judge's disappointment over Steele's willingness to succeed him was understandable. Even if the board had firmly decided not to appoint Lindsey under any circumstances, it was altogether human for the Judge to feel that a friend should not accept an appointment to take over his life work. The Judge's feeling of injury was undoubtedly exacerbated by the circumstances of his ouster; nevertheless, as in the 1906 election episode, it would have been wiser for the Judge to have kept his silence. Instead, angered further by some comments of Judge Steele that he construed as an attack on his juvenile court philosophy, Lindsey assailed him in *The Dangerous Life* as an inexperienced opportunist who was trying to curry favor with the worst reactionary forces in Colorado. At least the scorching comments by the Judge were leavened by one bit of unconscious humor. "I entertain no personal animosity," he wrote.[7]

Given his foibles and more serious limitations, what was it about Ben Lindsey that made him one of the major figures in the history of twentieth-century American reform? His fame cannot rest on his role as a sociological theorist, a legal historian, or a lawyer's lawyer, for he was none of these. Where then did his greatness lie?

To a large degree Lindsey's fame must rest on his contributions as a politician. The word is chosen deliberately. When Lincoln Steffens sent Lindsey the draft of his manuscript that eventually became "The Just Judge" in *McClure's Magazine*, he had written, "Lindsey is not a mere philanthropist, he is a politician." The Judge was horrified at the choice of words and successfully implored Steffens to delete the latter part of the statement. Lindsey was undoubtedly correct when he surmised that to the average reader such a statement would be the equivalent of saying, "Lindsey is not a mere philanthropist, he is a common thief."[8]

The Judge understood, of course, that Steffens intended the remark as high praise. Used in that sense it was one of the most perceptive comments ever made about Lindsey. Time after time the Judge demonstrated his ability to organize support and get things done. In Denver, during the early years, he organized boys' gangs so successfully that he was sometimes called the chief boys' gang leader in town. At the state level Lindsey was indisputably the outstanding contributor to the drafting and passing of reform legislation in Colorado during the first two decades of the twentieth century. His pre-eminence, of course, was in the field of children's legislation. From his accession to the judgeship to the codification of child welfare legislation in 1923, he frequently played the key role in drafting bills and an equally crucial part in mobilizing the political support needed to enact them into law. Many of the basic statutes he wrote with his own hand after arduous research and correspondence. This legislation, in codified form and with new amendments, includes much of the juvenile court law of Colorado today. Some of it is still in the Judge's own words. Outside the field of child welfare legislation the Judge also played a major role. He sponsored several labor reform measures and drafted many progressive election laws and city charter amendments between 1905 and 1913.

On the national level Lindsey's role as politician, as Steffens used the word, was more indirect but also significant. To the American public he was the embodiment of the juvenile court movement. He corresponded, lectured, and appeared before legislative bodies in every section of the country in support of juvenile court legislation. The concept of parental and adult responsibility for contributing to child delinquency was a Lindsey innovation adopted by almost every state. The general trend in the country has been to place greater emphasis on civil proccedings as the preferred form of enforcement of such laws, on the grounds that jailing a parent may create more problems than it solves and that assessment of responsibility in cases involving adults is often difficult. Lindsey recognized these problems at an early date and drafted the so-called civil contributory laws for Colorado within a few years of the adoption of the criminal statute.[9] On the national level, as in Colorado, the Judge did not confine his support of reform legislation to the field of child welfare. He was also a constant national spokesman for other liberal causes such as prison reform, the abolition of capital punishment, woman suffrage, and birth control. Only in his support for the cause of Prohibition did he have subsequent reason to reverse his judgment, a verdict in which most of the American people concurred when the Eighteenth Amendment was repealed in 1933.

Lindsey's place in history must also be assessed in terms of his chief role in life, that of a juvenile court judge. Because of his involvement in so many different phases of liberal movements, one can almost lose sight of the fact that the judgeship of the Juvenile Court of Denver was the post in which he spent roughly half of his adult life. A perceptive listener, after hearing for some time about Lindsey's wide interests and varied activities, asked the crucial question, "How did he do with the kids?"

The state of the remaining records of the Denver Juvenile Court for the Lindsey era is such that the question must be answered impressionistically. As far as Lindsey's conduct of the court itself is concerned, the reports of nationally prominent journalists, from Lincoln Steffens in 1906 to Franklin P. Adams in 1915, were highly favorable and invariably praised the Judge's ability "to talk the boys' own language," to use group-therapy techniques (before the term was invented) in the famous Saturday morning sessions, and to make the court as much a community-action center as a judicial forum. Perhaps the quality most consistently noted by those who saw Lindsey in action was his success in persuading boys to "open up" and tell him what they would not reveal to their parents or other adults. Oscar Chapman, who served as chief probation officer in Lindsey's court in the 1920's and who later went on to obtain a national Cabinet appointment, confirmed this impression in the 1960's when he used the phrase "almost uncanny" to describe the Judge's talent for winning the confidence of adolescents. One of the most unexpected sources of favorable comment was Lindsey's successor on the Denver Juvenile Court, Judge Robert W. Steele, a man who certainly had reasons for feeling hostile toward the Judge. Not surprisingly, Steele's compliment was tempered by criticisms. He described the records of the court as "chaotic" when he took over, and he was critical of Lindsey's admitted practice of dispensing with legal formalities in certain adoption cases and keeping only personal notes as "records." Nevertheless, Steele magnanimously added, he felt that Lindsey's ouster from the judgeship was unjustified and largely motivated by personal antagonism, and that Lindsey "was the best qualified man in the state" for juvenile court work.[10]

The highly favorable verdict on Lindsey as a juvenile court judge was not unanimous. The chief source of dissent from the prevailing view was that segment of the Denver press that was hostile to Lindsey, most consistently the *Denver Republican* and occasionally the *Post*. Sometimes there were charges that a sentence was harsh or that Lindsey was high-handed. The Judge always denied such assertions, of course. He seemed to be particularly sensitive to criticism in connection with his sentencing of boys to a term in the State Industrial School at Golden. On more than one occasion he defended such sentences on the grounds that they were given only when a boy had violated his probation or when a term in the reformatory at Buena Vista was the only alternative. Lindsey's statement was probably true, but his defensiveness caused him, characteristically, to overstate his case. More than once he asserted that Golden "was the same as a public school and in no sense a prison." It was true that the State Industrial School was not a maximum security institution. It was also true that it had a comparatively enlightened administration. But it was not "the same as a public school."[11]

By far the more common criticism of the Judge was that he was too lenient, a not unexpected charge. The underlying assumption of juvenile court work is that probation is the preferred method of handling delinquent children, and it seems clearly to have been Lindsey's first preference. Under the circumstances the *Republican* and sometimes the *Post* would eagerly watch for any allegations that Lindsey's "softness" was responsible for a growth in the crime rate and enthusiastically spread the word when they discovered a case in which one of Lindsey's probationers had failed. A hostile Denver periodical called *Clay's Review* frequently portrayed the Judge as a mindless do-gooder whose psychological and sociological orientation had proved to be an ineffective substitute for the stern hand of the law in dealing with juvenile offenders. The Judge's reply to such stories expressed curiosity that his enemies never found anything newsworthy in the vast majority of cases in which his probationers "made good."[12]

Unfortunately the state of the records for the Lindsey era of the Juvenile Court of Denver is such that only a few broad generalizations are possible. At all times the Judge seems to have preferred informal settlements of complaints. In the early years of the court, when the staff was quite small, he sometimes negotiated the settlements personally. In later years he encouraged probation officers and school principals to reach as many amicable agreements as possible without filing formal charges against an accused delinquent. Since these settlements never became formal cases at all, the official records are of no help in evaluating this important part of the work of the court. The records of the filed cases in the later period indicate that Lindsey continued to put most first offenders on probation. Since a filed case in the 1920's was one that had received a preliminary screening and was considered by a probation officer serious enough to justify an official hearing, Lindsey's granting of probation in slightly more than half of the cases indicates a continuing strong inclination to give delinquents a second chance. Conversely there were enough commitments to demonstrate that the Judge was not simply an easy mark who never held delinquents responsible for their conduct.[13]

The records that have been preserved allow no very solid conclusions about the handling of the cases themselves. The docket files often contain only formal pleadings which give no information on the social history of the cases. The huge *Delinquency Record* tomes contain such categories as nature of delinquency, "habits," and home conditions, but even when these spaces have been completely filled out the information given is often minimal. Sometimes, for example, the nature of the delinquency is described simply as "incorrigible," "leading an immoral life," or "taking things." Lindsey himself, on more than one occasion, admitted that the case records were inadequate and placed much of the blame on insufficient appropriations, a charge that seems to have been well founded. "If anything must suffer because of this [financial] handicap," he wrote in 1924, "it has been the practice to let it be the written records rather than the actual needs of, and personal work with, the individual."[14]

Certain institutional changes that affected Lindsey's role as a juvenile court judge over the years should be mentioned. In the early years of the century, when Lindsey was guiding the court in its formative stages, Denver was almost a frontier community and was only beginning to extend its social services. The essence of the Judge's humanitarian genius lay in his vigorous creativity in filling the gaps. In those years he was, as a fellow reformer with whom he corresponded observed:

> probation officer, visitor, president of the Boys' Club, advisor to the Woman's Auxiliary, director of the fresh air fund, manager of the beet farm, inspector of the bathing rooms, and, in short, general manager and overseer of the entire field.[15]

Lindsey worked closely with charitable and religious groups during this period. As a result of their cooperation, and partly through the use of his own limited funds, the Judge and his court became a kind of social welfare clearing house. Among the achievements of the court (one is tempted to say "the agency") in the early years that Lindsey itemized in his famous booklet *The Problem of the Children and How the State of Colorado Cares for Them* (1904), were: "baths given probationers, positions secured, needy children relieved, number of garments supplied (second-hand), number of garments supplied (new)."[16] By the 1920's the growth in school attendance, the compartmentalization of social welfare activities, and the routine enforcement of child labor laws helped to reduce Lindsey's more dramatic activities which had played such a large part in making him a national charismatic figure. Ironically the Judge, through his many campaigns for social legislation, had been a major force in effecting the change.

In weighing Ben Lindsey's influence on his America, one must go beyond his career as a judge and even beyond the laws he wrote or supported and the causes to which he lent his name. Why, aside from his fantastic energy, did the Judge make such an emotional impact on the American people? Why was this man, who had been forced by economic circumstances to be a high school dropout, who could sometimes be vain, who was occasionally careless with facts, named in a national poll in 1914 as one of the greatest living Americans? Why, as the daughter of Senator La Follette had written in 1910, was there no person in the entire country whose name evoked such an immediately favorable response or whose endorsement of a cause carried the same "finality of conviction"? In the answer to these questions lies much of the final greatness of Ben Lindsey.

The secret of Lindsey's success in winning such a favorable national response was based in very large measure on his role as spokesman for the American conscience. Walter Lippmann was right when he commented that *The Beast* was a uniquely effective piece of muckraking because Lindsey appealed for justice in the name of children. But there was more to it than that. The Judge also cried out with equal eloquence on behalf of adults. If he elicited the reader's sympathy for "Tony Costello" as the child-victim of "the system," he also did not fail to mention Tony's father, whose lungs were being destroyed by the effects of lead poisoning and who was lying helplessly on his deathbed, forgotten by his former employer and ignored by society at large. Lindsey's graphic illustrations of such tragedies had the ring of authenticity. Their existence called for the emergence of a Jeremiah, and Lindsey played the role well.

He played it well because it came from the heart. The absence of mothers' pensions, the sharp practices of life insurance companies, the humiliations of poverty were not matters that he had learned about from books. They were a part of his own life. Inadequate safeguards against accidents in shops and factories, the absence of workmen's compensation laws, the meaninglessness to the poor of "equal protection of the laws"—all these were injustices that he observed at close hand. When the Judge attacked these evils and cited moving personal experiences to illustrate them, he gained a large national audience. Thousands of others knew them too. A later generation would have said of Lindsey, "He told it like it was."

Lindsey's political enemies never understood this source of his strength. When they gleefully discovered some omission or inaccuracy in his speeches or writings and broadcast it through Denver and beyond, one cannot but wonder if they ever asked themselves why such revelations failed to do any significant political damage to Lindsey for so many years. Undoubtedly a large part of the answer was that the voters saw in the Judge a moral crusader who was, on the great issues of the times, essentially right.

These observations apply chiefly to Lindsey's role as a crusader for children's legislation and conventional political reform measures. Any final estimate of the Judge must also consider his place in the history of sexual reform. At times when he felt depressed the Judge would say to his wife, "If I'm remembered at all, it will be for companionate marriage." It was an overstatement. In later years historians began the process of recognition, notably Louis Filler in *The Muckrakers: Crusaders for American Liberalism* and Eric Goldman in *Rendezvous with Destiny*. In 1965 the Judge's role in the juvenile court movement was depicted in the national television series "Profiles in Courage." In 1970 *The Beast* was reissued for the first time since its original publication sixty years earlier.

Nevertheless Lindsey's melancholy prediction contained a large grain of truth. Probably most college history students since the 1930's, if they remember Lindsey's name at all, came across it in Frederick Lewis Allen's lively account of the twenties, *Only Yesterday*. In recent years writers such as Vance Packard and Margaret Mead have referred to the Judge's writings in popular accounts of the "new" sexual revolution, and a competently written study of the 1950's called *Marriage, Morals and Sex in America* has a final chapter entitled "From Lindsey to Kinsey." The Judge's name also has appeared more consistently in the bibliographies of texts on marriage and the family than it has in books about child welfare legislation, political reform, or even juvenile delinquency.[17]

What is the relationship of *The Companionate Marriage,* the chief repository of Lindsey's ideas about sexual reform, to his general stature as a reformer? As far as the basic proposal is concerned, it would doubtless impress many young readers today as conservative and even irrelevant. If a couple is uncertain about making a commitment to permanent marriage but is willing to live together, why bother to institutionalize the arrangement at all? The Judge's subsequent elaboration on the companionate marriage program, made in response to hostile comments that he was advocating "free love," stressed that such marriages would be dissolved only after a state commission had made an effort to preserve them. Those who are not committed, for psychological, religious, or other reasons, to the ideal of permanent marriage will probably continue to prefer an informal arrangement that can be terminated at will to one in which it would be necessary for them to place their reasons for "discord" before a governmental commission. In any event, there seems to be no groundswell in favor of legislating for companionate marriage. Occasionally a concern over the growth of population has led to suggestions for some kind of licensing for parenthood; but a strong belief in the right of individual decision-making in this area, combined with the lack of any agreement over the principles on which such licensing would be based or the procedures by which it would be enforced, make it unlikely that any formal and legally enforced distinction between "individual marriage" and "parental marriage," as Margaret Mead has labeled them, will be recognized in the near future.[18]

The significance of *The Companionate Marriage* goes beyond the specific proposal, however, and beyond the context of the Judge's symbolic role as the most widely recognized spokesman for the "sexual revolution" in the twenties. *The Companionate Marriage,* like Lindsey's more traditional muckraking efforts, also made an appeal to many readers' common sense and feelings against injustice. Many of the laws and practices in the United States regarding divorce, birth control, and alimony which Lindsey described in the 1920's *were* cruel and absurd. Some of them, at least in regard to divorce and alimony, still are.[19] There are passages in Lindsey's book that seem timely in the last third of the twentieth century. A recent (and continuing) debate about dispensing the Pill in college health centers brings to mind a passage from this book of almost half a century ago:

> The discovery of contraception may prove to be the most revolutionary thing that has ever happened to human society. We are just at the beginning of it. The day will come when contraception, in contrast with the clumsy methods in use at present, will amount to no more than the swallowing of a pill. . . .[20]

Elsewhere in the book, as we have seen, Lindsey advocated giving contraceptive information and devices to all who wanted them. In the 1960's a popular syndicated columnist asked a number of physicians about their views on the same subject. Most of them agreed with the suggestion. There was no mention of Lindsey's name, and undoubtedly some alarmed readers shook their heads and assured one another that nobody would have dared publicly discuss such a proposal "ten years ago."

The long resistance to governmental participation in family planning, especially by any form of subsidization of birth control, is also a measure of Lindsey's vision in uncompromisingly advocating it in the 1920's. As late as the 1950's President Dwight Eisenhower declared that he could think of no field in which it was less appropriate for government to act—a statement he retracted in later years. The change in national attitudes was reflected on the twentieth anniversary of the founding of the United Nations in 1965, when President Lyndon Johnson's remark that family planning was the most *important* element in international economic development caused hardly a ripple. Those who remembered the tempestuous careers of such pioneers in the birth-control movement as Ben Lindsey and Margaret Sanger must have been amused at the respectability in which such suggestions were now clothed.

Other aspects of *The Companionate Marriage* also challenged the old order and appear now to be gaining wider acceptance. Lindsey's pervasive insistence that sexual conduct should generally not be a subject of the criminal law was far ahead of its time. In recent years even the organized bar has been coming around to the view that the courts should not concern themselves with the private sexual conduct of consenting adults, though only one state (Illinois) has gone as far as to repeal the section of its criminal code which made homosexual activity between consenting adults a crime.[21] Lindsey's call for candor in discussing all aspects of sexual questions has fared better than his proposal to abolish criminal sanctions for private sexual acts, but even here the struggle has often been uphill. For years the Hays Code forbade any reference in approved motion pictures to the "social diseases," as syphilis and gonorrhea were delicately called, and the Surgeon General of the United States was considered quite daring in 1939 when he used the word "syphilis" in a national radio broadcast. Even in the 1970's, as some school board members had good reason to know, there were those who believed that courses in sex education and marriage counseling were part of a Communist conspiracy. Substitute the word "Bolshevik" for "Communist" and we are back in the 1920's, reading attacks on the Judge.

In any list of leading American reformers of the twentieth century, Ben Lindsey deserves to rank high. Among those who recognized the fact during his lifetime were Theodore Roosevelt, Jacob Riis, Brand Whitlock, Walter Lippmann, Bertrand Russell, Upton Sinclair, John Dewey, and Franklin D. Roosevelt. Havelock Ellis once wrote to Lindsey: "I trust you are encouraged by knowing that you have on your side the sympathy and approval of the best people all over the world." H. G. Wells advised the Judge: "I follow your conflict with the old order by means of press cuttings. . . . You are doing great work." When it became clear that Lindsey's career was in jeopardy after the Ku Klux Klan victory in the 1924 election in Colorado, George Bernard Shaw wrote to him: "So much the worse for the United States and for humanity. . . . Anyhow, the law that what is done cannot be undone holds valid of good as well as of evil; and nothing can unmake your record."[22]

These Lindsey advocates did not come from a single mold, and in fact were profoundly different from one another in many respects. Yet they had two qualities in common. All retained a liberal optimism about improving the human condition, and each in his own way was a fighter. Since they were also men of the world, they probably perceived that Lindsey had his limitations. But they also recognized his greatness as an evangelist of American liberalism who fought the good fight, who kept the faith, and who was in the vanguard of any movement to free the human spirit and make easier the life of man on earth.

EPILOGUE

A month after the Judge's death, the presiding judge of the Los Angeles Superior Court invited Mrs. Lindsey to the traditional memorial service held by the court in honor of its recently deceased members. It was a matter that the Lindseys had previously considered. Upon receiving Judge Emmet Wilson's invitation, Mrs. Lindsey sought the help of a friend in drafting a reply. The key paragraph of her letter stated:

> In recent months, Judge Lindsey had discussed with me the regular memorial service held by the Judges. He specifically requested me to ask that his name be deleted from such a service. He felt that it would be a mockery for the majority of his colleagues to honor him in death while in life they failed to extend to him even the conventional amenities due any colleague.[1]

The allusion, as the letter went on to make clear, was chiefly to the persistent refusal of Lindsey's colleagues to allow him to preside over the Juvenile Court of Los Angeles.

As an alternative to the official memorial service Mrs. Lindsey arranged a public memorial service for the Judge. It was held on Sunday, May 9, 1943, in the First Unitarian Church in downtown Los Angeles. After several eulogies by the Judge's friends and associates, the service was concluded with the reading of a letter recently received by Mrs. Lindsey:

> My dear Mrs. Lindsey:
>   Among Ben Lindsey's accomplished tasks were the development of our modern juvenile court system and a constructive approach to the whole problem of juvenile delinquency. He is remembered by thousands of Americans who today have reason

to feel a direct, personal indebtedness. The memory of Ben Lindsey is best honored in the name of youth. In so honoring him, I speak for those young Americans who now face supreme sacrifice that the ideals of this nation might live.

Very sincerely yours,
Franklin D. Roosevelt.[2]

In death, as in life, the Judge remained a maverick. Shortly before he died he and Mrs. Lindsey agreed that there would be no conventional funeral and that his body would be cremated. A few days after his death, friends joined in scattering most of his ashes in the garden of the family home in Bel Air. Mrs. Lindsey, who was a bit of a maverick herself, decided upon a final personal gesture in remembrance of the Judge's work in Colorado: she kept a small portion of his ashes and quietly returned with them to Denver for a brief visit. There, one evening, accompanied by a former associate of the Judge, she sprinkled the remainder of the ashes over the site of the old courthouse where he had presided for more than a quarter of a century. At the time the area was the site of a small park, the demolition of the courthouse having been completed in 1933. The gesture was doubly appropriate. The Judge would doubtless have been pleased at this defiance of the legislation lobbied through by the funeral directors' segment of the establishment, which is dedicated to preventing such quixotic disposal of the dead. But Lindsey, who did so much to work for recreational facilities for the youth of Denver, might even be more pleased by a scene that is regularly enacted by the site of a part of his mortal remains. A few years after Mrs. Lindsey disposed of the remainder of his ashes, an adjacent area became the location of an outdoor winter ice rink where succeeding generations of youngsters skate happily and unknowingly by the remains of the Kids' Judge of Denver.

NOTES

CHAPTER 1: THE MAKING OF A REFORMER

1. L. T. Lindsey to James Dinkins, July 11, 1865, Benjamin Barr Lindsey Collection (cited hereafter as BBLC), Manuscript Division, Library of Congress, Box 146. Judge Lindsey's two autobiographical works—*The Beast* (New York, 1910), written in collaboration with Harvey O'Higgins and cited hereafter by title only, and *The Dangerous Life* (New York, 1931), written in collaboration with Reuben Borough and cited hereafter by title only—are the chief sources of information about Lindsey's early years. BBLC is excellent for the years after 1901, when Lindsey became a judge, but has comparatively few materials on the earlier period. Unless otherwise indicated, the account of the pre-1901 period is drawn from *The Beast* and *The Dangerous Life*. *The Beast* has been reissued in the Americana Library series after being out of print for sixty years (Seattle and London, 1970).

2. Lindsey later observed, "The schooling I received there would amount to about the first year of high school." Lindsey to Selena S. Martin, October 24, 1907, BBLC, Box 11. Hereafter when the name Lindsey alone is used, the reference is to Ben B. Lindsey.

3. Lindsey's letters to his parents are located in BBLC, Box 79. *Cf.* especially Lindsey to L. T. Lindsey, October 28, 1884.

4. C. T. Bates to Lindsey, letter dated "February, 1888," BBLC, Box 79. Lindsey did not reveal his father's suicide in any of his published writings. The details about the discovery of the body and the manner of suicide are based on the author's interview with the late Mrs. Ben B. Lindsey, the Judge's widow, in Los Angeles, May 23, 1966.

5. It is not entirely clear why an attorney from the tramway company came to see Lindsey and Parks. Since a case involving the tramway company is discussed immediately afterward in both *The Beast* and *The Dangerous Life*, it is possible that the two cases were confused. Perhaps Stevenson acted as an emissary of the "corporation lawyer" who represented the surgeon.

6. Simply stated, the first two doctrines saved an admittedly negligent employer from payment of damages if the injured employee was also negligent, or if a second employee's negligence contributed to the accident. The assumption of risk doctrine held that an employee "assumed" the risk of certain types of accidents when he accepted a hazardous occupation.

7. *In re Senate Bill No. 142 to Regulate Jury Trials in Civil Cases*, 26 Colo 167, 56 Pac. 564 (1899).

8. *City of Denver v. Hyatt,* 28 Colo. 129, 63 Pac. 403 (1900).
9. C. T. Bates to Lindsey, April 10, 1890; C. T. Bates to Lindsey, December 23, 1894. BBLC, Boxes 79, 80.
10. C. T. Bates to L. T. Lindsey, August 23, 1886, BBLC, Box 79.

CHAPTER 2: THE KIDS' JUDGE

1. *The Beast,* p. 87.
2. Ibid., pp. 90–91. *Cronin v. City of Denver,* 29 Colo. 503, 69 Pac. 1124 (1902).
3. Lincoln Steffens, *Upbuilders* (New York, 1909), pp. 198–200.
4. *The Beast,* pp. 100–101. *Denver Post,* May 24, June 1, 1902.
5. Lindsey to Paul H., January 25, 1902, BBLC, Box 82.
6. *The Beast,* pp. 100–110; Steffens, *Upbuilders,* pp. 208–216.
7. Lindsey to Timothy D. Hurley, January 17, 1902, BBLC, Box 82; September 20, 1902, BBLC, Box 84. Hurley was editor of the *Chicago Juvenile Record* and chief probation officer in the Chicago court. Lindsey described his study of the Massachusetts and Illinois legislation in a letter to James F. Hill, a Michigan legislator, in a letter dated January 17, 1903, BBLC, Box 85.
8. For background materials on Lindsey's role in drafting the probate and juvenile laws of 1903, *cf.* Lindsey to County Judges Association, December 6, 1902, and numerous letters sent and received by the Judge, in BBLC, Box 1. *Cf.* "Remarks of Vice-President Hunt" and "Address by Judge Ben B. Lindsey: The New Probate Code," *Report of the Sixth Annual Meeting of the Colorado Bar Association, July 1–2, 1903,* vi (Denver, 1903), 43, 112–137.
9. The 1903 legislation, with commentaries by Judge Lindsey, is reprinted in *The Problem of the Children and How the State of Colorado Cares for Them* (Denver, 1904), and in Lindsey, ed., *The Juvenile Court Laws of the State of Colorado as in Force and as Proposed and Their Purpose Explained* (Denver, 1905). The legislative and judicial history of the laws after their enactment, as well as the later Lindsey bills, can be traced in James H. Pershing, "Juvenile Court Law and Procedure in Colorado," *Report of the Twenty-seventh Annual Meeting of the Colorado Bar Association, September 19–20, 1924,* xxvii (Denver, 1925), 232–297. Cf. Stanley H. Johnson, *The Juvenile Court of Denver, Colorado: Digest and Analysis of Its Law and Work* (Denver, 1933). In this chapter, unless otherwise indicated, I have used the Pershing account in tracing the history of the legislation. Direct quotations are from copies of the original bills, of which complete files are in BBLC, Boxes 290–297.
10. *Denver Post,* May 1, 1903. The force of the Adult Delinquency Law was briefly weakened in *Gibson v. People,* 44 Colo. 600, 99 Pac. 333 (1908), when the Supreme Court of Colorado construed the law to apply only against parents, guardians, or others having formal custody of the child. The constitutionality of the law was not questioned, however, and the legislature subsequently affirmed Lindsey's intention that the statute should be applied against *all* adults who contributed to a child's delinquency.
11. Lindsey to Lincoln Steffens, March 18, 1907, BBLC, Box 101.
12. 60 Colo. 230, 153 Pac. 224 (1915).
13. *Ex parte Songer,* 65 Colo. 466, 177 Pac. 141 (1918).

14. *Abbott v. People,* 91 Colo. 510, 16 Pac. 2d 435 (1932).
15. The legislature made no further effort to confer felony jurisdiction over adults on the Juvenile Court.
16. For a comparison of Lindsey's proposed 1905 dependency statute and the law finally enacted, *cf.* Lindsey, *The Juvenile Court Laws of the State of Colorado,* pp. 44–46, and *Session Laws of Colorado, 1905,* Chapter 81.
17. Author's interview with Judge Philip B. Gilliam, Denver, Colorado, August 5, 1966. The first state to adopt the chancery proceeding as a means of supervising parents was Kentucky, in 1907. Julian H. Mack, "The Juvenile Court," *Harvard Law Review,* xxiii (December 1909), 104.
18. For brief descriptions of the working of the Master of Discipline Act, *cf.* Lindsey to Thomas C. Hennings, March 7, 1914; Lindsey to Katherine B. Davis, March 3, 1920. BBLC, Boxes 45, 61. *Cf.* Pershing, *op. cit.,* pp. 270–272.
19. Lindsey to William Stapleton, editor of the *Denver Republican,* May 10, 1906, BBLC, Box 96.
20. Johnson, *op. cit.,* p. 26.
21. *The Beast,* pp. 110–111. *Denver Post,* August 3, 1904, August 21, 1905. Lindsey to superintendent of Denver Orphans' Home and to Mother Superior, St. Vincent's Orphanage, both dated June 27, 1905, BBLC, Box 4.
22. Judge William Healy, U.S. Court of Appeals, Ninth Circuit, to Mrs. Ben B. Lindsey, March 27, 1943, BBLC, Box 196.
23. Henry J. Haskell, "The 'Kid Judge' of Denver," *The Outlook,* lxx (June 24, 1905), 497. *Cf.* Frances M. Björkman, "The Children's Court in American City Life," *Review of Reviews,* xxxiii (March 1906), 305, for a different version of the same episode.
24. Lindsey to "Dear Boys," January 22, 1910, BBLC, Box 116.
25. Haskell, *op. cit.,* p. 498. Lindsey, "Some Experiences in the Juvenile Court of Denver," *Charities,* xi (November 1903), 403.
26. Steffens, *Upbuilders,* pp. 132–136. The chapter on Lindsey in *Upbuilders* is simply a reprint of the original Steffens articles entitled "Ben B. Lindsey: The Just Judge," which appeared in *McClure's Magazine* (October–December 1906), xxvii, 563–581; xxviii, 74–88, 162–176.
27. Lindsey to Judge George T. Gann, March 25, 1907, BBLC, Box 101.
28. Lindsey to Governor J. B. Orman, November 3, 1902; Orman to Lindsey, November 7, 1902. BBLC, Box 84.
29. *The Dangerous Life,* Chapters 6, 7. *Denver Post* and *Denver Times,* July 29, 1905. M. A. Capp, warden of the State Reformatory, to Lindsey, January 27, 1915; Lindsey to Alexander Nisbett, commissioner of safety of Denver, January 29, 1915. BBLC, Box 50. The records of the State Industrial School and the Juvenile Court contain no precise figures or references concerning this practice.
30. On the factual background of the Wright case and Lindsey's role in it, *cf.* the majority and dissenting opinions of the Colorado Supreme Court in *Lindsey v. People,* 66 Colo. 343, 181 Pac. 531 (1919) and "Can a Child Trust the Law?: The Case of Judge Lindsey," *The Outlook,* cx (August 11, 1915) 845. The legal aspects of Lindsey's fine are discussed in "Must We Recognize a New Privilege in the Law of Evidence?" *Harvard Law Review,* xxxii (November 1919), 88, and in "Note," *Yale Law Journal,* xxix (January 1920)

356. On Upton Sinclair's suggestion that newsboys pay the fine, *cf.* Lindsey to Upton Sinclair, November 27, 1915, BBLC, Box 51. The poem appeared in the *Brooklyn Eagle,* November 20, 1915.

31. Lindsey to Annie Besant, October 6, 1909, BBLC, Box 22. The claim of the Juvenile Court of Denver to be regarded as the first juvenile *and* domestic relations court is based on the Lindsey laws giving it the power to deal with parents and other responsible adults contributing to delinquency or dependency. *Cf.* Charles L. Chute, "The Juvenile Court in Retrospect," *Federal Probation,* XIII (September 1949), 4.

CHAPTER 3: FIGHTING THE ESTABLISHMENT

1. Lindsey to Board of Commissioners, May 5, 15, 22, 1902, BBLC, Box 83.
2. *Rocky Mountain News,* June 11, 1902. *The Beast,* pp. 113, *passim.*
3. *The Beast,* p. 124 (Lindsey's italics).
4. *Ibid.,* p. 127.
5. *Ibid.,* pp. 35–36, 44, 209, *passim.* Lindsey qualified some of his criticisms of the Supreme Court. He expressly commended the dissenting record of his old friend Justice Steele. Of Chief Justice Campbell, who had written the opinion invalidating the eight-hour law, Lindsey commented: "No charge of corruption against Judge [*sic*] Campbell is here made or implied. Even the laboring men . . . recognized that Judge Campbell's decisions were those of an honest prejudice, due to his training and his temperament." *Ibid.,* p. 213 n. On Campbell's economic conservatism, *cf.* David Lonsdale, "The Fight for the Eight Hour Day," *Colorado Magazine,* XLIII (Fall 1966), 339–353.
6. *The Beast,* pp. 91–93.
7. In Lindsey's two partial autobiographies, *The Beast* and *The Dangerous Life,* he used the fictitious name Charles Gardener in lieu of Fred Parks. In both books he stated that he did so "for old times' sake." The explanation is not satisfactory, since the identity of the Judge's partner was common knowledge in close-knit Denver, a fact attested by Parks's strong public reaction to Lindsey's charges against him, as reported in the Denver press. *Cf. Denver Post,* September 19, 1909, for Parks's comments.
8. *The Beast,* Chapter 10.
9. *Ibid.,* pp. 188–202.
10. "The Beast and the Jungle" appeared in *Everybody's Magazine* (October 1909–May 1910), XXI, 431–452, 579–596, 770–784; XXII, 41–53, 231–244, 391–406, 528–540, 632–644. On Sinclair's part in its publication, *cf.* Upton Sinclair, *The Autobiography of Upton Sinclair* (New York, 1962), p. 148.
11. *The Beast,* pp. 3–4.
12. *Ibid.,* pp. 151–152.
13. Lindsey to William Allen White, July 3, 1911, BBLC, Box 32.
14. Lindsey to Billy Sunday, September 15, 1909, and January 18, 1915, BBLC, Boxes 49, 22.
15. Lindsey to Julia Lathrop, October 24, 1907, BBLC, Box 11.
16. *Rocky Mountain News,* March 10, 1906. Lindsey to Joseph W. Folk, June 8, 1914, BBLC, Box 46.

17. Dalton Brown to Lindsey, October 22, 1909, BBLC, Box 112.

18. Anna Louise Strong to Lindsey, October 27, 1911, BBLC, Box 34. Carl D. Thompson to Lindsey, November 9, 1909, BBLC, Box 112. Upton Sinclair to Lindsey, October 18, 1908, BBLC, Box 106.

19. *Rocky Mountain News,* July 28, 1907.

20. Lindsey to Anna Louise Strong, October 31, 1911, BBLC, Box 34. *Cf.* Lindsey to L. M. Hodges, May 25, 1907; BBLC, Box 100.

21. *The Beast,* pp. 154–156. Steffens, *Upbuilders,* p. 203.

22. *Rocky Mountain News,* December 1, 1902. Arthur Bray to Lindsey, December 17, 1902, BBLC, Box 1. Lindsey, "Child Labor Legislation and Methods of Enforcement in the Western States," *Annals of the American Academy of Political and Social Science,* xxiii (May 1905), 97–98.

23. *Burcher v. People,* 41 Col. 497, 93 Pac. 15 (1907).

24. *Colorado Statutes Annotated,* iii (Denver, 1911), 2569, 2583. On Lindsey's role in drafting and lobbying for the law, *cf.* E. K. MacColl, "John Franklin Shafroth, Reform Governor of Colorado, 1909–1913," *The Colorado Magazine,* xxix (January 1952), 43, and Lindsey to Helen H. Lytle, May 24, 1920, BBLC, Box 62.

25. Lindsey, "The Mothers' Compensation Law of Colorado," *The Survey,* xxix (February 15, 1913), 716; *The Dangerous Life,* pp. 340–341 n. Neither the Child Labor Act of 1911 nor the Mothers' Compensation Act of 1913 was a complete victory for Lindsey. In the former law, he had to accept elimination of protection for children working in the beet fields in order to obtain its passage. The Mothers' Compensation Act required appropriations, and the legislature did not create the fund to carry out some of the law's intentions for six years.

26. An excellent and thorough account of the strike is Graham Adams, Jr., *Age of Industrial Violence, 1910–1915* (New York and London, 1966), pp. 146–175.

27. For a reliable survey of President Wilson's ineffectual role in the strike, *cf.* Arthur S. Link, *Wilson: The New Freedom* (Princeton, 1956), pp. 457–459.

28. Lindsey to George W. Perkins, May 17, 1914, BBLC, Box 285.

29. Lindsey to E. W. Scripps, May 22, 1914; Jane Addams to Lindsey, June 10, 1914. BBLC, Box 285.

30. *New York Times,* May 23, 1914. It appears that Lindsey's Denver office erroneously informed the *Times* that a meeting had been set.

31. *Ibid.,* May 24, 1914.

32. *Ibid.,* May 29, 1914. For the complete transcript of the hearings, *cf. Final Report and Testimony Submitted to Congress by the Commission on Industrial Relations,* 64th Congress, 1st Session, Sen. Doc. 415 (Washington D.C., 1916).

33. *New York Times,* May 23, 26, and 29, 1914. Upton Sinclair returned to New York City, picketed the Rockefeller offices, and was sent to jail for three days. *Cf.* Sinclair, *Autobiography,* p. 200.

34. Lindsey to E. W. Scripps, June 16, 1914; Lindsey to William Allen White, June 15, 1914. BBLC, Box 138. A reprint of "Remarks" by the Hon. George J. Kindel in *Congressional Record,* June 13, 1914, may be found in BBLC, Box 285.

CHAPTER 4: A NATIONAL FIGURE

1. Clipping from *The Outlook* dated June 24, 1905, BBLC, Scrapbook 3.

2. Lindsey, "My Recollections of My First Speech," unpublished manuscript dated February 28, 1914, BBLC, Box 137.

3. Peter G. Slater has very perceptively analyzed the inconsistencies in Lindsey's writings on the nature of the child but, in the opinion of this writer, underestimates the dominance and persistence of the environmentalist motif in the Judge's writings. *Cf.* Peter G. Slater, "Ben Lindsey and the Juvenile Court of Denver: A Progressive Looks at Human Nature," *American Quarterly,* xx (Summer 1968), 211–223.

4. Lindsey, "Moral Training," *Journal of Proceedings and Addresses of the Forty-seventh Annual Meeting of the National Education Association* (Winona, Minn., 1909), p. 943. Lindsey, "Childhood and Morality," *ibid.,* p. 150.

5. Lindsey to Elbert Hubbard, Jr., May 29, 1915, BBLC, Box 46.

6. Lindsey, "Moral Training," p. 942.

7. *Ibid.,* p. 941.

8. Walter Lippmann, *A Preface to Politics* (New York, 1913), p. 254.

9. *The Dangerous Life,* pp. 177–178.

10. *Denver Post,* November 25, 1902.

11. Clipping from the *Toledo* (Ohio) *News-Bee* dated "February, 1908," BBLC, Scrapbook 9. The interview dealing with industrial safety legislation appeared in a clipping from the *Laramie* (Wyoming) *Boomerang* dated February 15, 1909, BBLC, Scrapbook 10.

12. Lincoln Steffens to Lindsey, March 18, 1906; S. S. McClure to Lindsey, June 25, 1906, BBLC, Box 7.

13. Jacob Riis to Lindsey, April 14, 1904, BBLC, Box 88. Lindsey to Riis, October 17, 1904; Lindsey to Theodore Roosevelt, December 9, 1904; Lindsey to Riis, January 13, 1905. BBLC, Box 3. A. H. Lewis, ed., *A Compilation of the Messages and Speeches of Theodore Roosevelt, 1901–1905* (Washington, D.C., 1906), p. 838.

14. A. E. Winship to Lindsey, May 24, 1906, BBLC, Box 97. E. A. Fredenhagen to Lindsey, April 21, 1905, BBLC, Box 3. Lindsey to John H. Greusel, December 24, 1907, BBLC, Box 13. A year after the adoption of the first "Lindsey bills" in Colorado, the Judge counted forty-four addresses in thirteen states given in support of them. *Denver Post,* March 20, 1904.

15. Grace Abbott, "Abstract of Juvenile Court Laws," in S. P. Breckinridge and Edith Abbott, *The Delinquent Child and the Home* (New York, 1912), pp. 247, 263–264. S. P. Breckinridge and Helen R. Jeter, *A Summary of Juvenile Court Legislation in the United States* (Washington, D.C., 1920), p. 1. Lindsey to Lincoln Steffens, May 31, 1906, Lincoln Steffens Collection, Columbia University, New York City.

16. *New York World,* April 22, 1910. Grace A. Johnson to Lindsey, March 2, 1911, BBLC, Box 126.

17. *Cf.* Aileen S. Kraditor, *The Ideas of the Woman Suffrage Movement, 1890–1920* (New York and London, 1965), especially Chapter 3.

18. Lindsey to Hans P. Freece, June 23, 1908, BBLC, Box 16. Lindsey to

Ida M. Tarbell, March 25, 1909; Lindsey to H. H. Gerardy, January 25, 1909. BBLC, Box 19. Lindsey to George Creel, February 16, 1915, BBLC, Box 140.

19. Lindsey to Mrs. Frances P. Parks, June 5, 1912, BBLC, Box 145.

20. Broadside, National Purity League, 1909, BBLC, Box 112. Announcement, American Anti-Cigarette League, May 29, 1904, BBLC, Box 2.

21. Henry F. May, *The End of American Innocence* (New York, 1959), pp. 9, *passim*. Lindsey to J. H. Finney, November 15, 1912, BBLC, Box 40.

22. Lindsey to editor of the *Salida Mail,* October 31, 1903, BBLC, Box 85. Lindsey to Florence Weaver, June 15, 1907, BBLC, Box 10.

23. Lindsey to E. W. Scripps, November 2, 1912, BBLC, Box 35.

24. Lincoln Steffens, *The Autobiography of Lincoln Steffens* (New York, 1931), p. 571.

25. Francis Heney to Lindsey, June 9, 1908; Lindsey to Lincoln Steffens, June 22, 1908. BBLC, Box 104.

26. Lincoln Steffens to Brand Whitlock, April 25, 1910, quoted in Ella Winter and Granville Hicks, eds., *The Letters of Lincoln Steffens* (New York, 1938), I, 245. Steffens, *Autobiography,* p. 571.

27. Lindsey to Kate Campbell Robertson, June 8, 1914, BBLC, Box 138. Lindsey to Anti–Capital Punishment Society of America, January 9, 1915, BBLC, Box 140.

28. Lindsey to Lincoln Steffens, June 30, 1906, BBLC, Box 126.

29. Brand Whitlock to Lindsey, January 8, 1910, quoted in Allan Nevins, ed., *The Letters and Journal of Brand Whitlock* (New York and London, 1936), I, 127–128. Jacob Riis to Lindsey, December 29, 1909; Lindsey to Mrs. Robert M. LaFollette, December 4, 1909; George W. Musser to Lindsey, December 20, 1909. BBLC, Box 114.

30. "A Reformed Boy" to Lindsey, November 2, 1909, BBLC, Box 28. Mutual Improvement League to Lindsey, August 2, 1912, BBLC, Box 39. Beryl B to Lindsey, January 24, 1909, BBLC, Box 19.

31. Lindsey to Max Eastman, May 25, 1915, BBLC, Box 141. Lindsey to Alexander Berkman, April 18, 1916, BBLC, Box 142. Lindsey to A. J McKelway, August 13, 1909, BBLC, Box 21. Lindsey to Thomas A. Edison February 8, 1915, BBLC, Box 140.

32. Edward L. Thorndike to Lindsey, September 28, 1904, BBLC, Box 4 Lindsey to G. Stanley Hall, February 10, 1908, BBLC, Box 103. Lindsey to E. W. Scripps, March 22, 1911, BBLC, Box 126.

33. Fola La Follette to Lindsey, October 2, 1910, BBLC, Box 122.

CHAPTER 5: THE BULL MOUSE AND COLORADO PROGRESSIVISM

1. *The Beast,* pp. 233–236. *Denver Post,* April 5, 1905. The headless ball (also called the Massachusetts ballot), by listing candidates according to offi rather than by party, was supposed to discourage voting the straight par ticket.

2. Colin B. Goodykoontz, ed., *Papers of Edward P. Costigan Relating the Progressive Movement in Colorado, 1902–1917* (Boulder, Colo., 1941), P 13–14.

3. Oliver Knight, ed., *I Protest: Selected Disquisitions of E. W. Scripps* (Madison, Wisc., 1966), p. 186. Copies of a part of the Causey-Scripps correspondence relating to the origins of the *Denver Express* are found in BBLC, Box 95. *Cf.* Goodykoontz, *op. cit.,* pp. 22, 206, 262.

4. Lindsey to Alva Adams, July 3, 1906; Alva Adams to Lindsey, July 13, 1906. BBLC, Box 7.

5. *The Beast,* pp. 265–267. Lindsey to Lincoln Steffens, August 23, 1906, BBLC, Box 8. *Denver Post,* August 21, 1906. *Rocky Mountain News,* August 22, 1906.

6. *The Beast,* pp. 270, *passim. Denver Post,* October 5, 1906. Lindsey to Lincoln Steffens, October 14, 1906, BBLC, Box 129.

7. Lindsey to Joseph W. Folk, Lindsey to Robert M. La Follette, November 16, 1904. BBLC, Box 3.

8. Lindsey to Theodore Roosevelt, August 1, 1916, BBLC, Box 53. Theodore Roosevelt to Lindsey, August 11, 1916, BBLC, Box 143.

9. Robert M. La Follette to Lindsey, September 22, 1910, BBLC, Box 122. George Mowry, *Theodore Roosevelt and the Progressive Movement* (Madison, Wisc., 1946), p. 127.

10. Lindsey to "Dear Bunch," March 11, 1912, BBLC, Box 132. The italics are Lindsey's.

11. Lindsey to Lincoln Steffens, November 7, 1908, BBLC, Box 17. Same to same, November 21, 1908, BBLC, Box 106. The *Rocky Mountain News* and the *Times* also eventually endorsed Lindsey.

12. Lindsey to William Allen White, May 28, 1910, BBLC, Box 119.

13. Lindsey to Brand Whitlock, December 14, 1911, Brand Whitlock Papers, Manuscript Division, Library of Congress, Box 24.

14. Lindsey to William F. McCombs, October 26, 1911, BBLC, Box 129. McCombs to Lindsey, October 31, 1911, BBLC, Box 34. Lindsey to E. W. Scripps, November 2, 1911, BBLC, Box 34.

15. Lindsey to Robert M. La Follette, October 26, 1911, BBLC, Box 129.

16. Lincoln Steffens to Lindsey, October 10, 1910, BBLC, Box 28. *Denver Express,* August 30, 1910. Upton Sinclair to Lindsey, September 10, 1910, BBLC, Box 122.

17. Lindsey to Theodore Roosevelt, November 2, 1911, BBLC, Box 129. Roosevelt to Lindsey, December 5, 1911, BBLC, Box 130.

18. Knight, *I Protest,* p. 355.

19. E. W. Scripps to Lindsey, January 4, 1912, BBLC, Box 35.

20. Edward P. Costigan to Lindsey, April 16, 1912, BBLC, Box 36. In this letter, written at Lindsey's request, Costigan included an excerpt from a letter he had written on the subject to J. S. Temple on February 6, 1912.

21. Woodrow Wilson to Lindsey, February 28, 1912, BBLC, Box 131.

22. Lindsey to E. W. Scripps, April 8, 1912; Lindsey to Hiram Johnson, April 10, 1912. BBLC, Box 132. Knight, *I Protest,* p. 449.

23. Lindsey to Theodore Roosevelt, February 8, 1912, BBLC, Box 131. Lindsey to Gifford Pinchot, April 26, 1912, Gifford Pinchot Papers, Manuscript Division, Library of Congress, Box 154. Medill McCormick to Lindsey, May 24, 1912, BBLC, Box 37. Theodore Roosevelt to Lindsey, July 20, 1912, BBLC, Box 132.

24. Lindsey to E. W. Scripps, December 29, 1911, BBLC, Box 130.

25. *Rocky Mountain News,* June 26, 1912. Lindsey to Gilson Gardner, June 4, 1912, BBLC, Box 38. Goodykoontz, *op. cit.,* Chapter 4, *passim.*

26. Lindsey to William Allen White, November 22, 1912, BBLC, Box 40. The Colorado Supreme Court subsequently declared the recall of the judicial decisions measure unconstitutional. *Cf.* Duane A. Smith, "Colorado and Judicial Recall," *American Journal of Legal History,* VII (April 1963), 198–209, which describes Lindsey's role in preparing the bill.

27. Allen F. Davis, *Spearheads for Reform: The Social Settlements and the Progressive Movement, 1890–1914* (New York, 1967), p. 206. *Rocky Mountain News,* January 9, 1913. Lindsey to George Perkins, February 4, 1914, BBLC, Box 45. Lindsey to Hiram Johnson, January 9, 1915, BBLC, Box 49.

CHAPTER 6: OVER THERE

1. Handbill, *Friends of Russian Freedom.* Lindsey to J. S. Temple, December 11, 1908. BBLC, Boxes 9, 107.

2. Lindsey to David Starr Jordan, December 19, 1912, BBLC, Box 41.

3. *New York Times,* November 25, 1915. Rosika Schwimmer to Mrs. Ben B. Lindsey, April 1, 1943, BBLC, Box 197. A definitive history of the Ford Peace Expedition is yet to be written. For a low-keyed but reliable brief account, see Allan Nevins and Frank Ernest Hill, *Ford: Expansion and Challenge, 1915–1933* (New York, 1957), Chapter 2. Louis P. Lochner, *Henry Ford: America's Don Quixote* (New York, 1925) is an account by a principal participant. Burnet Hershey, *The Odyssey of Henry Ford and the Great Peace Ship* (New York, 1967) is a lively journalistic account. I am indebted to Edith Wynner of New York City, who is completing a biography of Rosika Schwimmer, for access to the Schwimmer-Lloyd Collection in the New York Public Library, which has numerous press clippings on all aspects of the trip and its aftermath.

4. Lindsey to Anne Morgan and Theodore Roosevelt, November 27, 1915, BBLC, Box 51.

5. Theodore Roosevelt to Lindsey, November 30, 1915, BBLC, Box 51. Lindsey to Henry Ford, November 25–28, 1915, Ford Peace Plan Papers, Library of Congress, Boxes 1, 2.

6. Lindsey to Anne Morgan, November 27, 1915; Lindsey to Charles A. Beard, November 30, 1915. BBLC, Box 51.

7. *Denver Post* and *New York Times,* April 13, 1915. Lindsey to Harvey O'Higgins, May 25, 1915, BBLC, Box 141. *Cf.* affidavits and memoranda relating to the Women's Protective League and reprints of its circulars, in Women's Protective League File, BBLC, Box 289.

8. Upton Sinclair to Lindsey, June 1915; Charles and Mary Beard to Lindsey, June 15, 1915. BBLC, Box 50. The *Denver Post,* October 26, 1915, refers to an offer of $17,000.

9. Roger W. Babson to Louis Lochner, November 30, 1915, Ford Peace Plan Papers, Library of Congress, Box 2.

10. Henry Ford to Members of the Party (Lindsey's copy), December 11, 1915, BBLC, Box 141. Elmer Davis to Lindsey, April 26, 1931, BBLC, Box 167. R. B. Bermann to Central News, Ltd., December 13, 1915, Ford Peace Plan Papers, Library of Congress, Box 4.

11. Lindsey to E. G. Liebold, March 31, 1916, BBLC, Box 53. Lindsey to E. G. Liebold, September 15, 1916; Lindsey to Harvey O'Higgins, September 20, 1916. BBLC, Box 143. George Creel to Lindsey, October 20, 1916, BBLC, Box 144.

12. *Washington Post,* February 6, 1916. *Denver Post,* March 12, 1916.

13. Lindsey to George Creel, July 27, 1916, BBLC, Box 143. Lindsey to E. W. Scripps, November 13, 1917, BBLC, Box 57.

14. Lindsey to George Creel, October 17, 1917, BBLC, Box 57. British Bureau of Information to Lindsey, October 17, 1918, BBLC, Box 146.

15. Ben B. Lindsey and Harvey O'Higgins, *The Doughboy's Religion and Other Aspects of Our Day* (New York, 1920), pp. 35, *passim.*

16. *Ibid.,* pp. 7–8, *passim.*

CHAPTER 7: PROPHET OF THE JAZZ AGE

1. It is also quite likely that he was motivated by a desire to supplement his modest judicial salary, which never exceeded $4,000 a year, by means less arduous than chautauqua lecturing.

2. Frederick Lewis Allen's delightful *Only Yesterday* (New York, 1931) still provides the best social history of the sexual revolution of the twenties. Two contemporary treatments of the subject, which drew heavily on Lindsey, were V. F. Calverton, *The Bankruptcy of Marriage* (New York, 1928) and Floyd Dell, *Love in the Machine Age* (New York, 1931).

3. Lindsey, "Why Girls Go Wrong," *Ladies' Home Journal,* xxiv (January 1907), 13.

4. May, *The End of American Innocence,* especially Part Four.

5. Lindsey to F. A. Davis Company, July 1, 1912, BBLC, Box 39.

6. Havelock Ellis, *Sex in Relation to Society* (Philadelphia, 1910), pp. 63, 190, 413, 443, 505, *passim.*

7. Lippmann, *op. cit.,* Chapter 5, *passim.*

8. Lindsey to Walter Lippmann, November 10, 1913; Walter Lippmann to Lindsey, November 20, 1913. BBLC, Boxes 43, 136.

9. Harvey O'Higgins and E. H. Reede, *The American Mind in Action* (New York, 1924). *Cf.* Harvey O'Higgins, "In Praise of Hypocrisy," *The Outlook,* cli (January 16, 1929), 522–526, 556–557, which contains favorable references to Judge Lindsey as an advocate of "the New Sex."

10. The journalist was William L. Chenery, whom the author interviewed at Big Sur, California, December 14, 1964. The second conversation was with Lindsey's literary collaborator, Wainwright Evans, at La Luz, New Mexico, February 5, 1969.

11. Conversation with Wainwright Evans, La Luz, New Mexico, February 4, 1969.

12. Here, as elsewhere, I refer to all opinions and anecdotes in the Judge's books as his alone, since Evans, though he did all the actual writing and was listed as co-author, kept himself entirely out of the text.

13. Ben B. Lindsey and Wainwright Evans, *The Revolt of Modern Youth* (New York, 1925), pp. 32–33, 157.

14. *Ibid.,* pp. 186–187.

15. *Ibid.,* pp. 123–127.

16. *Ibid.,* pp. 198–200.
17. *Ibid.,* p. 125.
18. *Ibid.,* p. 127.
19. *Ibid.,* pp. 15, 291–292.
20. *Ibid.,* pp. 358–359. Ironically, *The Revolt* appeared at a time when eugenics was coming under strong attack by natural scientists and sociologists. Thus, what Lindsey was presenting as the wave of the future was already being regarded as dogmatic and old-fashioned in scientific circles. *Cf.* especially Chapter 11, "The Decline of Galtonian Eugenics in the United States," in Donald K. Pickens, *Eugenics and the Progressives* (Nashville, 1968).
21. Lindsey and Evans, *The Companionate Marriage* (New York, 1927). The title used for the articles was "The Moral Revolt." The book title, *The Companionate Marriage,* is used hereafter to refer to the articles and the book interchangeably. Bertrand Russell to Lindsey, April 26, 1927, BBLC, Box 154. Conversation with Wainwright Evans, La Luz, New Mexico, August 15, 1970.

CHAPTER 8: COMPANIONATE MARRIAGE: IMAGE AND REALITY

1. Julian Messner to Lindsey, October 29, 1927, BBLC, Box 158. *Omaha World-Herald,* April 4, 1928. Unidentified United Press clipping dated March 1, 1928, BBLC, Scrapbook 29.
2. M. M. Knight, "The Companionate and the Family: The Unobserved Division of an Historical Institution," *Journal of Social Hygiene,* IV (May 1924), 257–267. M. M. Knight, "Companionate Marriage," *Encyclopedia of the Social Sciences* (New York, 1935), IV, 113–115. The present writer was a student and graduate assistant of Professor Knight at the University of California, Berkeley, in 1945.
3. Wainwright Evans to Lindsey, February 2, March 17, 1927, BBLC, Boxes 154–155. Lindsey to Wainwright Evans, May 9, 1927; Wainwright Evans to "Dear Henrietta and the Judge," July 15, 1927. BBLC, Boxes 156–157.
4. *The Companionate Marriage,* Preface, p. v.
5. *Ibid.,* pp. 139–141. *The Revolt of Modern Youth,* pp. 175–176.
6. *The Companionate Marriage,* pp. 243, *passim.*
7. *Ibid.,* pp. 257, *passim.*
8. *Ibid.,* pp. 21–31.
9. *Los Angeles Examiner,* May 13, 1928 (emphasis added). *St. Louis Star,* March 20, 1928. The cartoon of the black and white children, which is not identified as to source, appears in BBLC, Scrapbook 29. Will Rogers' comment appeared in his daily squib in more than fifty newspapers (*e.g.,* the *New York Times*) on March 30, 1928.
10. Lindsey to Wainwright Evans, September 20, 1926 (personal letter in possession of Mr. Evans). *San Francisco News,* January 10, 1928. *Seattle Star,* March 9, 1927.
11. X to Lindsey, March 15, 1927, BBLC, Box 155.
12. The letters from private sources, both friendly and hostile, are found chiefly in BBLC, Boxes 72–77, 153–164. The letter quoted is dated March 12, 1927, and is in Box 155.

13. *Saturday Review of Literature,* IV (December 24, 1927), 468. Walter Lippmann, *A Preface to Morals* (New York, 1929), pp. 309, *passim.*

14. Miss Addams' remarks appeared in an unidentified press clipping dated March 28, 1927, BBLC, Scrapbook 27. The duty of the state to try to save marriages, especially when children were involved, was one of Lindsey's most fervent convictions. *Cf.* Lindsey, "The House of Human Welfare," *The Forum,* LXXVIII (December 1927), 101, and *The Companionate Marriage,* pp. 259–260.

15. X to Lindsey, October 9, 1928 (spelling and punctuation in the original), BBLC, Box 76.

16. Lindsey to X, October 18, 1928, BBLC, Box 76.

17. X to Lindsey, March 14, 1927, BBLC, Box 73.

18. Lindsey to Upton Sinclair, May 7, 1929, BBLC, Box 77. In 1930, a federal Court of Appeals reversed Mrs. Dennett's conviction. The case was a turning point in the direction of a more liberal construction of federal anti–birth control laws and regulations. *Cf.* Sidney Ditzion, *Marriage, Morals and Sex in America* (New York, 1953), pp. 395–396.

19. Lindsey to X, August 22, 1928, BBLC, Box 161. Lindsey to X, October 17, 1928 (Lindsey's emphasis), BBLC, Box 162.

20. Havelock Ellis to Lindsey, March 20, 1927, BBLC, Box 155. Bertrand Russell to Lindsey, April 26, 1927, BBLC, Box 154.

CHAPTER 9: "THE BLUE MENACE"

1. *Springfield* (Mass.) *Republican,* March 20, 1928. *Cf.* Norman Hapgood, ed., *Professional Patriots* (New York, 1928), pp. 8–9, *passim.*

2. *The Companionate Marriage,* pp. 320, 372. For a treatment of the disillusionment of some prewar Progressives regarding Prohibition, see Andrew Sinclair, *Prohibition: The Era of Excess* (Boston, 1962), pp. 311–312. For Lindsey's views on Prohibition as class discrimination, see *Rocky Mountain News,* October 9, 1921; *Denver Express,* October 22, 1921.

3. *The Beast,* pp. 228, 245.

4. Lindsey to William Allen White, June 19, 1914, BBLC, Box 138.

5. *The Revolt of Modern Youth,* pp. 166–167, 282. *The Companionate Marriage,* p. 181.

6. *The Revolt of Modern Youth,* p. 293 (Lindsey's emphasis).

7. *The Companionate Marriage,* p. 223. Richard Hofstadter, *Anti-Intellectualism in American Life* (New York, 1964), p. 121.

8. *The Companionate Marriage,* pp. 383–384. *The Revolt of Modern Youth,* p. 313.

9. *The Companionate Marriage,* p. 206.

10. Lindsey to H. G. Wells, May 14, 1927, BBLC, Box 156. *Portland* (Oregon) *Journal,* April 28, 1928. *Chicago Tribune* (European edition), July 1, 1929.

11. James T. Farrell, *The Young Manhood of Studs Lonigan* (New York, 1934), Chapter 21.

12. The Judge followed the common practice of American courts by cooperating with private charitable and religious institutions of the same faith as the dependent children's parents. Thus he attempted to place Catholic chil-

dren in Catholic homes just as he tried to place Jewish and Protestant children in homes of their faiths.

13. Although a book-length treatment of the Klan in Colorado has not yet been written, three excellent, useful scholarly studies are David M. Chalmers, *Hooded Americanism: The First Century of the Ku Klux Klan* (Garden City, New York, 1965), Chapter 18; Kenneth T. Jackson, *The Ku Klux Klan in the City, 1915–1930* (New York, 1967), Chapter 15; James H. Davis, "Colorado Under the Klan," *The Colorado Magazine*, XLII (Spring 1965), 93–108. Also helpful is Lindsey's own published account, "My Fight with the Ku Klux Klan," *Survey Graphic*, LIV (June 1, 1925), 271–274, 319–321.

14. R. E. Strickland to L. D. Wade, Imperial Kligrapp, Knights of the Ku Klux Klan, January 25, 1922. A facsimile of the letter may be found in BBLC, Box 151. Lindsey also quoted a part of the letter in the article for *Survey Graphic* referred to above. He did not indicate how a copy came into his possession. Given the record of the Klan's campaign against him, there is no particular reason to doubt the authenticity of the letter.

15. *New York World,* June 1, 1924.

16. *People ex rel. Graham et al. v. Lindsey,* 80 Colo. 465, 253 Pac. 465 (1927), the crucial decision by the Supreme Court of Colorado, contains a fairly extensive summary of the original trial. The *Denver Post,* April 1–17, 1925, is extremely helpful in following the trial. Various briefs and transcripts are available in the State Archives of Colorado, Denver. I am deeply indebted to Philip Hornbein, Jr., of Denver for a copy of the printed brief submitted to the Supreme Court of the United States in the petition for certiorari; it contains a transcript of the proceedings in the trial court. A good brief summary of all the litigation appears in the *New York Times,* January 25, 1927. For Judge Lindsey's version, *cf. The Dangerous Life,* pp. 393–395, *passim.*

17. Justice Charles Butler was ill, however, and did not participate in the decision. Two members of the Court still dissented on the propriety of Mrs. Graham's being allowed to sue but concurred in the opinion of the Court that all votes cast in J-6 ought to be invalidated.

18. Justice Sheafor's language was not always a model of precision. Although he took as his premise the claim that fraud had been committed in J-6, he also asserted that election irregularities could be so enormous, as they were in this case, that "it is not necessary that actual fraud be committed." Sheafor did not explain the difference between "fraud" and "actual fraud."

19. Havelock Ellis to Lindsey, April 26, 1927, BBLC, Box 155.

20. Roscoe Pound to Lindsey, May 6, 1927, BBLC, Box 156.

21. O. N. Hilton to Lindsey, July 11, July 28, 1927, BBLC, Box 156. In the earlier letter, Hilton refers to Unter's "full statement" of confession made on March 24, 1927.

22. The original copy of the Unter "confession" is located in BBLC, Box 157. It is accompanied by a corroborative statement signed by one Howard Kebler, who allegedly served as Unter's "guard" while he was under the control of Denver authorities and Klansmen. The Kebler and Unter statements are adequately summarized in an account in the *Denver Post,* September 18, 1927. It is not clear why more than a month elapsed before they were released to the press.

CHAPTER 10: DEFEAT

1. *Rocky Mountain News,* July, 10, 1927.

2. *Denver Post,* July 10, September 14, September 17, 1927. *The Dangerous Life,* p. 398. *Denver Post,* September 19, 1927. *Rocky Mountain News,* October 3, 1927.

3. For testimony regarding Van Cise's initiation of the Lindsey disbarment, see Respondent's Brief *Contra* Motion for Judgment on the Pleadings, No. 12130, Supreme Court of Colorado, n.d., pp. 42–43, State Archives of Colorado, Denver, Colorado.

4. For a good summary of the Stokes settlement and the events leading to it, see *New York Times,* July 30, 1926.

5. *Ibid.,* June 26, 1926.

6. *Ibid.,* July 30, 1926. There is an interesting exchange of letters between Lindsey and Untermyer in which Untermyer reminded Lindsey that the decision made in Untermyer's office to attack the validity of the transfer of assets by Stokes, Sr., was responsible for "at least 85% of the final recovery." Nevertheless, Untermyer added, "your aid to her was of real value." The New York lawyer went on to chide Lindsey gently for having been willing to settle for considerably less, but Lindsey denied having so advised Mrs. Stokes. In spite of this disagreement, the Lindsey-Untermyer exchange was quite cordial. Samuel Untermyer to Lindsey, December 2, 1926; Lindsey to Samuel Untermyer, December 6, 1926. BBLC, Box 153.

7. Untermyer's letter to Lindsey accompanying the $10,000 check stated, in part: "Regardless of the fact that my *voluntary* offer to you was on the basis of a settlement that did not materialize in its entirety, and in recognition of your assistance and of my regard and friendship for you, I am herewith enclosing you my check . . . as originally arranged between us." (Emphasis added.) Samuel Untermyer to Lindsey, December 2, 1926, BBLC, Box 153. Although Untermyer may have used the word "voluntary" to protect himself against any future claims, the word would seem to give support to Lindsey's later contention that the idea of a "gift," as Lindsey called it, or a "fee," as Van Cise called it, originated unilaterally with Untermyer. It should also be noted that this letter was written almost a year before Van Cise commenced proceedings against Lindsey.

8. The colloquy is quoted in full by Justice Butler of the Colorado Supreme Court in his dissenting opinion in the 1933 reinstatement case cited in note 11, below. *Cf. The Dangerous Life,* pp. 403–404.

9. The only options left would be to ask the Supreme Court to reverse itself, in effect, by petitioning for a rehearing, or to try to find a federal ground on which to bring the case to the Supreme Court of the United States. Both options had been tried unsuccessfully in the ouster case. In the disbarment case Lindsey decided, probably correctly, that either approach would be futile.

10. *People ex rel. Colorado Bar Association v. Lindsey,* 86 Colo. 458, 283 Pac. 539 (1929).

11. *People ex rel. Colorado Bar Association v. Lindsey,* 93 Colo. 41, 23 P. 2d. 118 (1933). Chief Justice Whitford was off the court by 1933. A newly elected Justice, Benjamin Hilliard, also dissented from the court's refusal to

reinstate Lindsey and expressed his general agreement with Butler's views on the merits of the original disbarment. For reasons stated below, in Chapter 11, it is more appropriate to treat Justice Hilliard's separate dissenting opinion in another context.

12. Clarence Darrow to Lindsey, December 17, 1929, BBLC, Box 164.

13. John Dewey to Lindsey, December 15, 1929, BBLC, Box 164.

14. Roger Baldwin to Lindsey, December 10, 1929, BBLC, Box 164.

15. Bertrand Russell to Lindsey, January 14, 1930, BBLC, Box 165.

16. Lincoln Steffens to Lindsey, December 22, 1929, BBLC, Box 78.

17. Lindsey to Wanda Munson, July 27, 1920, BBLC, Box 63. Lindsey to E. Haldemann-Julius, April 18, 1926, BBLC, Box 153. Ruth Biery, "Judge Lindsey Defends Flapper Movies," *Photoplay* (November 1927), pp. 29, 41. Lindsey, *The Child, the Movie, and Censorship* (New York, 1926). Cecil B. De Mille to Lindsey, June 10, June 23, 1927, BBLC, Box 156.

18. John E. Biby, State Board of Bar Examiners, to Lindsey, September 14, 1927, BBLC, Box 157. Miles Dodge, assistant secretary, State Bar of California, to Lindsey, May 1, 1928, BBLC, Box 159.

19. Thomas Mann's statement appeared on a printed handbill advertising the Dutch edition of *The Companionate Marriage,* BBLC, Box 162. On Lindsey's influence in Germany, *cf. Baltimore Sun,* January 20, 1929; *Des Moines Tribune,* February 11, 1929. The comment by the Indian journalist appeared in the *Madras Mail,* April 22, 1929.

20. The best account of the episode in the cathedral is in the *New York Times,* December 8, 1930. *Cf. The Dangerous Life,* pp. 345, *passim.* Author's interview with Wainwright Evans (who was present in the cathedral), February 4, 1969.

21. William T. Manning to Lindsey, February 8, 1927, BBLC, Box 154.

22. Author's interview with Dr. Harry Benjamin, San Francisco, California, September 3, 1969. *Cf.* Harry Benjamin, "Reminiscences," *The Journal of Sex Research,* vi (February 1970), 8–9.

23. *Nation,* cxxxi (December 17, 1930), 665. *New Republic,* lxv (December 17, 1930), 124. Newspaper clipping dated December 29, 1930, BBLC, Scrapbook 33. *Cf. New York Times,* December 9, 1930.

24. *New York Times,* December 18, 1930.

25. Clarence Darrow to Lindsey, undated letter in 1931 folder; Upton Sinclair to Lindsey, October 7, 1931. BBLC, Box 168.

26. Author's interview with Reuben Borough, Los Angeles, California, October 24, 1969. *Cf.* Reuben Borough, "The Little Judge," *Colorado Quarterly,* xvi (Spring 1968), 371–382.

27. Borough, *op. cit.,* p. 381. Lindsey to James Randolph Walker, December 9, 1932, BBLC, Box 170.

CHAPTER 11: VINDICATION, AND NEW CRUSADES

1. Franklin D. Roosevelt to Lindsey, March 6, 1913, BBLC, Box 135. Lindsey to Roosevelt, February 18, 1932; Roosevelt to Lindsey, March 15, 1932. BBLC, Box 169.

2. Marvin H. McIntyre to Lindsey, January 8, 1934, BBLC, Box 173. Lindsey to Louis M. Howe, April 10, 1933, BBLC, Box 172. Franklin D. Roos-

evelt to Lindsey, October 20, 1933, and copies of letters from George Creel to Roosevelt and Donald Richberg, November 7, 1933. BBLC, Box 286.

3. *People ex rel. Colorado Bar Association v. Lindsey,* 93 Colo. 41, 23 P. 2d 118 (1933).

4. *Rocky Mountain News,* June 7, 1933.

5. Lindsey, "The House of Human Welfare," *The Forum,* LXXVIII (December 1927), 801–816. *Cf. The Dangerous Life,* Chapter 15.

6. Brochures, form letters, and correspondence relating to the proposed Institute of Human Relations may be found in BBLC, Box 171. Duplicate copies of some of the materials are also available in a small Lindsey Collection in the Department of Special Collections, Library of the University of California at Los Angeles (cited hereafter as LCLA).

7. Author's interview with William H. Neblett, Los Angeles, California, July 6, 1965.

8. Lindsey's NRA appointment was announced by Creel in a communication to the *Los Angeles Times,* February 14, 1934. Mimeographed press release dated May 30, 1934, BBLC, Box 176.

9. Author's interviews with Mrs. Albert Mellinkoff, Los Angeles, California, May 23, 1966, and subsequently. I am indebted to Mrs. Mellinkoff for the loan of additional materials relating to the 1934 election. For other materials, *cf.* BBLC, Boxes 179–180, and duplicates in LCLA.

10. Script dated August 27, 1934, for delivery over Station KFWB, BBLC, Box 178. Strictly speaking, Roosevelt's comment was not a presidential endorsement of Lindsey's candidacy. The comment was made in a private letter in 1932, before Roosevelt was President or Lindsey a candidate. The White House never repudiated the "endorsement," however, and relations between Roosevelt and Lindsey always remained cordial. *Cf.* Franklin D. Roosevelt to Lindsey, September 2, 1939, BBLC, Box 194.

11. Author's conversation with Mrs. Mellinkoff, July 14, 1970. Upton Sinclair to Albert Mellinkoff, August 8, 1934 (letter in possession of Mrs. Mellinkoff and viewed by the author). On Sinclair's own campaign, *cf.* Charles E. Larsen, "The E.P.I.C. Campaign of 1934," *Pacific Historical Review,* XXVII (May 1958), 127.

12. Copies of the pamphlets are in BBLC, Box 289, and in LCLA.

13. Statement dated October 30, 1934, signed by Mrs. Stokes and witnessed by Albert Mellinkoff, on loan to the author from the late Mrs. Ben B. Lindsey. Lindsey received 576,324 votes; Judge Adams, 245,653. Sinclair was defeated in the race for governor.

14. Lindsey to Judge Samuel Blake, June 13, 1934, BBLC, Box 177. Judge Samuel Blake to Lindsey, November 5, 1934 (copy in possession of Mrs. Mellinkoff and viewed by the author). Conversation with Mrs. Mellinkoff, July 14, 1970. A letter from the author to Judge Blake, July 20, 1970, requesting him to give his version of these events, met with no response.

15. Excerpt from statement released to Los Angeles newspapers by Judge Lindsey, January 7, 1936. Author's interview with Judge Robert W. Kenny, Los Angeles, California, April 13, 1965. Author's interview with retired Judge William Palmer, Oakland, California, May 26, 1966.

16. *People ex rel. Colorado Bar Association v. Lindsey,* 97 Colo. 599 (1935). The action was taken by the Supreme Court "on its own motion." The

story that the Judge's November birthday was a convenient excuse for moving up the date of reinstatement was told to the writer by Judge Philip Gilliam of the Juvenile Court of Denver, August 5, 1966.

17. Lindsey to Dr. G. S. Lackland, August 6, 1937, BBLC, Box 189. Lindsey to Dr. G. Hardy Clark, May 26, 1938, BBLC, Box 190.

18. Lindsey to District Attorney Buron Fitts, January 14, 1936, BBLC, Box 185. Marshall W. Taggart to Lindsey, May 15, 1936, BBLC, Box 186. *Los Angeles Examiner,* April 23, 1938. Fred B. Wood, legislative counsel, State of California, to Lindsey, September 20, 1938, BBLC, Box 191. Form letters, Lindsey to parents of numerous child actors and actresses, October 17, 1938, BBLC, Box 192. *San Francisco Chronicle,* January 19, 1939.

19. The bill was co-sponsored in the California Legislature by Senator Ed Fletcher (R., San Diego). Judge Robert W. Kenny to author, February 19, 1965. Lindsey to Harriet Buhler, assistant counsel, legislative counsel, State of California, December 20, 1938, BBLC, Box 192. Same to same, July 6, 1939, BBLC, Box 194. The best newspaper summary of the proposed Lindsey legislative program is in the *Los Angeles Times,* December 21, 1938. Copies of the proposed bills are located in BBLC, Boxes 290–291, and in LCLA.

20. *The Companionate Marriage,* pp. 259–260. Lindsey, "The House of Human Welfare," *passim.* Lindsey, "The Constructive Work I Have Undertaken in the United States," reprinted from *Report of the Fourth Congress of the World League for Sexual Reform* (Vienna, 1931). *The Dangerous Life,* pp. 331–336, *passim.*

21. The original Lindsey law appears in *Statutes of California, 1939,* Chapter 737. For its subsequent history, see Louis H. Burke (a former judge of the Conciliation Court in Los Angeles), "The Role of Conciliation in Divorce Cases," *Journal of Family Law,* I (1961), 209–226.

22. "Thousands of Problem Marriages Saved," *Los Angeles Metropolitan News* (official newspaper for the County of Los Angeles), July 2, 1970.

23. Lindsey to Harriet Buhler, July 6, 1939, BBLC, Box 194. *San Francisco Chronicle,* January 19, 1939.

24. Lindsey to Robert W. Kenny, March 9, 1939, BBLC, Box 193. Other Lindsey bills defeated in the 1939 session of the legislature dealt with the simplification of adoption procedures and the extension of chancery jurisdiction to all adult criminals. Strictly speaking, the latter was not a "children's bill," although Lindsey included it with the other bills.

25. Lindsey, "Court of Mended Hearts," *Liberty,* February 3, 1940, p. 55. Frank Murphy to Lindsey, February 3, 1940; Frances Perkins to Lindsey, February 29, 1940. BBLC, Box 195. The *Reader's Digest* article was condensed from Frank J. Taylor, "A Court to Prevent Divorce," *New Republic,* CIII (August 19, 1940), 239–240.

26. *Los Angeles Times,* August 11, 1939, July 24, 1940. *Los Angeles Examiner,* August 30, 1940.

27. Author's interview with Mrs. Mellinkoff, July 14, 1970. Unpublished transcripts of the hearings by the Lindsey committee and its final report are in BBLC, Box 288, and in LCLA. For newspaper coverage of the committee report, *cf. San Francisco Chronicle* or *Los Angeles Times,* December 8, 1940.

28. Kenneth I. Fulton (secretary to Governor Olson) to Lindsey, December 14, 1940; Lindsey to Governor Olson, January 6, 1941. BBLC, Box 195.

For a good summary of the Whittier episode and its aftermath, *cf.* Robert E. Burke, *Olson's New Deal for California* (Berkeley and Los Angeles, 1953), pp. 178–180.

29. Correspondence relating to the Lindsey-Bates controversy may be found in BBLC, Box 251. *Cf. Los Angeles Times,* especially January 18, 19, and 28, 1941. For the report of the committee that investigated the Court of Conciliation, see *Los Angeles Times,* March 27, 1941, which also briefly reviews the Bates-Lindsey feud.

30. Alvin Weis, president of the Yuba-Sutter Bar Association, to Lindsey, March 4, 1941, BBLC, Box 254. Box 254 also contains a considerable file of correspondence on the efforts by Judge Lindsey and his friends to block the DeLap-Rich bill, including copies of the letters and telegrams sent by clergymen to members of the legislature. On the defeat of the DeLap-Rich bill, *cf.* State of California *Assembly Journal,* June 14, 1941, p. 4369.

31. BBLC, Box 254.

32. Lindsey to Senator Jack B. Tenney, March 24, 1943, BBLC, Box 196.

33. *Los Angeles Times, Los Angeles Examiner,* and *New York Times,* March 27, 1943.

CHAPTER 12: MAVERICK JUDGE

1. *Denver Post,* March 13, 1915. Theodore Roosevelt to Lindsey, March 20, 1915, BBLC, Box 140. *Los Angeles Times,* February 22, 1934; November 21, 1934. *Saturday Review of Literature,* IV (December 24, 1927), 468.

2. *Twenty-Five Years of the Juvenile and Family Court of Denver* (Denver, 1926), p. 27. *Cf.* Lindsey to Bernard Flexner, December 11, 1908, BBLC, Box 107.

3. Florence Kelley to Lindsey, September 6, 1912, BBLC, Box 39. Lindsey to Owen Lovejoy, April 10, 1911, BBLC, Box 127. Paul Kellogg to Lindsey, March 6, 1911, BBLC, Box 126.

4. For examples of widely publicized photographs of the Judge conferring with young women, *cf. Physical Culture Magazine* (February 1925), p. 30.

5. Louis Filler, *The Muckrakers: Crusaders for American Liberalism* (Chicago, 1968), p. 374. Adolf A. Berle, Jr., to Paul Kellogg, April 23, 1925, Survey Associates Collection, Box 94, Social Welfare History Archives Center, Minneapolis, Minnesota.

6. *The Beast,* pp. 268–269.

7. *The Dangerous Life,* pp. 282, *passim.*

8. Lindsey to Lincoln Steffens, August 10, 1906, BBLC, Box 8.

9. For a recent critical analysis of *criminal* statutes that deal with contributing to the delinquency or dependency of a minor, *cf.* Paul W. Alexander, "What's This About Punishing Parents?" *Federal Probation,* XII (March 1948), 23–29. The revised Standard Juvenile Court Act, prepared by the National Probation and Parole Association, the National Council of Juvenile Court Judges, and the United States Children's Bureau, recommends the civil proceeding only.

10. Author's interview with Oscar Chapman, Washington, D.C., November 2, 1965. Author's interview with Judge Robert W. Steele, Denver, Colorado, August 16, 1966.

11. *Denver Republican,* April 27, 1906, January 14, 1911.

12. *Ibid.,* August 23, 1909. *Denver Post,* April 14, 1910. *Denver Republican,* May 5, 1910.

13. For statistics on "cases" settled informally in the later period by probation officers, school authorities, and others, it is necessary to rely on occasional references by Lindsey, since any records that might have been kept have not been preserved. In fiscal year 1924, according to the Judge, more than two thousand complaints were handled without a case being filed. *Twenty-five Years of the Juvenile and Family Court of Denver,* p. 49. Such a figure would amount to about three times the number of formal cases handled by the court. It would also help to explain the large number of cases placed on probation or simply dismissed in the early years of the court when a greater proportion of complaints became filed cases. *Cf.* Lindsey, *The Problem of the Children and How the State of Colorado Cares for Them,* pp. 152–154.

14. *Twenty-five Years of the Juvenile and Family Court of Denver,* p. 56.

15. T. D. Hurley to Lindsey, April 11, 1905, BBLC, Box 92.

16. *The Problem of the Children and How the State of Colorado Cares for Them,* p. 126.

17. *Cf.* Vance Packard, *The Sexual Wilderness* (New York, 1970), pp. 425–426; Margaret Mead, "Marriage in Two Steps," *Redbook,* cxxvii (July 1966), 48–49; Sidney Ditzion, *Marriage, Morals and Sex in America,* Chapter 11.

18. Mead, like Lindsey, suggested that parental marriages should be much more difficult to terminate. Mead, *op. cit.,* pp. 84–86. Some authorities seriously question the value of preserving certain marriages for "the sake of the children." *Cf.* Herma Hill Kay, "A Family Court: The California Proposal," *California Law Review,* lvi (October 1968), 1205–1248. For a treatment of some young persons' reactions to the concept of companionate marriage, see Ernest R. Groves and Gladys Hoagland Groves, *The Contemporary American Family* (Philadelphia, 1946), pp. 519–520.

19. A contemporary article on divorce and alimony in the United States contains almost all the criticisms made by Lindsey more than forty years ago: Christopher Lasch, "Divorce American Style," *New York Review of Books,* February 17, 1966, pp. 2–3.

20. *The Companionate Marriage,* p. 313. The words in the quotation were attributed to a physician who was purportedly describing his liberal views on his own daughter's upbringing. The "physician" may have been a literary device to express Lindsey's own views. Author's conversation with Wainwright Evans, August 16, 1970.

21. The examples that Lindsey used in his books and articles in attacking repressive legislation all involved unconventional heterosexual episodes. Privately, the Judge early expressed the view that homosexuality was a "malady" which did not necessarily imply "viciousness of heart" and should be treated with sympathy and compassion. He believed, however, that the state had a legitimate concern with the subject and a duty to try to cure such persons. Lindsey's attitude was fairly liberal for his time (and is not wholly illiberal today), but it would hardly meet with the approval of the Gay Liberation Front. *Cf.* Lindsey to Kate Campbell Robertson, June 8, 1914, BBLC, Box 138.

22. Havelock Ellis to Lindsey, March 20, 1927; H. G. Wells to Lindsey,

March 30, 1927. BBLC, Box 155. George Bernard Shaw to Lindsey, December 17, 1924, BBLC, Box 152.

EPILOGUE

1. Mrs. Ben B. Lindsey to Judge Emmet Wilson, May 4, 1943. A copy of the letter is in the possession of Mrs. Albert Mellinkoff and was seen by the author.

2. Franklin D. Roosevelt to Mrs. Ben B. Lindsey, April 29, 1943, BBLC, Box 197.

A NOTE ON SOURCES

The Benjamin Barr Lindsey Collection is one of the largest in the Manuscript Division of the Library of Congress. It contains manuscripts and reprints of the Judge's writings, special containers dealing with the 1914 coal strike and Ford peace mission, and an extensive correspondence with a cross-section of leading political and literary figures. Unfortunately only about one-third of the correspondence is indexed. Both the indexed and unindexed correspondence are arranged chronologically, however, which eases the researcher's task somewhat. One of the great merits of the collection lies in the fact that Lindsey kept carbon copies of a substantial amount of his outgoing correspondence as well as the letters he received. In spite of the scope of the collection, materials relating to Lindsey's childhood and early manhood are scanty. The preserved correspondence grows rapidly after 1901, when he first became a judge. Duplicates of a small portion of the collection, emphasizing the California years (but not restricted to them), may be found in the Department of Special Collections of the Library of the University of California at Los Angeles.

Other collections in the Library of Congress which contain some original copies of letters duplicated in the Lindsey Collection, as well as additional correspondence relating to the Judge, include the Ford Peace Plan Papers, the Gifford Pinchot Papers, the Brand Whitlock Collection, the Theodore Roosevelt Collection, and the Woodrow Wilson Papers. The Lincoln Steffens Collection at Columbia University and the Survey Associates

Papers at the Social Welfare History Archives Center at the University of Minnesota have a few choice items, but they are small in number. Some of the most pertinent correspondence in the Edward P. Costigan Papers, located at the University of Colorado, has been published in Colin B. Goodykoontz, ed., *Papers of Edward P. Costigan Relating to the Progressive Movement in Colorado, 1902–1917* (Boulder, Colo., 1941). Duplicates of parts of the Costigan Papers are also contained in the Lindsey Collection in the Library of Congress. Scattered references to Lindsey are also found in the Hiram Johnson Papers at the Bancroft Library of the University of California at Berkeley, in the papers of Governors John Shafroth and William Sweet in the Colorado State Historical Society, and in the Schwimmer-Lloyd Collection in the New York Public Library. The Western History Division of the Denver Public Library has an excellent collection of Denver newspapers for the Lindsey period. The Lindsey Collection in the Library of Congress includes thirty-five scrapbooks of newspaper clippings from all over the world.

The remaining records of the Juvenile Court of Denver were transferred in 1970 from the basement of the City and County Building in Denver to the State Archives. The records relating to delinquent boys and girls comprise three categories of documents: *Delinquency Records, Clerk's Minutes,* and filed dockets. Noticeably absent from these records are many of the "social history" materials relating to the filed cases as well as data dealing with a much larger number of "cases" settled informally. For statistics on the latter category it is necessary to rely on occasional data supplied by the Judge.

Of published reminiscences about Lindsey, the chief sources are his own two semi-autobiographical works, *The Beast* (New York, 1910) and *The Dangerous Life* (New York, 1931). Both books provide valuable insights into the Judge's personality, but also reflect his tendency to exaggerate his accomplishments. Specialists in Colorado history accept Lindsey's description of conditions in the state on the eve of the Progressive era as basically correct, but are skeptical about his accuracy in matters of detail and doubtful regarding some of the conversations he reports in *The Beast*. On the latter point see Allen Breck, *William Gray Evans, 1855–1924, Portrait of a Western Executive* (Denver, 1964). Two of Lindsey's friends reminisced about the early Denver days: Lincoln Steffens in his *Autobiography* (New York, 1931) and George Creel in *Rebel at Large* (New York, 1947). The Judge's literary collaborator, Reuben Borough, left a fascinating personal memoir of Lindsey in "The Little Judge," *Colorado Quarterly,* xvi (Spring 1968), 371–382.

Although Lindsey's name has been mentioned in scores of books and periodicals, his contributions have not always been recognized in scholarly works and professional journals. The establishment of the California Children's Court of Conciliation is a case in point. Indisputably Lindsey was both the chief draftsman and outstanding lobbyist for the legislation that created this court. To the extent that the adoption of any new law can be credited to a single person, Lindsey deserves credit for the 1939 statute. Yet most of the literature about the court either omits any reference to the Judge or implies that he had nothing to do with its establishment. One is reminded of the practice of Soviet encyclopedists who are required to make an "unperson" of a fallen leader. In articles about the California court in two respected law journals, Lindsey's name is not mentioned, even though the authors find space to discuss the historical antecedents of the court and to refer to the fact that the law creating it was passed in 1939. *Cf.* Louis H. Burke, "The Role of Conciliation in Divorce Cases," *Journal of Family Law,* i (Spring 1961), 209–226; Frank B. Blum, "Conciliation Courts: Instruments of Peace," *Journal of the State Bar of California,* xl (May-June 1966), 33–48. An article in another reputable journal takes what might be called a middle ground on Lindsey's role by stating: *"It is understood* that the plan was conceived and the bill drafted by the famous Ben B. Lindsey, who became its first judge and continued as such until his death." *Cf*. Charles L. Chute, "Divorce and the Family Court," *Law and Contemporary Problems,* xviii (Winter 1953), 49–65 (emphasis added). A writer for one of the oldest social science journals in the United States came close to implying that Lindsey's role in the creation of the Court of Conciliation might even be a complete myth. He commented: "In California, a plan *allegedly* conceived by Judge Ben B. Lindsey went into effect in 1939." Jacob T. Zuckerman, "The Family Court—Evolving Concepts," ccclxxxiii (May 1969), 119–128 (emphasis added). A book bearing the imprimatur of a distinguished university press, and with a foreword by one of the most honored family court judges in the United States, partially explains the absence of a court of conciliation in San Francisco on the basis of "distrust of the ideas of Judge Ben B. Lindsey, whose idea the statute *is said to have been.*" Maxine Virtue, *Family Cases in Court* (Durham, N.C., 1956), p. 9 (emphasis added).

The same pattern of disregard may be found in the treatment of Lindsey's other legislative accomplishments. One typical example will suffice. It is especially appropriate because of the law involved. The article dealt comprehensively with state laws making it a criminal offense to contribute to the delinquency of a minor. Lindsey drafted and lobbied for the first general state law *in the United States* to establish this principle, the Colorado Adult Delinquency Act of 1903. He also corresponded with lawyers, judges, and legislators on its behalf, and made personal appearances in several states to lobby for it. Yet the article, which is otherwise excellent and even definitive, does not even mention Lindsey's name. *Cf*. Frederick J. Ludwig, "Delinquent Parents and the Criminal Law," *Vanderbilt Law Review,* v (June 1952), 719–736.

Undoubtedly the major reason for such slights to Lindsey in more recent publications is simply inadequate research. Most of the Judge's contemporaries are now dead, and it is reasonable to assume in most cases that no malice is involved. Authors are known to rely on published works of recent vintage, and even scholars copy other scholars. The Judge was never a member of a legislative body, and the bills he drafted in Colorado and California never formally carried his name. As a minimal first step in discovering his influence on certain items of legislation, it would be necessary to consult newspaper files, many of which are not indexed. Even state histories of Colorado have often given Lindsey only the most cursory treatment. In spite of the Judge's national prominence, he has not fared a great deal better in American history textbooks. One of the most widely read and best written one-volume histories of the United States refers to Lindsey only once (in connection with companionate marriage) and misspells his name even in that brief notice. *Cf.* Samuel Eliot Morison, *Oxford History of the American People* (New York, 1965), p. 908.

Two early and memorable examples of scholarly works which treated Lindsey's contributions are Louis Filler, *Crusaders for American Liberalism* (1939), and Eric Goldman, *Rendezvous with Destiny* (1953). Two recent and creditable examples are Peter G. Slater, "Ben Lindsey and the Juvenile Court of Denver: A Progressive Looks at Human Nature," *American Quarterly,* xx (Summer 1968), 211–223, and Murray and Adeline Levine, *A Social History of Helping Services* (New York, 1970), Chapter 9. Two first-rate doctoral dissertations which explore Lindsey's role in the Progressive era in considerable depth are Frances Huber, *The Progressive Career of Ben B. Lindsey, 1900–1920* (Ann Arbor: University Microfilms, 1963), and J. Paul Mitchell, *Progressivism in Denver: The Municipal Reform Movement, 1904–1916* (Ann Arbor: University Microfilms, 1967). For an excellent survey of recent historical writing on Colorado progressivism containing a number of references to Lindsey, see *The Colorado Magazine,* xlv (Winter 1968), 1–78.

Without repeating the expressions of appreciation in the Preface or the acknowledgments in the footnotes, a final word should be written about the invaluable contributions of the dwindling but helpful group who generously shared their reminiscences of the Judge with me. Whatever the limitations of oral history may be, I am grateful to a score of persons for supplying information that could not have been found in newspapers, books, articles, or preserved correspondence.

INDEX

Deterrent to crime, punishment as, 6

De Voto, Bernard, 177, 249

Dewey, John, 105, 106, 215

Dime novels, 85

Disbarment of Lindsey, 204, 208–217

Divorce, 163–165, 167–169, 178; legislation on, 239–241

Domestic relations cases, 54, 237

Doughboy's Religion and Other Aspects of Our Day, The (Lindsey), 142–143, 149

Draft cards, burning of, 6

Dreyer, August, 222

Drugs, use of, in '60's and '70's, 6

Eastman, Max, 105, 140

Edison, Thomas A., 106, 132, 135

Education: Lindsey's ideas on, 105–106; relevancy of, 4

Eisenhower, Dwight D., 266

Election of 1912, presidential, 118–127

Ellis, Havelock, 145–146, 159, 173, 182, 200

Elmer Gantry (Lewis), 162

Employers' liability, lack of, in Colorado, 20

EPIC (End Poverty in California), 232–233

Equity: civil proceedings in, 40–41; failure of, in California, 242

Eugenics, 159–160

Evans, Wainwright, 151, 160–161, 164–165, 175

Evans, William G., 59, 60, 61, 62

Everybody's Magazine, 64, 103, 116, 117

Fabian, Warner, 150

Family, changes in the, 163–164

Farrell, James T., 189

Fee system, elimination of, 36

Fellow servant, doctrine of, in Colorado, 20

Field, E. B., 62

Filler, Louis, 254, 263

Fitzgerald, F. Scott, 150

Flaming Youth (Fabian), 150

Flanagan, Father Edward, 244

Flexner, Bernard, 40

Folk, Joseph W., 67, 113

Folks, Homer, 91

Ford, Henry, 129–130, 136, 138, 139

Ford Peace Mission, 130–133, 135–139

Francis, Charles, 194, 195

Fredenhagen, E. A., 93

"Free divorce," 146

"Free marriage," 146

Free Silver movement, 25

Freudianism, 146, 149

Fundamentalism, 183, 186–189

Future of Nakedness, The, 252

Gambling, in Denver, 29–30

Gardner, Gilson, 126

George, Henry, 25, 66, 114

Gilliam, Philip B., 40, 248

Glenn, John M., 250

Golden, Colorado, industrial school at, 28

Goldman, Emma, 105

Goldman, Eric, 263

Graham, Cora, 196–197

Graham, George, 20, 21

Graham, Royal R., 194, 195, 196

Graham v. Lindsey, 194–203

Guggenheim, Simon, 69

Gurley, Boyd, 117, 118

"Hague System," 128

Hall, G. Stanley, 106, 145

Hanna, Louis B., 137

Harding, Warren, 143

Harmon, Judson, 122

Harriman, Karl, 160

A NOTE ON THE AUTHOR

Charles Larsen was born in San Francisco and studied at the University of California, Berkeley, and at Columbia University, where he received a Ph.D. He has been a Fulbright Scholar and is now Professor of History at Mills College in Oakland, California. Mr. Larsen's articles and reviews have appeared in several historical journals, including the *Journal of American History*, the *American West*, and the *Pacific Historical Review*.